WHEN VALUES COLLIDE

The Catholic Church,
Sexual Abuse,
and the Challenges
of Leadership

Joseph P. Chinnici, O.F.M.

ORBIS BOOKS
Maryknoll, New York 10545

Founded in 1970, Orbis Books endeavors to publish works that enlighten the mind, nourish the spirit, and challenge the conscience. The publishing arm of the Maryknoll Fathers and Brothers, Orbis seeks to explore the global dimensions of the Christian faith and mission, to invite dialogue with diverse cultures and religious traditions, and to serve the cause of reconciliation and peace. The books published reflect the views of their authors and do not represent the official position of the Maryknoll Society. To learn more about Maryknoll and Orbis Books, please visit our website at www.maryknollsociety.org.

Copyright © 2010 by Joseph P. Chinnici, O.F.M.

Published by Orbis Books, Maryknoll, New York 10545-0302.

Manufactured in the United States of America.

Library of Congress Cataloging-in-Publication Data

Chinnici, Joseph P.
  When values collide : the Catholic Church, sexual abuse, and the
challenges of leadership / by Joseph P. Chinnici.
      p. cm.
  Includes bibliographical references and index.
  ISBN 978-1-57075-873-7 (pbk.)
  1. Child sexual abuse by clergy. 2. Catholic Church—Clergy—Sexual
behavior. 3. Catholic Church—Discipline. 4. Franciscans. I. Title.
  BX1912.9.C475 2010
  261.8'3272088282—dc22
                                        2009046179

CONTENTS

Seeing Me,
Your head turned ever so slightly forward,
And the line of Your Glance
Pulled Gently into the Future.
And I, Looking Back
Saw Providence
Shattering Stone Jars,
So that oil could soothe Jerusalem.

Joseph P. Chinnici
April 21, 1997

INTRODUCTION

The Catholic Church, Sexual Abuse, and Leadership

GOD'S CHURCH EARNS PRAISE: "Christians are fine people, and only of Christians can this be said. How great is the Catholic Church! They all love each other; they do their utmost to help one another. The church devotes itself to prayer, fasting and hymns the world over, and God is praised by its unity and peace." So people talk. Someone who hears this eulogy may fail to realize that the evil aspects which are mingled with the good have been passed over in silence. So the hearer comes along, attracted by such acclaim, and finds bad people mixed with the good, a kind he was not told about before he came. He is so shocked by false Christians that he shuns good Christians.

SAINT AUGUSTINE OF HIPPO
Expositions of the Psalms[1]

THIS BOOK ORIGINATED IN a distinct experience and inter-pretation of Church and society as they intersected in the last twenty-five years with the scandalous abuse of minors by Roman Catholic churchmen. I have been involved in many of the events narrated here. Being the son of two faithful Catholics, a brother of two brothers and two sisters, a professed member of a religious order in the Church, and a priest, I approach the interpretation of the sexual abuse scandal from a particular point of view. On June 8, 1988, the Franciscan Friars of the Province of Saint Barbara elected me to their top position of leadership, that of Provincial Minister. The Province is that enti-ty of the Order of Friars Minor (popularly known as one branch of the Franciscans) that covers the states of California, Oregon,

Washington, Arizona, and New Mexico. The Franciscan Friars are a fraternal community, some members being ordained cleric friars, others being non-ordained lay friars, and all of whom are "brothers." In 1988 we numbered well over two hundred and fifty. At the time of my election I had already been a professor of history for twelve years. I was forty-three years old and would serve as the chief executive officer of the province until January 1997. A vicar provincial, my assistant, and six consulters were also elected. We in turn appointed a secretary who would bring our leadership team to nine. Abruptly, we—I, along with our entire group of brothers—found ourselves in a "dark wood" at the center of one of the multiple spasms of clergy sexual abuse which shocked the Church in the early 1990s and have continued into our present times. Our experience is now twenty years old, "yet its ominous shadows still obscure or haunt present-day lives."[2]

The sexual abuse of minors by Roman Catholic clergymen remains an appalling crime. Attention has justly been given, and more attention needs to be given, to both the individual and the family victims of that crime. Their experience, which is both searing in its clarity and purifying in its demands, is a truth claim, one which should continue to shape the face of the Church. Additionally, I, like many others in the Church, am horrified and angered not only by what was discovered within my own religious community but also by the revelations over the last twenty years of both the extensiveness of the problem and the denial or mismanagement of the crisis by some in positions of authority. Yet, while deploring what has happened and trying to be as sensitive as possible to the victims, this work addresses the sexual abuse of minors by clergy from a different perspective.

I am concerned about how the crisis looked from the perspective of some in leadership. Here I appeal to my own experience, not as exemplary or ideal, but as a reality that sheds some light on larger questions that were confronted throughout the Church. Indeed, from all accounts, the motivations, perceptions, and actions of those in positions of hierarchical leadership have been placed at the center of the debate over how the Church has handled this crisis. As will be explained in the historical portions of this work, the course of the sexual abuse scandal changed over time from a focus on the crimes of individual priests to an overriding systemic issue: the ecclesial culture that permitted the denial of the crimes and aided the mismanagement and malfeasance of some in hierarchical positions of leadership. I consider the naming of this "culture of denial" to be a central insight that the whole scandal has revealed. More should be expected from the Church. But subsuming the history of the crisis into such a total abstraction does not move the discussion forward. In fact, in the course of the abuse scandal, multiple cultural and institutional systems and values in the familial, ecclesial, legal, psychological, financial, political, civil, and canonical worlds collided. And this collision itself reflected a much wider and more extensive public struggle over authority, responsibility, and power, who has them and how they are used to interpret and to shape events and people in both the Church and the society. If we are to address the deeper and more lasting issues, these broader dimensions need to be considered.

From 1988 to 1994 some in positions of ecclesial authority and leadership worked with victims and professional laity to develop alternate institutional strategies. These strategies attempted both to purify the Church of abusive activity and to bridge the differences between colliding systems and values in the clerical and lay worlds. Although different assessments may be given to these actions and they may be judged terribly inadequate by today's standards, their development was historically significant. After describing in broad fashion the public course of the sexual abuse scandal from 1950 to the present, this book will analyze one of these institutional strategies in detail, that of the Franciscan Friars of the Saint Barbara Province. It will present this example, not as a model for action or as one without its shortcomings, but as a dense local event revelatory of much larger patterns at the center of the crisis. The case study of this one religious group—its leadership, the questions they confronted, the collision of values that they experienced, and the structures they used to try to resolve these conflicts—reveals that at the heart of the sexual abuse scandal was not simply the criminal activity of individual priests. Rather the crisis presented to leadership the much deeper and more institutional challenge to create mediating structures of reciprocal exchange where the failures of relational power could be confronted and its positive energies released. This is the deeper issue that continues to confront those in positions of leadership.

Eventually, it was precisely because these mediating structures were developing and were at the same time rejected by some in positions of leadership that the crisis mutated into one of systemic scandal. Particularly in the wake of the extensive revelations of hierarchical mismanagement in the Archdiocese of Boston in 2002, alternative mediating approaches were swept up in the condemnation of the larger patterns of the abuse of power. As a consequence, the hierarchical and communal forces within the Church and society and operative throughout the crisis have now sorted themselves into partisan factions. The voice of those developing mediating structures has softened to a public institutional whisper. Looking at this entire history from the viewpoint of someone who was in leadership at the time of the development of other approaches may help us go more deeply into the fundamental issues that remain unresolved. My hope is that this book will help move our national discussion and actions beyond partisanship and also enable the continuing story from the viewpoint of the victims to be more clearly heard, assimilated, and collaboratively addressed.

When Values Collide seeks to approach the events not simply by mapping the historical, organizational, and psychological terrain, but also by exploring the spiritual topography of the valleys, underbrush, and mountains that many participants tried to negotiate. The sexual abuse scandal within Roman Catholicism has left many bishops, priests, religious leaders, educated and committed laity, young inquirers, and prominent people in the society with a host of questions that touch not simply management and organization but also faith and the human spirit. Many in the Church have experienced profound ecclesial scandal. They have been alienated not simply by sexual abuse but by the actions of those in authority. They have discovered that the Church, the Body of Christ, is composed of the good and the not-so-good at all levels of its existence. Their awareness of how the Church works has changed. Its institutional patterns of relationship are now honeycombed for some with bitter experiences and memories. In the wake of scandal, the faith of good people has groped for ways to find self-expression and continued institutional commitment.

To acknowledge this difficult experience and intellectually to articulate an understanding of faith from within it is one of the tasks of ecclesial leadership—be the leaders bishops, priests, lay ministers, or members of the historical and theological academies. "Should anyone ask you the reason for this hope of yours, be ever ready to reply" (1 Pet. 3.15). Yet if the aftermath of the sexual abuse scandal has seen the growing invisibility of mediating structures in Church and society, the violent intensity of the crisis has all but obscured any substantial theological reflection on the impact of the crisis on the life of faith and the spirituality of the believer. The focused attention on episcopal leadership has publicly isolated other religious voices speaking from the broad and wide tradition of Catholic theology and spirituality. In the midst of this experience of ecclesial impasse, this book seeks to find a way forward. Is there something we can learn from history that will strengthen our faith and help us give a stronger witness in society? "History is a great teacher of justice and of truth. She permits us to distinguish things and their concrete conditioning."[3]

And our contemporary history has taught us some hard truths. This book, then, addresses something much larger than the immediate institutional challenge of the sexual abuse of minors. It is the story of faith seeking understanding by pondering how God might be present in the Church through the distressing history of these times.

Throughout this work I make reference to the spiritual and theological inheritance of a major stream of reflection in the Western Catholic Christian Tradition. In the midst of their experience of the crisis, the Franciscan friars turned to their own sources. As their leader, I tried to discover in Francis of Assisi and Bonaventure a spiritual and theological vision that could help all of us negotiate the difficult terrain of a collision of values and ecclesial scandal. This book is the fruit of my own reflection and the discussions of our brothers after twenty years. The focus of Francis of Assisi on the mediating structures of a fraternity of brothers and sisters and the humble presence of the poor Christ within the community of the Church illuminates our contemporary struggles in a new way. Francis's own spiritual vision indicates the broad outlines of an ethics of reciprocal exchange that begs for structural expression within the Church. Bonaventure's ecclesial vision, his focus on the Order of Love, and his synthesis of history and faith provides some theological depth to the analysis. Confirmation of some of these insights can be found in the pastoral reflections and theological teaching of St. Augustine. This present work will return frequently to this Augustinian-Franciscan spiritual and theological inheritance as providing a much longer frame of meaning to help us in our current pilgrimage. I realize there are other viable traditions of interpretation. I present the one with which I am most familiar to show that the contemporary Church possesses in the storehouse of its collective memory ideas, concepts, approaches, and experiences of faith from the past that give us life in the present. As I mention throughout, the discovery of a path forward needs to be the work of the whole Church.

Chapter 1 presents in summary fashion a history of the phases of the sexual abuse scandal as it has rocked the contemporary Church in the United States. This chapter paints a background landscape to the foreground focus on the experience of one case study of the sexual abuse of minors by priests and allows that one case to illuminate a much larger picture. Chapters 2 and 3 examine in detail the personal and communal experience of the Franciscan Friars, Province of Saint Barbara, as they confronted the difficulties of the sexual abuse of minors by members of their own community. The purpose of these pages is to invite the reader firsthand into a leader's experience of the collision of values which shaped the scandal.

Having invited the reader into the experience from the viewpoint of leadership, Chapter 4 moves the story once again outward into a broader field of interpretation. The scandal is treated as the symbolic center point of the much larger battles over power between the hierarchical and communal dimensions of the Church. I argue that a fundamental consequence of the abuse crisis has been the loss of a shared ethical space of reciprocal exchange between people. Particular attention is called to the challenge of relational power. The crisis has deep roots in the affections and needs to be examined at that level. Chapters 5 and 6 describe the Franciscan tradition with its focus on the centrality of becoming brother and sister and the absolute primacy of the Order of Love; this tradition is presented as one way of visioning the recovery of a space of trust between people. Chapter 7 discusses the continuing problem of dominating power as culturally related to ownership, money, and freedom. The insertion into the public discussion of the distinctive Franciscan tradition of "dispossession" or the practice of "poverty" is one means forward. Chapter 8 examines the difficult problem of scandal. It tries to identify some pointers from the Franciscan tradition that might help those confronted with a rethinking of their faith in the wake of deep ecclesial scandal. The last chapter, a short conclusion, purposely does not provide an overall summary but instead points to a continuing practice of certain key dimensions of faith. A path forward from the present is briefly indicated: the creation of new mediating structures, penitential conversion, and a daily practice in a time of colliding values of humility, charity, reciprocal exchange, mourning, dispossession, *pietas,* and prayer.

Throughout all these chapters other perspectives surface that may prove helpful both to the members of the Church and the citizens of our society. Inasmuch as each believer is also a citizen of this world and that the "earthly city" and the "heavenly city" in large measure influence each other, actions that help address the internal power difficulties of the Church will also help address the conflicts over power that permeate our society at large. Repeatedly this book implies that the Church has now entered a new era. It is an era in which we are aware that as members of the Body of Christ in time we are ambiguously mixed up in the affairs of the world. It is an era in which we are called in a new way to witness to the power and peace, the humility and piety, the generosity and compassion, of God-with-us. This vision moves beyond that of a Christendom that no longer exists. This way has been opened up for us by our experience of the scandal of sexual abuse here in the Church in the United States. But it also points in a direction important for the formation of a global Church undergoing similar travails. Once one has crossed the Rubicon of scandal, one cannot go back again except through pretense and a flight from history.

Joseph P. Chinnici, O.F.M.
Franciscan School of Theology, Berkeley, California
Feast of Blessed John Duns Scotus,
November 8, 2009

1. THE CHURCH IN RELATION TO THE TIMES

THE SOUL DOES NOT HAVE illumination, except when considering the Church in relation to the times.

SAINT BONAVENTURE
Collations on the Six Days[1]

WHEN LOOKED AT FROM the viewpoint of the historian, the sexual abuse scandal has been one of the most festering issues ever faced by the Roman Catholic Church in the United States. The sheer numbers attached to the crisis are staggering. Studies commissioned by the hierarchy and released in 2004 and 2006 confirm that between 1950 and 2002, 10,667 victims/survivors came forward and 4,392 priests had allegations of abuse against them. Named were 4.2 percent of diocesan priests and 2.7 percent of religious priests; allegations of sexual misconduct touched 4 percent of the priests in each region of the country, and, as of March 2004, well over half a billion dollars had been spent in litigating claims.[2] In 2006 those dioceses and eparchies responding to the requests of the National Review Board for information paid out $332,970,559; the cost to religious congregations amounted to $65,627,135.[3] In July 2007 the Archdiocese of Los Angeles alone agreed to a $660 million settlement. One recent estimate places the total cost of settlements at over $3 billion.[4]

As to the origins of the crisis, the John Jay Study commissioned by the bishops reports that the origins of the abuse lay deep in the generation born between 1920 and 1949 and ordained between 1950 and 1969. Graphing the incidents of sexual abuse known or reported to the Church by 2002 indicates a steady increase in abusive activity in the 1950s and

1960s, an apogee in 1970, and a slow and steady decline only after 1980. Approximately one-third of all reports were made in 2002, the incidents named dating back some thirty years. There appears to have been a clear decline in abuse during the 1990s.[5] The 2006 Annual Report indicates that 1970–1974 was the most common time period for abuse by diocesan priests, with the peak for religious priests being slightly extended.[6] The extensive public exposure of this activity began to surface at the United States Catholic Conference and National Conference of Catholic Bishops only in 1982 and became evident to the national press in 1984–1985.[7] In the next decade, despite the steady exposure of the problem in the public media and national attempts to address it, the leadership as a whole responded only gradually until the crisis reached a climactic explosion in 2002 in Boston. These general outlines are fairly well known.[8] Yet the disparity between when the abuse occurred and when it surfaced so as to become a public issue is historically jarring. Over its fifty-year history, the crisis of the sexual abuse of minors has undergone considerable change. In sketching a chronological summary of the overall developments from 1950 to 2008 we can identify five distinct phases which go from public invisibility to systemic anger.

1950–1982: Public Invisibility

As FAR AS THE clerical abuse scandal is concerned, we might refer to the period previous to the first public exposures in the mid-1980s as a time of public invisibility. This should not surprise us. It is in the nature of social eruptions, both positive and negative, to undergo extended periods of gestation: civil rights litigation and protest began long before Rosa Parks refused to move to the back of the bus. However, it was only in 1955 that the kindling burst into a national flame. By the time Michael Harrington identified the underbelly of the economy of an affluent America between 1958 and 1962, the social problem of the poor had long since become entrenched in the structures and institutions of the society. Similarly, the Vietnam War had been gestating for over a decade before the public mobilized to critique it. Historians now trace the public feminist revolution of the mid-1960s to its roots in the cultural patterns of the postwar period.[9] In hindsight, what is astounding about clerical sexual abuse is that while the amount of violent and abusive activity was increasing, the public institutional silence surrounding it was deafening. Neither the elite culture of the psychological establishment, nor the legal culture protective of the common good, nor the criminal authorities, nor the religious culture structured around hierarchy and traditional social arrangements could see the pattern clearly.[10] Within the Church, this social fact of public invisibility was doubly compounded by the inherited concept of "holiness" as an institutional mark of the Church embodied in a "holy priesthood," pure and removed from the affective struggles of sexuality.[11] In addition, because such abusive activity was classified as "sinful," it became an issue to be addressed by repentance and conversion. The mechanisms for its removal, the confessional and spiritual direction, were privatized. This privatization abetted the guilt, silence, and isolation dominating the victims' awareness. All of this reflected in part the regulatory system surrounding sexual and familial mores, which the society itself promoted.[12] It is important to recognize that institutional pathways and choices, once made, remain embedded in the memory, laws, customs, and structures of organizations until they are often violently excised from the social fabric of relations.[13] The very real problem of sexual abuse lay hidden just beneath the surface of public social consciousness.

During the 1960s and early 1970s, dramatic changes were occurring in gender arrangements and concern for sexual orientation, in the relationships between clergy and laity, the priesthood and family life, in the practice of celibacy and the formative structures of seminary and ministerial life, in the power equilibrium between civic and religious authorities, and in the role of the media and the professional elite in shaping public institutions. The factors are too many to identify in this short survey. Suffice it to say that these extensive changes in role expectations, personal identities, and social relationships reflected a context of gradual upheaval in codes of behavior and cultural restraints. That which was private was beginning to go public; the personal was becoming the political.[14] Within the Church, embedded as it was within this culture, there were simultaneously during the 1960s both an outbreak of abusive activity and a continuation of the previous public patterns abetting its invisibility.

Culturally, the sexual abuse reporting laws began to change in response to the society in the mid-1960s.[15] The Federal Child Abuse Prevention and Treatment Act passed in 1974. In the decade after that period, precisely when the charged debates over family life, abortion, and homosexuality filled the air, public forces started to mobilize around child abuse.[16] The atmosphere created by the "rights revolution" and a general awareness of patterns of cultural victimization swept the country.[17] That which was previously handled privately or denied entirely was now going to be addressed through the mobilization of social institutions and professional power structures.[18] The cultural consensus was in the process of creating a new public ethical horizon. The same process was occurring within the Church. One of the largest factors was the emphasis from the Vatican Council on the "priesthood of all believers" and the role of the laity in the Church. A more influential and assertive cadre of lay leaders, committed to the experience and values of family life, began to have a stronger moral voice in the community.[19] The invisible sin of child abuse could no longer remain privatized; it was now about to explode into the public arena through the outside forces of the courts and the media.[20] How would the Church deal with it? The era of invisibility had ended.

1982–1988: Initial Recognition and Institutional Response

DURING THE SECOND PHASE, from 1982 to 1988, local situations began to congeal in the minds of some into a national pattern of clergy sexual abuse. The National Conference of Catholic Bishops became aware of some local cases in 1982.[21] The journalist Jason Berry exposed the court proceedings around the criminal activity of Father Gilbert Gauthe, a priest of the Diocese of Lafayette, Louisiana, in the pages of the *National Catholic Reporter* in June 1984.[22] In May–June 1985 a team of canonical, legal, and psychological experts presented the national hierarchy with a white paper on the prevalence of the sexual abuse of minors in the Church. This now famous report described several case scenarios and dealt extensively with "insurance considerations, civil law considerations, criminal law considerations, clinical/medical considerations, selected spiritual concerns, public relations concerns." The issue in the judgment of the authors was systemic and demanded a systemic response.[23]

These first cases became known to the wider public within the context of litigation and media exposure, a situation that reinforced the inherited patterns of decision making and established pathways of institutional privatization. Legal classifications and organizational strategies such as reliance on the statutes of limitations, risk management, financial liability, confidentiality of settlements, attorney-client privileges, insurance claims, personnel policy development, medical interventions, guidelines for reporting criminal offenses, and media damage control clouded the ethical horizon of decision making. The ecclesial problem of sexual abuse of minors was framed not within the context of the vision of *Lumen Gentium* or *Dei Verbum* or *Gaudium et Spes* or *Dignitatis Humanae* or *Justice in the World* (1971 Synod) but within the operative ecclesiology provided by the interpretive systems of canon and civil law. With respect to the treatment of priest offenders, the dominant model was a mix of the privacy of the therapeutic-psychological and the secrecy of the confessional-ecclesiastical with a heavy dependence on personal consultations and Church-related treatment centers.[24] When the United States Catholic Conference issued its first public statement, February 18, 1988, the spokesman was the General Counsel; attention was drawn to the widespread prevalence of abuse in the society, and no mention was made of the priesthood. These juridical and institutional perspectives shaped the national internal Church response.[25] The disjunction between the cultural consensus about the intensity of the problem, the need for open disclosure, and the managerial reactions of the Church were becoming increasingly apparent to some in the society at large.

This initial institutional and juridical response has received a far-reaching and legitimate critique. It was a continuation of established institutional pathways. Certainly the patterns of privatization prevalent during the period of invisibility had some influence. In addition, the entanglement of the Church in the systemic and bureaucratic approaches of the Great Society probably formed a deep background for the initial managerial framing of the crisis. The reliance on experts in canon and civil law and the public policy focus surrounding the issues of abortion, taxation of church property, and struggle over the civil rights of homosexuals contributed to an overly legalistic interpretation of events. The hierarchical response may also have been shaped by what many considered to be a hostile press unsympathetic to the Catholic practice of priestly celibacy or the Church's moral teaching in the areas of contraception, abortion, and homosexuality. The deeply ingrained fear of anti-Catholicism strengthened defensiveness.[26] Lastly, the contentious arguments over apostolic authority reflected in birth control, women's ordination, and moral probabilism so positioned the leadership in relationship to the laity as to make the ceding of some positional authority an extraordinary act. The initial response then, while perhaps typically ecclesiastical and perhaps characteristic of any closed professional system, was at the same time revelatory of broader social, cultural, political, and ecclesial patterns in the society itself. New ethical horizons are not easily created on an organizational level by people shaped through custom and habit.[27] What is needed is a "triggering event" engendering a "constitutive moment" when significant new institutional choices are made and established "cultural patterns" are broken.[28] That moment would not occur for some years.

1988–1994: Mobilizing Alternative Institutional Approaches

ALTHOUGH THESE INSTITUTIONALLY ENTRENCHED patterns certainly continued, some changes in the established approach began to occur on multiple levels in the late 1980s. The cases now emerging were largely historic in nature, beyond the statutory limits of most state laws. The first priests began to return from treatment centers. Rising to the surface were questions of diagnosis, placement, disclosure, and pastoral intervention with victims.[29] Older treatment techniques rooted in a twelve-step approach came under criticism; newer, more forensic approaches, which had been mentioned in the 1985 report and had developed in the criminal justice system, finally came to the awareness of some leaders.[30] Insurance carriers reduced the coverage claims in cases of sexual malpractice.[31] Lawyers committed to the cause for the redress of victims' injuries developed more sophisticated legal strategies.[32] Most important, grassroots organizations alienated by the bureaucratic approaches of the initial stage, deeply concerned with the defense of victims' rights and seeking some quantifiable admission of organizational failure, mobilized. Survivors' Network for Those Abused by Priests (SNAP) had its roots in a neighborhood on the South Side of Chicago and was officially formed as a broader advocacy group in 1992, almost simultaneous with another group for victims, The Linkup.[33] During that same summer the *Boston Globe* ran seventeen front-page stories on James Porter, the Fall River priest who would plead guilty in the following year to multiple charges of child sexual abuse.[34] Studies of the impact of priestly abuse of minors on parishes and the diocesan Church community raised to an acute level the dimensions of the problem that went beyond law and individual victims into communal relationships of trust.[35] The Church as a whole appeared to be entering deeply into a spiritual crisis.

In such a context of increased consciousness and programmatic action, the Office of Media Relations for the National Conference of Catholic Bishops, building on recommendations available since 1987, issued a statement in February 1992 intended to guide individual bishops in investigating, removing priests, reporting to civil authorities, and providing pastoral care to victims. The difficulties in establishing a uniform national approach, one that superseded the jurisdictional and canonical authority of the local bishop, were apparent. Some individual dioceses had already adopted significant local policies; others had not. The Canadian Catholic Conference, in response to the poor reaction to the discovery of abuse in the province of Newfoundland, developed a wide-ranging and systemic approach titled *From Pain to Hope* (June 1, 1992).[36] Probably the most influential and proactive response came from the Church in Chicago, where Joseph Cardinal Bernardin on September 21, 1992, enlisted the help of clergy and laity in establishing a comprehensive approach to victim assistance, the screening of candidates, an independent review process, and guidelines for return to ministry.[37] In November, while representatives of SNAP staged a protest outside their gathering, some bishops at the National Conference gathering met with a few adult survivors of sexual abuse.[38] A think tank, which was a subcommittee of the Bishops' Priestly Life and Ministry Committee, was called together in February to discuss sexual abuse. They reported to the bishops at the June 1993 meeting. That same month the first papal statement appeared, and the National Conference established its Ad Hoc Committee on Sexual Abuse.[39] Chaired by Bishop John Kinney, its membership included Cardinal Roger Mahony, Archbishop John Roach, Bishop John Favalora, Bishop David Fellhauer, Bishop Harry Flynn, and Bishop Terry Steib.[40] Within fifteen months, "Restoring Trust: A Pastoral Response to Sexual Abuse" appeared.[41] Much of this activity spanned the time during which Stephen Cook alleged abuse against Cardinal Bernardin; the cardinal submitted to his own review process, and Cook withdrew his allegation in February 1994.[42] It was precisely during this time period of the mobilization of alternative approaches that the case study of the Franciscan friars, which will be described in chapters 2 and 3 of this book, emerged.

1994–2001: Percolation and Institutional Splitting

PETER STEINFELS, ONE OF the most prominent and perceptive commentators on the long-term effects of the scandals, identifies the period after the collapse of the Cook allegation until the outbreak of the Boston scandal in January 2002 as one of relative reprieve.[43] It might be best perhaps to see it as one of grassroots percolation and at the same time the hardening of the divergent sides represented by victim advocacy groups and those within the leadership of the Church fearful of public scandal and committed to the protection of its hierarchical structures. While instances of clerical abuse received less prominence in the national press, they continued unabated in the first published analyses of the crisis.[44] Anger festered just beneath the surface as many local dioceses failed to implement the recommendations of the Ad Hoc Committee. Some very influential bishops opposed the plans, considering national policies to be an infringement of local autonomy.[45] During this period an unending line of court and out-of-court settlements still privileged lawyer-client confidentiality and sealed documentation.

The patterns of managerial reaction continued. In reaction to perceived patterns of institutional resistance, lay advocacy groups and "cause lawyers" furthered their networking to defend victims, change the legal structures, and force public disclosures.[46] Perhaps most indicative of the subtle change in the historical dynamics of the crisis was the extensive profile which the *Indianapolis Star* ran on the Diocese of Lafayette, Indiana, during the week of February 16, 1997.[47] Amid the details of terrible abuse and numerous stories of victims there was an unremitting focus on the activities of the local bishop. A shift had occurred from the malpractice of the abusers to failures of leadership.[48] Ecclesiologically, the central cultural problem had ceased to be that of clerical sexual abuse and was fast becoming one of organizational incompetence and patterned institutional abuse of authority.

Tellingly enough, the *Indianapolis Star* unfavorably compared the actions of the Lafayette diocese with the Archdiocese of Chicago, which indicated important differences in leadership. What had been framed twenty years previously within local-familial-personal-moral terms was now being framed consistently in abstract, legal, systemic, national terms, and around divergent styles in the exercise of episcopal authority.[49] Whereas the Bernardin board involved the laity in extensive consultation and in contact with the victims, the Lafayette bishop was pictured as anguished but removed and somewhat of a law unto himself.[50] Why the divergence? With respect to the Church, what was the relationship between these two different approaches? Could the Church achieve some consistency in its position? In these and other areas the ecclesial tensions over structures and vision seemed to intersect with the cultural polarizations around authority, sexuality, hierarchy, and the ethical use of power. The affairs and patterns of the world cut through the heart of the Church's social body. The historical knots were becoming increasingly taut. A nuclear explosion lay on the horizon.

2002–Present: The Economics of a National Explosion

IN JANUARY 2002 THE *Boston Globe*, based on newly released court records, began its series of articles on the systematic shuffling of predator priests from parish to parish. The names of John Geoghan, Paul Shanley, and Joseph Birmingham continued in the tradition of Gilbert Gauthe.[51] The National Review Board, which interviewed numerous people knowledgeable about the cases, concluded: "The picture that emerged was that of a diocese with a cadre of predator priests and a hierarchy that simply refused to confront them and stop them."[52] In February of 2002 the Voice of the Faithful, a lay group pushing for reform and accountability, was formed.[53] The cardinals met in Rome, April 23–25;[54] in late May, the Archbishop of Milwaukee, who had been accused of sexual impropriety with an adult male, resigned;[55] and the bishops gathered in Dallas, June 12–15, to approve their zero tolerance policy.[56] At the end of the year, Cardinal Law was forced to step down (December 13, 2002). It all happened very quickly and very intensely, revelation succeeding revelation in a now charged society.

In the national conflagration the nuances of different episcopal actions were lost.[57] When the 2002 scandal broke, a sizeable percentage of the bishops had established lay boards, but many of the most prominent ones, the ones most publicly visible on the national scene, appeared to have delayed. The efforts of the Bernardin board and the Ad Hoc Committee on Sexual Abuse disappeared from the public perception; years of careful pastoral work on the part of some clergy and laity were swept aside. The John Jay Report notes that approximately one-third of all the reports were made in 2002 after a delay of almost thirty years.[58] What was being dealt with were historic factual wrongs and selected institutional pathways constructed around a moral interpretation of the past in terms of memory, awareness, responsibility, and accountability. The dike of public exposure had finally broken.

Ripples from the Boston affair spread across the country.[59] At the heart of the issue were hierarchical accountability and the pursuit of justice for those long injured, along with justice measured publicly in the American system by monetary compensation for negligence. Many, feeling they had been consistently reduced to institutional invisibility, saw civil litigation as the only forum in which they could be heard and vindicated.[60] Others interpreted the rise in civil suits as primarily motivated by greed run wild, fueled by a cultural undercurrent of anti-Catholicism and aided and abetted by sensationalism in the media.[61] From January to June 2002 the Associated Press estimated that three hundred lawsuits were filed.[62] One of the most drastic actions occurred in California where the legislature in June 2002 passed a law removing for one calendar year (January through December 2003) the statute of limitations for the filing of civil suits in historic cases of sexual abuse.[63] This action of the legislature eventually precipitated what was referred to publicly in the courts as Clergy I, Clergy II, and Clergy III; it led in Los Angeles to the massive settlement of July 2007. Attempts to remove the statute of limitation on civil suits were also occurring in fourteen states during this period, and efforts continue to the present time.[64] Multiple dioceses declared bankruptcy.[65] In the wake of Boston, as was noted at the beginning of this chapter, countless cases have now been settled, and billions of dollars expended. The society and the Church had moved from institutional invisibility to systemic anger focused on hierarchical malfeasance, all of it measured in economic terms.

So goes the chronological overview, which future historians will clarify, modify, and interpret. The entire situation was a new development in the Church in the United States. Never before had so many elements converged to create a clash of religious, social, professional, political, and economic cultures—to name just a few: the clerical world, family life, media professionals, legal experts, monetary-business systems such as insurance, psychological and medical personnel and institutions, and the universal Church. And the presenting situations were factual criminal and civil misbehavior that demanded justice. The frail and sinful humanity of the Church had been irrevocably revealed.

This history poses for the contemporary believer and society many profound questions of the inevitable entanglement between the Church and the world: In its earthly journey, how can a holy Church be so riddled with sinful members? How can such institutional denial be allowed to continue at the highest levels of the Church? What values and attitudes really shape the relationship between the clergy and the laity? What social and religious factors make criminal activity invisible? How are private and public worlds related and the boundaries between them defined? Who exercises power in the Church and society? How is this power used or shared? What have we learned?

In what follows, I offer some perspective on these questions, particularly as they relate to issues of power, ownership, and prestige in the Church and society. Perhaps a careful examination of some key areas will yield some general answers. Above all, understanding these developments in the light of the Franciscan tradition, I reflect on how all of this history might shape and color the life of some believers, changing in great measure their theological, ethical, ecclesial, and spiritual horizon of belief.

But before those issues can be engaged, it is important to appreciate the density of the experience in its unfolding, its sheer uncertainty, and its many different spiritual and material layers. A simple narrative exposition can give the impression of a bloodless history. But no narrative exposition can wipe away the tears, anger, and alienation expressed by the victims and families of the sexual abuse scandal. Nor can any narrative remove the anguish experienced by the Church at large during these times. Parents, families, friends, church members, people in leadership, priests and bishops also experienced the suffering caused by some in a Church of sinners. Let us now turn explicitly to the challenges of leadership when values collide.

2. CONFESSIONS

WE FIRST NEED TO be trained to mortality in this exile of ours, and to have our capacity developed for gentleness and patience in affliction.

SAINT AUGUSTINE OF HIPPO
The Trinity[1]

My Creator and My Maker,
My Protector and My Purifier, My Beginning and My End,
in my stubbornness I dabbled with your Truth and Life.
In your mercy you showed me the way
through human instruments which you yourself had made.
My Lord, in becoming human,
you chose to embrace the shattering disappointments of
    human life,
the mourning for the lost home, the exile from heavenly bliss,
the separation from the beloved, the orphanage of life.
And from within each person,
you speak the words your Father said at the beginning of time
for all of us to hear, this day:
"Let there be light." (Gen. 1.3)

NO ONE IS IMMUNE from the history of the times in which they live, and the responses of faith that we make to any given situation are firmly embedded in the culture and Church in which we receive the Word of God. As noted in the introduction, on June 8, 1988, I, along with seven other friars and a provincial secretary, was elected to lead the Franciscan Friars of the Province of Saint Barbara. I served as Provincial Minister until January 1997. What none of us knew at the time of the election was that all of us would be led during the next twenty years into the depths of a Church that would experience profound pain in its members and deep scandal from within the ranks of its own leadership. We were about to encounter events that would challenge our faith and require a rereading of life in the light of the Word of God and our own religious and ecclesial vocations. In this chapter and the one following I would like to share with the reader some of the outlines of our collective story as we struggled to deal with the issues of sexual abuse committed by some of our own members. The story has many twists and turns, difficulties, and, in retrospect, some blessings. To that extent it may serve as a case study shedding some light on the national crisis of the church.

As an historian, it is clear to me that all of these events have multiple significations and multiple interpretations. The intentions of the participants are generally unknown, and a multitude of factors beg for consideration. With the sexual abuse crisis, we are, after all, dealing with an institutional and spiritual crisis of some depth, touching different sectors of the Catholic community.[2] I am approaching the interpretation from my own perspective as an historian and the responsibilities given to me in a temporary position of leadership. It is in the light of the general history of the abuse crisis (Chapter 1) and context of this personal narration (Chapters 2–3) that the subsequent chapters on community, hierarchy, and power (Chapters 4–6), ownership and freedom (Chapter 7), and scandal and the Church (8) will emerge. All of this will be interpreted through the lens of the Franciscan tradition of spirituality and theology.

The Collision of Values and the First Learnings

ANY INDIVIDUAL OR FAMILY victimized by clergy sexual abuse can make many ethical demands on religious leaders. Principal among them are the ethical demands that follow actions of betrayal and the abuse of a pastoral and spiritual relationship. The individual and the family need to be listened to, and the truth of their testimony needs to be believed. Actions must be taken. They may justly cry out with the psalmist, "Even my friend who had my trust and partook of my bread, has raised his heel against me" (Ps. 41.10; John 13.18). Or, "Give us our rights against our opponent" (Luke 18.3). For myself as a leader and those of us on our team the first learnings of these truths occurred in a context where various values collided. Before beginning a detailed and more specific narration I would like to present two cases in a very general way.

Our first instances of clergy sexual abuse of minors surfaced in March 1989, and then in the Spring of 1992. Initially, a Franciscan priest, a member of our Province, was accused of abusive behavior. The abuse was horrendous and touched an entire family. It had occurred at our minor seminary in Santa Barbara, St. Anthony's. Some of the accusations fell within the statute of limitations, and the civil authorities brought criminal charges. The friar was indicted. Although I felt canonically bound to provide a legal defense, the friar's lawyer advised him not to speak with me, and those of us in leadership were advised by legal consultants not to contact the family involved. This advice blocked our pastoral outreach to the victims. In retrospect, I am able to frame the question that unconsciously weighed on me even at that early stage. Why must the rules of the legal forum be allowed completely to trump the truths embedded in a pastoral relationship? The adversarial nature of the criminal proceedings and the protracted time for plea bargaining added to the isolation and harm done to everyone concerned. Our own reluctance to contact members of the faith community compounded this experience. I had a great deal to learn.

Eventually, the friar did not contest the indictment and served a six-month jail term, followed by six months in a therapeutic treatment program. He never returned to ministry. It was later correctly pointed out to me and to all of us in leadership that the failure to provide personal pastoral outreach ran contrary to the ecclesial ideal presented by St. Paul: "The body is one and has many members, but all the members many though they are, are one body; and so it is with Christ. . . . The eye cannot say to the hand, 'I do not need you,' any more than the head can say to the feet, 'I do not need you' " (1 Cor. 12.12, 21). In other words, the advice we had received and followed led to the direct collision between three significant normative guides to our lives as citizens and believers: the canon law, which governed the Church and religious superiors; the civil law and its expected behaviors, which governed society; and the rule of the Gospel about how members of the same faith community are to treat each other. It was a situation that many leaders and people in the early years of the abuse scandal may have found themselves in, to one degree or another.

We were blessed. Eventually, direct communication and the reestablishment of relationships came. It was an act of trust on both sides. Those of us in leadership were able to meet with the good family that had been so severely harmed. A painful but fruitful dialogue began about the need for candor and fidelity in pastoral relationships. The legal arena simply could not be allowed to control the situation. A comprehensive approach to clerical misconduct needed to be established, one that included therapeutic help for the victims, communication with those affected, the necessity of improving education among the friars, and a revision of the general province policies that had already been adopted.[3] Based on the insights produced from our meetings and our own growing experience with the issue of sexual abuse in the Church, between 1990 and 1992 the Franciscan province adopted firmer guidelines for pastoral outreach and intervention in situations of abuse and the education of our friars. We scrutinized and modified admissions policies, engaged professionals in the field of psychosexual development and sexual deviancy to educate the entire community and those in formation, and adopted a clear and precise policy on sexual misconduct. The new policy established an investigative team, directed the members of the province to "cooperate fully with all public, official investigating agencies," and mandated compliance with state laws regarding the reporting of child abuse. The policy called for communication with and pastoral and financial support structures for victims and family members. It issued strict guidelines evaluating and monitoring the public ministry of anyone accused.[4] In doing all of this, we were following in some measure steps that were being taken in other parts of the country.

In the Spring of 1992 another case emerged that brought an even greater collision of values. It placed offense upon offense. This violation had occurred years before in the 1970s, when the victim, a boy, was very young. At the time of the abuse the friar was director of the Santa Barbara Boys Choir, a position he had held while a teacher at St. Anthony Seminary. This charge did not fall under any criminal statute. The civil authorities could not be engaged. The offense was communicated directly to me. I was horrified. The priest-friar was placed on immediate administrative leave, and I sent him for a specialized psychosexual diagnostic evaluation with an understanding that the friar's future treatment and removal from ministry would be based on the testimony of the family and the most professional recommendations available. He admitted the abuse in question and within a few weeks entered into an established treatment center for sexual abuse. He would never again return to ministry.

Aggrieved parents justly pushed for open disclosure. At that time, our leadership team, in the context of an increasing national picture that the Church was not adequately responding to the sexual abuse crisis, committed itself to develop a course of action that was responsive to everyone involved and to the victims who were still anonymous. We knew that help could be provided on a personal level as individual victims came forward. That was a pathway with which we were familiar. We were now faced with an entirely new and central challenge. Because the friar who had committed the offense had supervised the Boys Choir, the clear question became: How many other boys had been abused? We clearly needed to ascertain this information, but how? Different approaches produced different unresolved challenges. Was it best to wait for specific information and the names of individual boys to be identified by the friar himself? In this case individuals could be contacted and some privacy protected. How long would this take? Or should we make an immediate blanket contact with all members of the Boys Choir, past and present, in the hopes of alerting the public and surfacing possible victims? How would this affect the current choir? How would the information be made available to people, and how would the families and the community be affected by the disturbing news that one of their boys may have been abused?

During this time, we consulted several lay professionals in the field of psychological intervention. They had no clear picture of the course to be taken. A blanket contact was unnecessarily invasive at this point as it would lack specificity and possibly be injurious to innocent people and other victims. Yet, this advice was at odds with our own growing but as yet tentative awareness of the demand for full public disclosure. Should we defer to the experts? These were the questions that were asked at the time. Members of the laity who were aware of the situation disagreed as to the course to be taken. Some argued that the crisis should be dealt with in as private a forum as possible; individual family units needed to be treated with great care. Others, who turned out to be correct, continued to push for open investigation. Many people could not imagine a clear pathway through the storm of colliding opinions and values.

The Franciscan administration, with myself as their leader, decided for the time being that further information was needed before an exact course of action could be determined. We wanted the names of individual victims, specific knowledge of the years of the abuse, a profile of the abusive activity; we wanted to be responsive to a deeper consensus in the laity. We needed to understand how to balance the protection of privacy against the need to make the abuse public. Yet, we chose to temporarily wait. Sensitivity to individuals and personal situations, the specificity of the information that was disclosed, the timing and method of action appeared to be important. This difficult situation in which so many values collided would last three months. We still had much to learn.

During this time, from June to September, awareness that so much harm had been tragically foisted on good people, a dawning horror that our own religious brothers had engaged in the worst type of misconduct, anger at them and that the activity had brought shame upon all of us, a desire for justice for those injured, and fear for what this might mean in the future plagued those of us charged with addressing the terrible wrongs that had been done. The facts were clear enough and could not be denied. Uncertainty and a sense of being overwhelmed joined hands with a resolute firmness to do what was necessary to help others and redress wrongs. Some new pathway needed to be developed, but what it was remained just over the horizon. For myself, a new depth began to emerge from the psalm: "Behold you are pleased with sincerity of heart, and in my inmost being you teach me wisdom" (Ps. 51.8). Some years later I was to read in Augustine: "But you, O Lord, Ruler of all things in heaven and on earth, who make the deep rivers serve your purposes and govern the raging tide of time as it sweeps on, you even use the anger of one soul to cure the folly of another."[5]

The Demand for Action

IN SEPTEMBER OF 1992 the situation in Santa Barbara clearly exploded beyond the boundaries of personal contact and individual family concerns. Common knowledge of people's distress, contact between members of the local community, anxious telephone calls, and private conversations definitively moved information and fears from the private sector to the public forum. The local people in Santa Barbara began to speak in unison about the need for public pastoral action. In addition, in

September, finally the name of someone else who had been abused came to the surface. Time and events had now brought the possibility of and the demand for a public systemic approach. Direct outreach into the community was now required. Members of the laity had taught us some great truths.

There were few models of action, but the partially successful and healing community work of Bishop Harry Flynn in Lafayette, Louisiana, was known to us and provided some indication of how to approach the situation through listening sessions and pastoral action.[6] Those in leadership in the Franciscan friars, myself included, decided on a three-pronged response. A specific letter offering support was sent to the recently identified member of the Boys Choir who had been abused; in early October, working as closely as possible with the local leaders of the Boys Choir, a blanket letter, signed by the Provincial Minister and the Board of Directors of the Boys Choir, was sent to all the members of the Santa Barbara Boys Choir who had been part of the choir from 1976 to 1991. The letter stated that some members of the choir had been abused, asked for any other injured parties to come forward, and promised that help would be provided. It further stated that we had retained "the services of an independent psychologist . . . to assist individuals and families of the Boys Choir in dealing with this matter." In addition, a friar trained in counseling was available to "all parties concerned for spiritual or counseling assistance."

Last, the letter announced a community meeting for October 28, at 7:00 p.m., "to answer questions, share common concerns, and express the many feelings [th]at inevitably emerge in this type of situation." The letter was publicly posted at the seminary where there was a local Sunday worshipping community, and anyone who wished to take advantage of the meeting was invited to do so. "That which was hidden had now become revealed" (Matt. 10.26). And that which was revealed demanded a public forum in which people could express their feelings and concerns. Personally, I hoped that the province's outreach and the open meeting attended by me, a representative of the Boys Choir, and a trained psychologist would go some way toward restoring trust.

All of this happened while the national scene was developing in new directions. The Archdiocese of Chicago released its new policies and procedures on clerical sexual misconduct with minors on September 21, 1992. The Benedictine community at St. John's Collegeville took an open and public approach to discover cases of misconduct by the Benedictines.[7] During the national meeting of bishops, Cardinal Roger Mahony met with adult survivors of clergy sexual abuse, and the National Conference of Catholic Bishops pledged "again our care and concern for all victims of abuse."[8] In retrospect, the Franciscan friars were only one such group trying to break from the past and to address a new situation of great harm marked by a collision of perspectives and values. As was discussed in Chapter 1, the period from 1988 to 1994 witnessed the development of numerous alternate approaches to the handling of the sexual abuse crisis. Ten years later this general evolution and its complexity would all but disappear, swept away in the wake of some leaders still trying to manage institutional cancer by clinging to an inheritance of invisibility, legal maneuvering, or managerial shuffling.

The Challenging Year of Work

ALTHOUGH IT WAS UNKNOWN at the time, the public meeting of October 28, 1992, would inaugurate a full year of activity to address the problem of the sexual abuse of minors. In detailing some of the events, three specific time frames will be singled out for consideration. Each period represents a unique range of problems that needed to be considered in a fast-evolving situation. I have included within this narrative of chronological events three reflections that occurred to me during this year and which I have pondered now for some time. For me, these indicate a few of the deeper spiritual and ecclesial issues underlying the crisis. Their meaning will be unpacked in the more systematic and theological portions of this book (Chapters 5–8). Once again: "The soul does not have illumination, except when considering the Church in relation to the times."[9]

October–December 1992: The Development of a Comprehensive Approach

On October 28, 1992, as the leader of the Franciscan Friars of Saint Barbara, I met with approximately seventy-one active Catholics to "discuss recent revelations of sexual abuse involving two Franciscan priests in separate cases," one that had occurred twelve years before and one three years before.[10] Although the meeting had been called to consider the abuse that occurred in the Santa Barbara Boys Choir, the parents of a newly disclosing victim spoke and revealed that the abuse had also extended to their son, a student of St. Anthony Seminary. A general investigation of the Boys Choir was not enough; the situation now demanded a comprehensive response to abuse at the high school seminary. During the meeting other grievances against the Church arose. The failure to admit women to the priesthood, the arbitrary use of authority, and historic instances of abuse in other parishes were all raised as topics by those present. Looking back on it, I would say that the sexual abuse of minors emerged initially from specific instances of what would become known later as widespread wrongdoing; it would also come to carry on a symbolic level the emotional freight of other frustrations associated with the institutional Church, a topic that will be pursued in Chapter 4. At the meeting on October 28, a persistent challenge arose from grievously offended parents and members of the community: "What are you going to do about it?" As the difficult gathering closed, I promised a timely response within about a month. There would need to be another meeting.

In the next month, several realities shaped the developing

response. As all the instances of abuse were historic in nature, a criminal forum involving public authorities was not available. Previous experience with juridical norms and adversarial legal procedures while bringing some resolution in the civil arena had also indicated that a juridical approach often severed or restricted in an unhealthy way the relationships between parties. Such approaches did not always provide a sense of being heard and understood. In addition, given the long relationship between the community of worship at the seminary and the Franciscan friars, it was necessary that any comprehensive plan would need to be in some measure collaborative. The overall goal was to help victims, address the misconduct, and at the same time rebuild trust between people. The national picture of abuse seemed to require a move beyond strictly clerical or canonical solutions to some type of systemic approach that would involve all the members of the Church in addressing a collective and public harm. "Now the body is not one member, it is many. If the foot should say, 'Because I am not the hand I do not belong to the body,' would it then no longer belong to the body? . . . The eye cannot say to the hand, 'I do not need you,' any more than the head can say to the feet, 'I do not need you.' Even those members of the body which seem less important are in fact indispensable" (1 Cor. 12.14–15, 21–22).

Both the local community of lay people and the provincial administration worked actively but independently during the next month to develop a comprehensive plan to address the abuse. In Santa Barbara, on November 18, a group of concerned laity gathered at St. Anthony Seminary. Those present reviewed the responses to sexual abuse in Newfoundland, Canada, by the Royal Commission and Archdiocesan Commission of Enquiry. There was discussion of the need for an Independent Commission for the local situation. On November 30 this lay group outlined their recommendations: Develop a plan to determine victims and offenders; develop a plan for assistance to victims; monitor, document, and report on implementation of plans; obtain agreement on removal of offenders from opportunities for abuse; make recommendations to the Franciscans about a future action program on this issue throughout the Saint Barbara Province.[11]

At the same time, the Franciscan friars consulted with experts and knew about the Royal Commission of Enquiry. They were moving separately but in a direction parallel to that of the laity. We were considering putting into place a model of lay-religious cooperation with an essentially pastoral purpose, one a little like Chicago's but focused on victims, families, and community members. On November 24, I wrote to the friars in Santa Barbara both to encourage them to persevere and to present our decided course of action: In the next ten days, "we will be presenting a comprehensive plan. . . . I think we can be very proud of the policies and procedures and the approach that we have taken up to this time. We will also present a way of dealing with the pastoral situation at Santa Barbara through education, through meetings with the people, retreats, workshops, and other forums. At the same time we recognize our duty to discover the precise truth of the allegations which are made and give people a forum in which they can express themselves. For that reason, we probably will be notifying many past students of St. Anthony Seminary and also conducting a Board of Inquiry which will attempt to deal with the situation in the best way possible. I believe that this is pastorally sensitive and appropriate for the occasion. In taking these steps we are following our own comprehensive plan of dealing with friar misconduct and trying to pick up the best elements which are present in so many other areas of the Church."[12]

The lay members of the local community in Santa Barbara and the Franciscan friar leadership came together on December 4, 1992. On behalf of the Franciscans I delivered our answer to the challenges that had been presented at the October 28 meeting. In the public presentation the development of our current policies was first reviewed and then further steps announced:

We pledged to create a separate review board to advise the province and to make recommendations "to insure the integrity of the friars' lives and ministries as these relate to minors." The "Comprehensive Approach" also committed the Franciscans within the next month to establishing a formal Board of Inquiry for St. Anthony Seminary: "The board will function independently of the provincial administration and will report directly to the Provincial Minister [my own official title]. The board has an essentially pastoral purpose, acting for the good of the victims, the well being of the community and the friars and the integrity of the Church. It is fact-finding, consultative and advisory, not adversarial or adjudicative." The Board's task was "to process the results of past pupil contacts and investigate the allegations of sexual misconduct with minors and related issues at the seminary." Composed of six members, the Board would follow Province policies on active care for victims. Its full composition and procedures would be solidified during the next month.[13] In contrast to the meeting of October 28, the gathering ended somewhat amicably, both sides satisfied that they had acted together as best they could, albeit from different positions and with still unresolved feelings.[14]

A Reflection on History and the Creation of All Things in the Word

The events that transpired so quickly between May and December 1992, coming as they did on the heels of the first case of the sexual abuse of minors, were profoundly disturbing for the Franciscan friars, for those in leadership, certainly for the families who had been traumatized, and for many in the local Catholic community. With respect to the Franciscans, facts did not permit the luxury of denial or avoidance or simply indifference. Our initial shock reflected in a small way the experiences of many others in the Church in the United States. And there would be more shocks to come. A new and undeniable awareness was emerging. What did this outburst of immoral and criminal behavior mean? How was it possible that such activity could occur within the Church, perpetrated by its own clergy charged with the spiritual care of people? How could it be that people who were seen as partners in the ministry, brothers in profession, priests who had performed many good deeds and were popular and well loved by many good people, in fact, good persons producing good fruit, how could they have performed such acts of betrayal? And where could one place one's confidence? The hierarchy appeared frightened; the moral integrity of one's brothers seemed compromised; the help of experts, vague; the ordinary mechanisms of the civil and social order working for justice, inadequate. Could a person trust himself, when his knowledge had been proven to be ignorance, his heart's affinities misplaced, his central identity judged by others complicit in a class of malefactors?

In such a situation, good and evil, Church and world, sacred and profane, appeared now no longer as separate spheres of existence, clearly located by precise moral judgments, obedience to positional authority, allegiance to the clear and distinct knowledge of the catechism, or acceptance of the established pathways of social order; good and evil were in fact invisibly and at times visibly entangled together in a Church and a world and a self that bore the flawed and sinful marks of a shared pilgrimage through time. They had migrated into the crevices of the human will, where they had always resided (Matt. 7.20–23).[15] It was an experience of profound dis-location, a descent into dis-order: "Suddenly the curtain of the sanctuary was torn in two from top to bottom" (Matt. 27.51).

In the midst of this experience, in late December of 1992, I was reading *Summer Meditations* by the Czech leader Václav Havel. I had been familiar with his much earlier essay "The Power of the Powerless," in which he had described how the small actions of truth on the part of many people could topple a society honeycombed with lies. Individual actions of protest, over time, could come together to form a whole movement or

people with a common purpose. For him, that movement gave
birth to the fall of communism in Czechoslovakia, the "velvet
revolution." Now, having witnessed the collapse of an old order
and the birth of the new, Havel reflected in his *Meditations* on
something he had not anticipated: When communism fell there
occurred the simultaneous public emergence of the human
propensity toward evil. He wrote: "The return of freedom to a
society that was morally unhinged has produced something it
clearly had to produce, and something we therefore might have
expected, but which has turned out to be far more serious than
anyone could have predicted: an enormous and dazzling explosion of every imaginable human vice. A wide range of questionable and at least morally ambiguous human tendencies, subtly
encouraged over the years and, at the same time, subtly pressed
to serve the daily operations of the totalitarian system, have
suddenly been liberated, as it were, from their straitjacket and
given freedom at last. . . . The authoritarian regime imposed a
certain order—if that is the right expression for it—on these
vices (and in doing so "legitimized" them in a sense). This order
has now been shattered, but a new order that would limit rather
than exploit these vices, an order based on freely accepted
responsibility to and for the whole of society, has not yet been
built—nor could it have been, for such an order takes years to
develop and cultivate."[16]

Havel's experience of birthing a new society and the time
that it would take gave me great courage. It is not that I believed
that the Church or American society was comparable to a totalitarian regime. They are not. The analogy in many respects
limped. Still, from my understanding of history I knew that the
older constricted order of things in the Church in some ways
had bred its own vices very much related to the patterns of
invisibility described in Chapter 1. During the 1960s, this order
collapsed, and many of us experienced the dissolution of something we had inherited—perhaps an attitude, or a vision, or an
understanding of faith, or an image of the Church, or a social

arrangement that suddenly appeared inadequate, unequal, even at times exclusionary. So also new "vices" began to be identified and behaviors that had been hidden suddenly became visible. The older public protestations of perfection and holiness and customary pathways of relating could no longer contain the new reality. Our ethical horizon changed. In such circumstances, a new creation was needed (Col. 3.10). The light needed to be separated from darkness, the inherited Christian world from the emergent Christian world (Gen. 1.3; John 1.5).[17]

As I experienced it, the scandal of the sexual abuse crisis seemed to cut even more deeply than these questions of institutional change. I would describe the experience as something like this: For the person who does not have the luxury of disengaging from history and who believes from within a community of faith, in a context where the containment of good and evil seems to have collapsed, it becomes necessary to try to discover an ordering of things that can encompass in justice and mercy the disorder of all things. Is it not true that standing within relationships that at times fail one searches for a relationship that endures forever? New depth is given to the biblical comment: "Though the grass withers and the flower wilts, the word of our God stands forever" (Isa. 40.8, cf. 51.6; Matt. 24.35; Heb. 12.27). In the situation of the discovery of sexual abuse in the Church, what would it mean if we said, on some level and without abandoning our love and faith in the Church, the Church wilts but "the word of God stands forever"? What does it mean to live from this Word of God? As the crisis unfolded I began to reflect:

> This Word creates; this Word blesses; this Word guides;
> this Word defends good and condemns wrong; this Word
> strengthens in distress, encourages in exile; this Word
> heals; this Word is merciful, compassionate, clear, far-
> sighted, patient, educative, just but not judgmental, life-
> giving. This Word takes flesh. Spoken from eternity, it can-
> not be silenced; it does not return void; it accomplishes its

task. It need not fear death, destruction, fruitlessness, lone-
liness, abandonment. This Word is determined, not anxious; fierce, not violent; passionate, not clinging, shaping
itself to each situation. (Cf. Wis. 7.7–8.1)
This Word is **Being.**
"Through him all things came into being, and apart from
him nothing came to be. Whatever came to be in Him
found life, life for the light of men." (John 1.3)

For some, as I would learn, to endure the pilgrimage of history and the "wide range of questionable or at least morally
ambiguous human tendencies" and still begin to see in history,
in people, and in oneself, the goodness of being, it is necessary
to anchor oneself most deeply in the "Word that stands forever" and in a community and people who try to speak this Word.
It is necessary to hear that this Word's speech to each human
being, no matter how shamed and no matter how much in need
of discipline and healing, is only "Yes" (Col. 1.18–22).

January–May 1993: Responsibilities

The Board of Inquiry into St. Anthony Seminary, which had
been announced at the meeting on December 4, met for the first
time January 14–15. Six people had been chosen by the provincial administration for this difficult task: A practicing lawyer
skilled in family law and mediation, Geoffrey B. Stearns, who
would chair the Board; three psychotherapists, two of them spe-
cializing in the area of child abuse, a third in treating adult male
survivors and sexual offenders; a lay member of the local worshipping community, a father whose son had gone to St.
Anthony Seminary; and a Franciscan friar from another
province. Together with myself they fashioned "a set of guidelines and procedures for the board, defining its mandate,
authority, priorities, and tasks."[18] The Board's task, as mentioned above, was essentially pastoral. Its mandate was to
"assess the nature and extent of the reported sexual abuse of

minors at St. Anthony's Seminary from the school year 1964–65 to the time of the seminary closure in 1987" and to report these findings to the Provincial Minister. It would "follow the provincial policies on active care for victims."[19]

Although it was first envisioned that the Board of Inquiry would function for only a few months, the task proved daunting and much more extensive than planned. The Board met monthly for three-day sessions for almost ten months. It worked assiduously to contact all former students, eventually making an effort to reach over 950 former seminarians. Letters and personal interviews were conducted, new outreach to members of the Boys Choir initiated, therapy process guidelines developed, a resource packet assembled for identified victims, parents of victims, and others. The Board met monthly with interested members of the local worshiping community. It forged a working relationship with the press. It interviewed former students who responded and who "indicated they had been victimized," weighing the allegations and maintaining the confidentiality of those who came forward. Eventually it would find that thirty-four boys had been abused.

One of the Board's chief tasks was to "facilitate victims requesting and receiving therapy paid for by the Franciscan province." Those who wished to "remain anonymous to the Franciscan Province" were assigned a code number. Rather than seek insurance monies, the Franciscans had decided to provide counseling out of their own resources so as to avoid any intrusiveness into the lives of identified victims. The Board advised the Provincial about friars who had already been identified as offenders and helped to locate appropriate evaluation centers and offender treatment programs. With respect to offenders who might be newly identified, the Board assessed and reported the offense to the Provincial Minister. With this information I in turn interviewed the friar, placed him on administrative leave, sent him to an established diagnostic evaluation center for sexual misconduct, and with the information available from all the sources disciplined him. All of this was standard procedure, and by then I had realized that presumption of truth needed to be in favor of the victim. Eleven individuals were eventually identified by the inquiry. Friars were removed from public ministry, evaluated and treated, placed in severely restricted ministry, and ordered to have no contact with minors. In these and other ways a collaborative relationship insuring substantial outreach to victims and appropriate disciplining of friars occurred.[20]

The full story and assessment of this collaboration, pastoral in nature and respectful of different competencies and responsibilities, is beyond the scope of this present work. However, two significant elements that have implications for the future analysis and also communicate some of the underlying issues should be noted. The first issue relates to the nomenclature and composition of the Board. When the Board began to contact former students, as, for example, in its initial letter of February 1993, it identified itself as "Independent Board of Inquiry Regarding St. Anthony Seminary." Why the word "Independent," a nomenclature that seemed purposely oblivious to the pastoral initiatives of the Franciscan Friars? With respect to composition, why did the Board consist of predominantly lay professionals, both Catholic and non-Catholic? These questions certainly occurred to many at the time, and I myself had initially objected to the use of the word "Independent." In describing what I learned at the very end of the process I noted: "We have learned that competent and professional lay people can establish an objective view of how offenders should be evaluated and then disciplined. We realize now the true value of a collaborative process of discovery and ongoing resolution. It is significant that the Board itself is composed of religious and lay people, people of different faiths, men and women of good will."[21] What I was to come to understand was that for the truth about abuses of power to emerge into the open, it is important to create safe places where anonymity and confidentiality, if requested, can be maintained, and where those who come forward can be assured, as much as possible, of objective listening. Institutionally, the Board could be described as a mediating structure. Such places are not necessary in all situations, but trust and relationships once lost or weakened must often be mediated through the actions of another.

Second, from the very beginning of the events in Santa Barbara, the local press covered the story. They too had their public responsibilities.[22] In an open society, maintaining confidentiality "without creating the appearance of perpetuating secrecy" presented a difficult challenge for the Board.[23] Almost immediately, after its second meeting on February 18 and after the initial contact letters had been sent, a local newspaper *The Independent* reported: "More of the friars who formerly staffed St. Anthony's residential school for boys or worked with the choir are coming under suspicion for possible child molestation. . . . [C]hair Geoffrey Stearns announced that as many as nine altogether may be implicated." The Board had made no comments as to the number of friars involved, and a month later the chair of the Independent Board of Inquiry corrected the information. Where it had come from, no one knew. The Board decided to issue a press release in March, communicating precise information and enlisting the "help of the media in disseminating the message that it wants to hear from any person, whether former student, member of the Boys' Choir or otherwise, who was the recipient of either physical or non-physical contact by a member of St. Anthony's staff or faculty, which hurt him or left him feeling confused, frightened, guilty or bad about himself." The news media were allowed to attend the monthly community meetings as long as they identified themselves; people were allowed to speak "off the record." In order to assure victims of safety and "prevent premature condemnation through speculation of innuendo of any friar" the Board kept all names confidential and refused to disclose any numbers until the final report.[24]

While the Independent Board of Inquiry struggled and eventually found its relationships with the local press constructive in terms of its own information, the Franciscan friars reading the news reports found the stories upsetting, embarrassing, almost searing. Headlines regularly appeared: "St. Anthony's Mails Out 400 Letters in Molestation Inquiry"; "Child Molestation Inquiry"; "More Accusations in St. Anthony's Child Molestation Inquiry"; "More Priests Accused by Ex-Students"; "Angry Audience Blasts Mahoney [sic] on Seminary Sexual Abuse Scandal"; "Molestation Inquiry Plugs On." Three friars who had been publicly named were identified in print; pictures of concerned parents and community members appeared; quoted comments expressed the anger and intensity of the unfolding situation.[25] The activities of the Board took center stage; only tangentially was it mentioned that the Franciscan friars had initiated the investigation or that it was in large measure collaborative. The news appeared to be all bad. The community of the city awaited monthly revelations of wrongdoing. The Old Mission Franciscan community, separate from the seminary but contiguous to it, felt its long and distinguished record in service to the local Church and people tainted; some members became silent, unable to respond to what was happening.

To address these public issues, the Franciscans and the Archdiocese of Los Angeles in March and April sponsored a three-part Lenten lecture series, "Breaking the Silence—Protecting the Innocent." Presented by recognized experts, one especially on community trauma, the series was designed "to help us understand the present difficulties that young people may face in their personal relationships."[26] The lecturers indicated particularly the effects of abuse: how the abused individual often feels guilty and responsible for the action, the long-term effects on intimacy, the disbelief of others. Sexual abuse, these experts noted, brings with it an internalized sense of betrayal, powerlessness, stigmatization. Local reports indicated that the series attracted only moderate interest. Still, on all sides, the question was clearly posed for everyone concerned: What does it mean in an open society to be transparent? What is the effect of this necessary openness: In the first and most important instance, upon those who have been wronged; in another way, upon those who have committed the wrong; yet also, upon those touched through word, image, relationships, and responsibilities by the whole affair? How does one approach the ripple effect of the actions of some on the lives of the many? Shame, isolation, confusion, humiliation, abandonment, anger, and silence, all cut in many different directions, with different modalities and levels of interiority. Leadership was not immune.

A Reflection and Prayer on the Incarnation

It is difficult to express the spiritual dimensions of this situation from the point of view of those who were directly engaged in dealing with it on an administrative and communal level. Those skilled in psychological healing tell us there are many necessary mechanisms of defense and mechanisms of engagement, constructive ways to approach challenges of collective suffering: strategies of speaking, personal counseling, group sharing, self-reflection, continuing education, solitary withdrawal, patient endurance—all can be put to effective use. For a person of faith, all of these tools are necessary. Yet one of the most important medicines for collective suffering is simply *presence,* a being-with characterized by solidarity in experience, an accompaniment offered through words, letters, prayers, silent partnership. The shared experience of poverty opens up the opportunity of healing presence, creating bridges for frayed relationships. Emerging from within experience there can be an intuitive sense of suffering with others, an unconscious communion that finds expression in a prayer of intercession for everyone involved, victims, family members, priests, friars, the people of God, and oneself. Something like the following came to me on March 12, 1993:

This morning, Lord,
I feel: lonely, frightened, guilty, abandoned, hurt, powerless,

discouraged, isolated, judged, confused, angry.
Our whole body is being torn and besieged.
Teach me compassion, Lord.

The experience of solidarity in suffering brings with it the recognition that presence to suffering human beings cannot be accomplished without help from another. People who are suffering do not need truths spoken from the outside, nor quick resolutions by power and authority, nor rejection of their persons by those who take refuge in idealized images of their own identity. Friendship is required, a grace given from above that touches one in a human way (cf. 2 Cor. 12.9). "A faithful friend is a sturdy shelter, he who finds one finds a treasure" (Sir. 6.14). And this requirement of presence in friendship can be accomplished only if there is a friend stronger than oneself willing to accompany everyone who is suffering. From out of this shared poverty of shame and this need for friendship, gratitude for stronger brothers and sisters occurs. And, most significantly, a different image of the "Word that endures forever" begins to take shape. The Word becomes flesh (John 1.14), one who shares our experience of poverty (2 Cor. 8.9), and from within this experience of shame, isolation, and humiliation (Phil 2.6–11; Isa. 53.4) does not disdain to call us "friends" (John 15.13–17), "brothers" and sisters (Heb. 2.11). And so we pray:

Most gracious God, in the immensity of your Wisdom and the gentleness of your touch, you guide us even when we wander; you heal us even as we cut ourselves; you enlighten us even as we feel ourselves in darkness. Are you not the Word who whispers even when our ears are closed: "By his powerful spirit he looked into the future and consoled the mourners of Zion" (Sir. 48.24). "He heals the brokenhearted, he binds their wounds" (Ps. 147.3). "The Lord is close to the brokenhearted and those who are crushed in spirit he saves" (Ps. 34.19). And did you not

say to your prophet and your Son: "He has sent
me to bring glad tidings to the lowly, to heal the brokenhearted (Isa. 61.1)." And did he not say to us: "Blessed are
they who mourn" (Matt. 5.4)? What more could your Son
do for us:

He renounced heaven, its control,
   And entered into exile, pilgrimage,
Heard people yell at him, the crowd attack him,
   Losing the free speech of his Father and Spirit,
Enduring the taunts of neighbors, the ridicule of those
         around him,
   Receiving denial and rejection from his best friends,
Enduring hunger, nakedness, cold, thirst, weariness, abuse,
   Entering into a land of death,
     Where God is only a star in the night,
     Or a shadow at noonday,
     Or a slight waft of incense beckoning from afar,
     Or hidden in the rock in the desert.
He knew, and he accepted ignorance,
He was eternal, and He entered into time,
He was perfectly loved,
   And He accepted rejection.
Why, Lord, would you do this?
Except that in the friendship who is God you might be
        with us. Amen.

June–November 1993: Responsibilities in Conflict

After an extensive March meeting, as the Independent
Board of Inquiry heard more stories of those who had been
abused, they reported their assessment to me and identified the
friars involved. The ensuing process of action has already been
identified: interview, professional assessment, treatment,
removal from ministry or placement in restricted ministry. It
was a process that continued throughout the year.[27] Since the

entire situation involved cases of a historic nature, ones outside of any statutory regulations, it was very dependent on open communication and trust between the Independent Board of Inquiry making the assessment and myself as the one charged to determine the disciplining of the friar. The Board complied with mandatory reporting laws, adhered to the strictest codes of confidentiality, and had each interviewee sign an Acknowledgment of Purpose and Scope of Operation.[28] It could be sensitive to those who came forward, but it had "no subpoena, disciplinary or other power over any reported offender." It "was not authorized or empowered to identify any offenders not previously known to the public."[29] Although it could invite friars to be interviewed, it could not coerce them to come.

As the leader of the friars, I in turn relied on the judgment of the Independent Board; I had no access to those coming forward, many of whom for good reasons chose to remain anonymous. With respect to those accused of misconduct, canon law, revised in the aftermath of the Second Vatican Council and which governed the office of Provincial which I held, protected each person's right to a good name and his right to privacy; it forbade a superior to induce a manifestation of conscience; it restricted the application of the vow of obedience to force an individual to cooperate in treatment.[30] *The Constitutions of the Order of Friars Minor,* presenting the governing norms of the friars, demanded that each friar, no matter what was done, was still to be treated with charity and justice. I could interview the friars and determine their fitness for ministry. Given the confidentiality under which the Independent Board worked, I could not identify the names of the accusers in speaking with the friars; in most cases I did not know who they were. I could describe the information received but could not force the friar to reveal his own activities. And what if the information from the Board and the information coming from the friar conflicted? How could accuracy be assured? I had learned that denial is so high in these instances that any prudential decision should always favor the protection of the minor. Yet, in doing so, it was possible to skate perilously close to the violation of some fundamental legal and moral norms protecting those who had been accused, guarding their human dignity.

In such a situation, if either the Board or the Province moved outside of its legal and moral constraints by violating confidentiality or rolling over human rights, the entire process would have entered into another and more problematic forum. Betrayal of responsibilities would have compounded the wrong and initiated a swirl of new but equally impossible conflicts. If the experience of legal procedures had indicated their adversarial and incomplete nature, the experience now of pastoral procedures revealed unanticipated difficulties. In actuality, the Board acted professionally within its human limits. The friars were cooperative in accepting professional evaluations, receiving the necessary removals from or restrictions on their ministerial work, and submitting to a continuing program of monitoring. The public was protected as much as humanly possible from any danger of present or future harm.[31] There was continuing cooperation between the Franciscan administration and the lay professional Board which was set up. One failure in the process was to be discovered only many years later.[32] Still, there could not but have arisen a sense of conflicting responsibilities, colliding values, and frustration with operating constraints. One specific area of conflict bears special consideration.

In the course of its work the Independent Board of Inquiry felt its obligations keenly. So also many other people felt the need for public accountability. The Board was listening to very difficult stories of abuse and meeting monthly with the larger community; its activities were being reported in the press; many were reading the news stories and speaking with each other. It was inevitable that in this situation some people would feel the need to judge not just the truth of what individuals were saying and doing, but also bring judgment upon the friars in question in order to assure themselves that the risks were being handled in an appropriate

fashion. To do this, in the case of Board members, the psychological and personnel files of the accused would need to be made
available; others in the community would need the names of the
accused to be made public. But how could this be done? The
Board, bound by confidentiality and by its own constraints, could
not reveal any names. They could exercise no authority over the
friar. Canonically and personally, bound by my constraints, I also
could not meet these demands. The system had its limits: The
process was pastoral not adversarial; no procedure existed that
could determine with exactitude the accuracy of the reports;
although in most cases privately admitting misconduct and
appropriately disciplined, individual friars with canonical and
legal rights still remained invisible to those who felt strongly
about an individual's need for specific public accountability. Yet
the system also preserved values of collaboration, compassionate
outreach, the dignity of each person, the confidentiality and safety of victims, the appropriate disciplining of those who had
offended, and the boundaries established by the civil, canonical,
and moral law. As much as possible, justice and mercy were
joined. These dilemmas that encompassed all participants were
complicated and made even more intense by a national image that
the Church was reluctant to address the malfeasance of its clergy
and an emotional atmosphere of fear, anger, defensiveness, mistrust. In the case of the sexual abuse of minors, so terrible is its
wake, a world of clearly defined responsibilities becomes mixed
inextricably with a world caught in webs of suspicion. Simmering
throughout the months of the investigation, the conflicting
responsibilities and demands came to a public climax when the
final version of the report was written in the Fall of 1993.

The report, which was to become known as *Report to
Father Joseph P. Chinnici, O.F.M., Provincial Minister,
Province of St. Barbara, Independent Board of Inquiry
Regarding St. Anthony Seminary,* was completed between late
October and mid-November 1993. The public release was pre-
ceded by several long and sometimes very difficult discussions

between myself, representing the Franciscan Friars, and the members of the Board. From the Board's point of view, its mandate was to assess "the nature and extent of sexual abuse of minors." From my point of view, to understand "extent" one needed also to make a distinction between the horrible misconduct that had occurred and the work and ministry of the good friars who had served well. Both sides, however, shared a common dilemma: How could the report be written so as to communicate such varied matters as the pastoral nature of the process, the accuracy of the presentation, the trauma of the victims, the protection of people's privacy, the public requirements of accountability, the integrity of different realms of responsibility, and people's adherence to their legitimate constraints? Last, how could the reality of collaboration, even if difficult, be maintained and projected for the benefit of everyone?

At first, it was anticipated that the report would be released in late October, but this proved to be impossible given the difficulties. When the delay was announced at an open community meeting, the *Santa Barbara News-Press* carried the following headline: "Sex Abuse Report's Delay Angers Accusers." The report stated, "Parents and former students who claim sexual abuse over decades by St. Anthony's Seminary priests erupted in anger this week when a Catholic official halted release of a report on the scandal until church investigators erase all hints of the priests' identities."[33] I was the "Catholic official." For some, it was a question of the release of the names of the offenders to the public. Trust was at a premium: Who would insure that it would never happen again? This was the conflict the press picked up. For me, there had been extensive communication with the Independent Board; all appropriate disciplinary actions had been taken. The questions involved touched basic issues of the protection of confidentiality for the victims and the human rights of those accused. The intersection of these different perspectives and responsibilities produced, once again, a collision of values.

After continued mutual discussion the Independent Board,

with respect to those areas touching different confidential responsibilities, decided to release a public report that used quantitative information and composite narrative case studies to communicate its findings. No names would be mentioned; nor could any not already in the public forum be inferred. The disagreements, once engaged, had in fact produced something substantial and integral to the entire process. The Board concluded: "We believe the process of meeting and conferring with the Provincial Minister has made for two strong, clear and effective documents: an internal confidential version for use by the Provincial and permanent board for ongoing monitoring and management of friar offenders; and this public version which describes the true nature and extent of the abuse without jeopardizing victims' security."[34] The release of the public report was set for November 29, 1993, but before addressing that event and its aftermath, one last reflection is in order.

A Reflection on the Law of Constraints and Mourning

What can happen when a person of faith is caught in a web of conflicting responsibilities? When, because of circumstances, each step that one takes appears in the eyes of others, and with some justice, to be inadequate? And the actions of others appear in one's own eyes to be less than understanding? There is a human necessity for action that cannot be avoided by those who assume or are given a "freely accepted responsibility," as Havel describes it. And yet positions and responsibilities between good people can easily collide. This is true even between members of the same religious family or Church: "All of them differ, one from another, yet none of them has he made in vain. For each in turn, as it comes, is good" (Sir. 42.25). The experiences that accompany the dilemma, if it is not completely ignored, are certainly ones of rejection by others, anger, frustration, and at times fury. On all sides there is a desire to restore the balance of justice and an indignation that such a balance cannot be accomplished as one sees it (2 Cor. 7.11). The complexity of the situation is beyond personal control.

Responsible agency (even if done out of mere duty) mixes with frightening weakness, partial justice with partial injustice, both in the situation and in oneself. I think Augustine in his second meditation on Psalm 30 describes something like the experience when he speaks about the "law of constraints." "What are these constraints," he asks, "from which we want our souls plucked free? Could anyone list them? Or heap them up, so that we can size them aright? Or suggest suitable means to avoid or escape them?" His short commentary lists four: "our ignorance of anyone else's heart, our tendency often to think badly of a faithful friend and to value an unfaithful one"; our inability to fathom how our own heart will be tomorrow; "the constraints of mortality itself," which occasion us to dislike what is unavoidable; our bad habits, so ingrained, so conflicting with the way we would like to be.[35] Dealing with the question of the sexual abuse of minors in the Church reveals that the law of constraints binds us all into a commonwealth of partial justices.

This law of constraints within a commonwealth of partial justices elicits a range of emotional and affective reactions that have already been named; these reactions in turn can lead to various administrative and professional temptations. First of all, there can arise a personal inner drive to break the relationships that are causing the difficulty by dominating the complexities through power, authority, expertise, or position. This can manifest itself by an excessive appeal to professional identity, so much so that all other perspectives are excluded and the image of reality becomes lopsided, its nuances subsumed into a single monolithic interpretation. This approach issues in the fracturing of any common good. Other types of temptations also arise. For example, outright denial of the situation or capitulation to expert opinions irrespective of one's own responsibilities. Even more attractive, especially when one is dealing with a religious conviction, is the flight into a self-referential enclave of people who are supportive and reassuring that one's own perspective and actions are without flaw, needing to be protected at all costs. My own experience indicates that these temptations are subtle and persistent. If not addressed appropriately they can severely impact how the dreadful reality of clerical sexual abuse is addressed. I am convinced that any future reflection on the history of the sexual abuse crisis that wishes to capture its deeper dimensions will need to take the reality and the emotional impact of the law of constraints seriously. And in the wake of the 2002 events in Boston I believe it must be seriously asked how the law of constraints may have led some in the Church to ignore the institutional alternatives that had been developing up to that time, eclipsing the memory of what had been happening on the part of many by subsuming it into a single interpretive framework dictated by the positional authority of the few. My own experience indicates that a better path for leadership, whether sacred or secular, is patient endurance, the studied recognition of goodness in the other, and the choice to stay in relationship. In the long run these attributes are more productive of the common good. It is a difficult pedagogy, as we shall see in subsequent chapters. On a human level, transformation occurs through commitment to the "law of giving and receiving" (Phil. 4.15).[36]

For a person of faith, in such a situation it can happen that God becomes obscure, the clouds of human conflict muddying the refreshing waters of the Spirit. In his comments on Psalm 30, Augustine, who experienced many constraints, both interior and exterior, those deriving from his ecclesial responsibilities and those deriving from the deeper crevices of his heart, knows that people can "be held fast not by glue but by their office."[37] He answers his own dilemma with the verse from the psalm: "My trust is in the Lord. I will rejoice and be glad of your kindness, when you have seen my affliction, and watched over me in my distress" (Ps. 30. 2,13). Constructively, confronting the law of constraints may elicit not simply the desire to dominate or bitter engagement but also mourning for lost salvation, what the ancients describe as mourning for a wholeness that can be achieved only through the final gift of eternal life. In a commonwealth of partial justices mourning over the incomplete becomes a constituent part of loving and doing justice; in an engaged humility, life is handed over to someone greater, to a final resolution at a future time (John 10.29). The situation lends itself to lamenting prayer: "Lord, in my present situation, I have no choice but to mourn. Help me to mourn in a way that leads to life, not death (2 Cor. 7.10–11). Give me the grace to take comfort from these words of your servant, Irenaeus:"

> To make is proper to God's kindness, and to be made is proper to human nature. . . . If then you hand over to him what is yours, that is, faith and subjection, you will receive his craftsmanship, and you will be a perfect work of God.[38]

And in the midst of such a prayer, a person waits as the consoling Spirit who grants dignity and personal agency descends from above (James 1.17).

> Lord,
>   You are so great, and we are so small,
>   You are so beautiful, and we are so ugly,
>   You are so just, and we are so sinful,
>   You are so strong, and we are so weak,
>   You are so good, and we are so evil,
> But in the bestowal of your goodness, we can be good.
> In the beauty of your love, we can be beautiful;
> In the work of your justice, we can be just;
> In the strength of your gentleness, we can be strong;
> In the gift of your mercy, we can be merciful;
> In you who are Light, we can see. AMEN.

3. INTERSECTIONS IN THE CHURCH AND SOCIETY

> We want to reach God's kingdom, but not to travel there
>   through death;
> yet constraint stands there saying, "This way."
> Do you hesitate to go that way, poor mortal,
> when by that same route God has come to you?
>
> SAINT AUGUSTINE OF HIPPO
> *Expositions of the Psalms1*

THE RELEASE OF THE public report on St. Anthony Seminary was scheduled for November 29, 1993, almost twelve months to the day after the pastoral plan to investigate the allegations of sexual abuse of minors had been announced. During that year much had been accomplished. The Independent Board of Inquiry had met every month to contact former students, gather data, listen to stories, review and evaluate the information received, and report the allegations to the Provincial Minister. I, in turn, had interviewed the accused friars, received outside evaluations of their behavior, removed some from ministry, and limited the activities of others. Simultaneously, the community of friars covering the Western United States, the worshipping community in Santa Barbara, the two papers *The News-Press* and *The Independent,* and the local radio and television stations had followed the developments. Many were anxiously awaiting the formal public presentation of the results. What exactly had happened at St. Anthony Seminary?

The Church in the United States as a whole had also been grappling in a new and intense way with the issues of clerical sexual misconduct with minors. As we have seen, in September of 1992 Joseph Cardinal Bernardin released a new policy for the Archdiocese of Chicago. He himself would fall under this policy when he was sued by Steven Cook on November 12, 1993. The cardinal would eventually be exonerated.[2]

In between these dates, while events in Santa Barbara took their course, the National Conference of Catholic Bishops convened a meeting of specialists on February 21–23 which coincided with the first meetings of the Independent Board of Inquiry.[3] In March, as significant revelations of abuse were occurring privately in Santa Barbara, *60 Minutes* aired its story of the sexual misconduct with several women of Archbishop Roberto Sanchez of Santa Fe, New Mexico.[4] On June 7, while the Franciscan friars and the Independent Board were grappling with mutual responsibilities, the *New Yorker* carried a long article, "Unholy Acts," detailing the "Catholic Church's failure to confront the crisis within its clergy."[5] The next day Pope John Paul II addressed a group of regional U.S. bishops at their international meeting in Rome. At the national June meeting of the entire episcopal conference, its committee of specialists reported: "The allegations of sexual misconduct against Catholic priests and the perceived inability of some authorities to respond with decisive pastoral leadership have resulted in a sustained crisis in the Church."[6] A specialized subcommittee was then formed to deal with the abuse question on a national basis.[7] Throughout the summer, as the Independent Board codified its recommendations for continued supervision of accused priests and the Franciscan friars considered how to form their own permanent review board, revelations continued on the national scene. On October 4, in one of the most notorious cases, James Porter appeared in court to "answer 46 charges of sodomy and indecent assault—charges that date back to his days as a priest in the Diocese of Fall River, thirty years ago."[8]

Unknown to most of the participants in these events, the local scene in Santa Barbara, the national scene in the United States, and the international scene in Rome were soon to intersect. Up to this time, the news in Santa Barbara had been largely confined to the members of the community who had been injured, a historic town, a single school seminary and its students, and to the knowledge of those directly involved in the investigation. What happened next would mark a new phase of history. The ensuing events would open up new dimensions to the meaning of "Church" and new challenges for the life of faith. Initially, it would create for the Franciscan friars an experience of painful national and international exposure, and for many who had been injured a mission for broader social and ecclesial justice.[9] As it developed, it would sweep everyone concerned into the uncharted territory of Church and society, where property, power, and prestige intersect. Before beginning our more systematic analysis of these deeper dimensions, it is to the story of how those intersections developed that we now turn.

A Contemporary Last Supper

ON NOVEMBER 29, 1993, on the feast of All the Saints of the Seraphic Order, in a blinding rainstorm, at the Goleta Community Center near Santa Barbara, California, the members of the Province of Saint Barbara, in conjunction with the members of the Independent Board of Inquiry, in the presence of approximately "fifty victims, parents, and concerned parishioners," in front of reporters from "all the network news shows as well as TV's *A Current Affair*," at 5:30 p.m., released for public consumption a seventy-two-page document revealing that eleven friars had abused thirty-four students of St. Anthony Seminary in the period from 1964 to 1987.[10] Although the extensive media exposure was not something that had been anticipated, the Franciscan friars had committed themselves to the public announcement of the Board's finding. We knew that this was an essential part of both healing and the reestablishment of credibility in the eyes of the community. The public trust had been violated by the offending friars; a public acknowledgment was a necessary part of the process.

Geoffrey Stearns, the chairman of the Board, began the session. He noted that the "report describes a wide range of sexually abusive behaviors perpetrated under a variety of circumstances, spread among the friars in a somewhat even fashion."[11] There had been a total of forty-four friars teaching at the seminary in twenty-three years. Of the eleven involved in abuse, one friar had seven victims, another eighteen; the others, either two victims or one. Six pages described the impact of the abuse on victims, with the following headings trying to summarize what the members of the Board heard: "No one would have believed me over a priest. Am I a homosexual or have I become a homosexual? Had I been a real man, I would have been able to stop the abuse. Even though I know I can trust my girlfriend, I am constantly haunted by the fear she will betray me. I idolized priests, I wanted to be like them. For three months I planned my suicide to make it look like an accident to my family. How can I bring a child into a world this unsafe?" Listed as effects on the life of faith among those abused were: "Loss of spirituality, rejection of Catholicism, rejection of God."[12] Included in the report was "a comprehensive set of recommendations concerning: (1) the prevention of further abuse through screening, training, formulation of guidelines and provision of support for friars; (2) methods of dealing with both known, and any newly reported offenders in a timely and effective manner; (3) ongoing pastoral response to, and support of victims and families; (4) a proactive stance for the Province towards laity in general, e.g., through ongoing education and other prevention work; and (5) scope and functions of the permanent board, referred to as the Independent Response Team, which will operate on a Province-wide basis."[13] The *New York Times* would later describe the case as "one of the largest involving sexual abuse by clergy ever disclosed."[14]

In response to the report, I, as the Provincial or leader, read the following statement: "On behalf of the Franciscan Friars of the Province of Saint Barbara, I come here this evening to do three simple things: to thank the Board of Inquiry for their work; to apologize to the victims and their families; to detail with full conviction a firm purpose of amendment for the evils of sexual abuse which have been committed by our brothers." Identifying the abuse "perpetrated by our own brothers on the victims and their families" as "truly horrific," I apologized to the victims and their families, adding, "I have only admiration for the strong character and goodness of the victims and their families; and I thank them for reminding us of our own sinfulness." I also acknowledged, as was mentioned in the last chapter, learning about "the safe and independent space" in which victims can come forward. I did not name the friars involved but described the steps taken to discipline them and pledged the Franciscans to work with a permanent assessment team who "will work with the Provincial Minister to monitor, and adjust as appropriate, the dispositions of the friar offenders."[15] I concluded: "We as Christians, followers of St. Francis, and members of the Roman Catholic Church, are not afraid of the truth; nor are we afraid to repent and reform. The Gospel of our Lord begins this way; and in this way, His way, is our dignity and peace."[16]

In the next two days, the tragedy which involved human beings in one small place became news affecting the impressions and lives of many other human beings scattered throughout the world. The local events were first carried on the evening television stations at 10 and 11 p.m. In an odd twist of timing, the Cardinal Archbishop of Los Angeles, who had earlier received a copy of the report, left that same evening for Rome on his *ad limina* visit. As would be apparent in the following days, our local events were going to affect the lives of many throughout the world. The next day papers across the United States carried the story in all of its details. A student from St. Anthony's was quoted in the *New York Times:* "I believe God has a twisted sense of humor, and He uses me for His amusement."[17] The press and television news in almost every major country made the local, global.[18]

I spent most of the day on November 30 responding to direct calls from CBS, CNN, NBC, the *New York Times*, *Los Angeles Times*, *San Francisco Examiner*, *Religious News Service*, and various local radio and television stations. The evening news networks headlined the story; the adjective "horrific" entered into the lexicon of television anchors; CNN made it worldwide. *The Asian Times* informed people far away. The Roman papers, *La Repubblica*, *Messaggero di Roma*, and *Corriere della Serra*, commented: "In reality, it is the latest trauma for the American Catholic Church, desirous of turning over a new leaf, combating sexual abuse cases in its midst, taken up more than ever with the ghosts of the past."[19] The Archbishop of a prominent Italian city called up the General Curia of the Franciscans demanding to know what was happening. Friars throughout the world were confronted: One spit at, another shunned, a third, when entering a room in a small city in the Holy Land, watched as everyone immediately departed. A universal web of mass communications united us all in an experience of global nakedness and the shame that accompanies it. Perhaps the words of the psalmist capture it best: "I have been made an outcast to my brothers and a stranger to the children of my mother. Holy Father, zeal for your house has consumed me and the abuses of those who have attacked You have fallen upon me. And against me they have rejoiced and have united together, and many scourges were heaped upon me and I knew not why."[20]

On December 2, 1993, in Santa Barbara, *The Independent* carried its coverage of the event of November 29. The article was accompanied by a full-page picture of representatives of the Province, the Board of Inquiry, and the broader Church. Seated behind a long table in the Goleta Community Center are ten men and one woman, four lay people and six friars, one promi-

nent friar from the local Franciscan community, one priest rep-
resenting the Cardinal Archbishop of Los Angeles, and one fam-
ily member who had been part of the Independent Board of
Inquiry. In the middle of the eleven people, on either side, sit the
Provincial (myself) and the chairman of the Independent Board
of Inquiry. The newspaper reporter notes the import of the icon:
"Lined up behind a long table it looked like a '90s version of
Leonardo da Vinci's *The Last Supper*."

In the weeks following November 29, newspaper articles,
personal encounters, phone calls, a national interview, and
countless letters overwhelmed the administrative offices of the
Franciscan friars.[21] The local event which had become global
elicited cries from many sectors of the Church community. Some
were highly offended: The Franciscan friars have brought public scandal to believers. One friar on the other side of the country wrote: "I deplore the public action and the wrongness. You
accomplished what good? Instead, needless scandal perpetrated.
I place my 50 years of priesthood to strengthen my condemnation of your actions."[22] Private conversations that I heard about
much later repeated the difficulties the exposure had caused for
episcopal leadership. A prominent and high-ranking church-
man, two weeks after the event, in the midst of a routine conversation, dismissed his priest counselor from the meeting. I was
left alone with him. While referring simply to the facts of abuse
with "you have your problems," he took the opportunity to
repeat a host of unfounded rumors and made sure he himself
remained untouched by any scandalous ripples. The responses
of many others in the Church—the criticism could be expressed
in a silent shunning or in overt disapproval—added to the quar-
ry of stumbling blocks for personal belief. In the media the cries
of some connected with victim advocacy groups expressed dis-
satisfaction that the names of offending friars were withheld:
"These men should have been turned over to law enforcement
immediately."[23]

Yet, for the most part, discordant voices were minor, even if well-placed and at the time deeply felt. Something greater clothed our global nakedness with garments of mercy (Gen. 3.21). Portions of the secular press and long-time critics of the bishops lauded the friars for the openness and forthrightness of the investigation.[24] Three archbishops wrote expressing their encouragement, compassion, and prayers; the Bishop of Oakland wrapped his cloak of protection around this son of St. Francis who had been the subject of another ordinary's humiliating words; parishioners, family, and friends reached out to friars; brothers turned to brothers in iron exchanges wrought by the strong arms of shared public shame; unknown laity and religious sisters in abundance expressed solidarity and gratitude; more than 160 supportive letters from the cities in the United States and from Paris and Jerusalem, Rome and Torino, the jungles of Colombia and the plains of Zaire, poured into the administrative offices:

- *From Arizona:* "I had a very hard time sleeping that night. But I awoke the next morning on the Feast of St. John of the Cross and joined the friars for Office of Readings and Morning Prayer. Little by little those initial feelings gave way to a deep serenity and realization that God is leading us through this."
- *From Minnesota:* "You know that your Franciscan brothers and sisters, in particular, will be asking the God of justice that justice, finally, be done, and that healing will happen to all of us."
- *From a former student:* "As a young person at St. Anthony's, I learned that Christian community was possible. I felt loved and supported and I found something to believe in and commit myself to with all my heart. It was my first real experience of moving beyond myself and growing in my capacity to love. Enlarged by this experience, I am better prepared to love and serve those people God entrust[s] to my care today."

• *From Africa:* "I have just heard a piece on the BBC about the abuse of minors scandal that has hit the Province and I just wanted to send you a word of encouragement. . . . Here our problems are different. . . . We live in a situation of total social, economic and political chaos: ethnic cleansing at least as bad as in ex-Jugoslavia, monetary 'reform' that has led me to the brink of despair when I see how it has swallowed up all the savings that I had amassed over the years, and two rival governments. And no end is in sight."

• *From California:* "I know what a terribly heavy cross this is for you to bear and I just want you to know of my brotherly solidarity with you and my prayers that through this terrible experience God will lead us all to still greater things in the life of the Church. 'Where sin abounds, grace does more abound.'"[25]

A Reflection on the Church as the Pilgrim Christ in the Modern World[26]

For those receiving this touch of communion, the international experience in the wake of November 29 revealed a force of goodness present in the field of the world and a Church and its members profoundly networked with each other, made even more interdependent by the exchange of suffering and joy that the modern means of communications both force and create. Apparently, all that it required was the "right occasion actually to emerge into being."[27] "Each individual," Augustine writes in his commentary on Psalm 122, "can cry out from his or her own country, but how is it possible to cry from every extremity of the world? Ah, but Christ's inheritance can."[28] If we are united in our Baptism, we are companioned in our suffering; and in the embrace of communal love, some redemption can occur. In sort of a counterstory not of sin but of grace, just as the revelation of abuse unmasked the weakness and criminal activity hidden from view, so also the act of public penance occasioned the personalization of forgiveness that is at the core of the formation of the global Church. A person need never be afraid to confess. "Help carry one another's burdens," Paul says in Galatians, "in that way you will fulfill the law of Christ" (Gal. 6.2).[29] Without public penance there is no possibility for this dimension of the law of Christ to come forward. The cries emerging from all over the world were those of tears and joy in the spiritual and material exchange of the Body of Christ, revealed for all to see in the breaking of the bread of repentance at a contemporary Last Supper.

Does such an experience say anything about the Church in its passage through the modern world as a single global body of networked members? In retrospect we now know that the scandal of the clerical sexual abuse of minors is not confined to the United States. It is a phenomenon of worldwide dimensions, manifesting itself in Canada, England, Ireland, South America, Germany, Italy, Africa, and the countries of Asia. We are now part of a world Church in all of its blessings and all of its sufferings. Being part of this global mystery of the Church in its pilgrimage through time is part of our contemporary experience. So also our membership with each other effected by our Baptism into Christ takes on universal dimensions. This leads, I think, to a broader understanding of the Incarnation.

One dimension of the mission of our Lord in taking on the human condition is to assume our failure as his own, to pray our own abandonment as his own prayer,[30] to take us inside of himself, to crack open his heart so that we will have room to live, so that we might live from his life, and in doing so, become in him, Church, members of a single body.[31] Jesus returns to be with us who are the disfigured members of his own body; he receives us into his own life so as to bear our afflictions, take on our guilt, forgive our sins, correct our failings, share our constraints, teach us the truth of God's true identity. And taken into his life, we are empowered to do this for each other. There is a different kind of love that comes with living in this charity of God's in Christ: It is the love that unites freely with those who are suffering. It is the love that chooses to be among us *quasi leprosus*, as if being with a leper who has "no stately bearing to make us look at him" (Isa. 51.1–5).[32] It is the love that chooses to take on the shame of our nakedness and the constraints of our humanity. It acknowledges the claim of someone else's existence, as a brother or a sister, on oneself and all others. This love is rooted in the power of the Spirit, and its manifestation is part of the witness of the contemporary Church.

The Church as a whole in our global world is reenacting the birth, journey into the poverty of being human, and passion of Christ. Entering into its own history, it is learning how to become present to its own disfigurement. And in that presence to itself, it is learning a new image of the God who is Love for the world. If all together, in Christ, are Christ's body, then we contribute by our actions to the journey of his full Body making its slow way up to Jerusalem to the final passion, death, and triumphant resurrection. This lies in the future; now we are pilgrims. For the wayfarer that I found myself to be with others throughout the world this experience and reflection occasioned a prayer of thanksgiving from within the richness of the Body of Christ's own poverty:

Lord, teach us to be like you, you who are charity.
You are disfigured in your members, sometimes beyond
    all recognition.
Stay with us,
In the Eucharist, in the sacraments, in our presence to
    each other. Amen.

Doing Penance, Handling Trauma

IN MAKING A PASTORAL response to the report of November 29, I promised for the Franciscan Friars that we would make "a firm purpose of amendment for the evils of sexual abuse which have been committed by our brothers."[33] All of us did not know what this entailed at the time; we knew only that it would probably take three different trajectories: continued care for the victims through therapy and some monetary compensation, oversight of the offending friars who had not left the order, and the reeducation and revitalization of our own corporate body. Institutionally, these developments required (1) an administrative structure that both helped victims and advised the Province on its policies and procedures, (2) a way to approach monetary settlements that would be compatible with our pastoral orientation and religious identity, and (3) a programmatic rebuilding of internal relationships. The work in all three areas would be our task for the next ten years, and a summary word may be said about each of these dimensions of "doing penance, handling trauma." Their importance will become apparent in future chapters.

1. Developing Administrative Structures

The Franciscan Friars had committed themselves to the formation of a review board, and in its report the Independent Board of Inquiry made significant recommendations for the establishment of a permanent Independent Response Team. The IRT, as it came to be known, was commissioned by the Provincial leadership almost immediately after the events of November 29. Designed to help victims and make a wide range of recommendations to the Province, its task was "to investigate, assess, advise and consult in instances of sexual abuse or sexual harassment by friars of the Province." Two members of the original board, two new therapists with expertise in child abuse and offender treatment, and a Franciscan sister composed the founding members. The IRT was to function in a pastoral manner for the good of everyone concerned. Funded by the Province but operating independently of the administration, it reported directly to the Provincial Minister/Chief Executive Officer. The Province also established its own Pastoral Agent, available upon request, for outreach to those who had been abused and to family members. The official protocol of guidelines and procedures in addition to new policies for the Province itself, after significant canonical review, were in place by the spring of 1995. At that time the IRT, which had adopted its own internal procedures, issued its first newsletter summarizing the first year's activities: "Interviewed victims and their families, who have approached us"; helped victims receive proper treatment; "interviewed and evaluated psychotherapists," for both victims and offenders, "with the goal of finding the most effective and qualified professionals"; advised the Province on monitoring, aftercare, and treatment programs for offenders; conducted educational workshops for new friars entering the order; supported "group facilitation for members of the seminary parish in Santa Barbara"; established a system of ombudsmen to "serve as field representatives around the seven Western states, in areas where Franciscan institutions are located"; provided resource material and information for the friars; created "guidelines for the assessment of the possible return of offending friars to limited ministry"; prepared a bulletin to update people "interested in what has been done since the press conference"; developed a brochure to be distributed in parishes and retreat centers run by the Franciscans. Within three years the IRT added to its list of accomplishments a "series of training sessions . . . to priests, brothers, employees, and Franciscan staff at parishes, retreat houses, and places of ministry, to explain the brochure and the function of the IRT."[34] In the work of the Independent Response Team can be seen the beginnings of an alternative and cooperative institutional pathway.

In tandem with these actions, the Franciscan Friars instituted a case manager who worked with the IRT "in regards to the overall supervision of the aftercare of the accused friars." It must be remembered that the actions of the friars in question were beyond the civil statute of limitations for criminal activity. It was left to the order to establish the appropriate disciplinary measures (dismissal, removal from ministry, restricted ministry, continual oversight and monitoring). Our guidelines paralleled the methods taken from the Association for the Treatment of Sex Abusers and the National Adolescent Perpetrator Network and established that friars, if they ever returned to ministry, would do so with maximum assurance of not reoffending.[35] In addition, policies were once again reviewed and updated; the interviewing of candidates for the order and formation policies incorporated significant sections on psychosexual development, boundaries, and human maturation; workshops on human sexuality and a required course on professional ethics for ministry ran throughout the formation program; and all the friars received training in "pastoral/professional responsibility." All of these actions incorporated and most went beyond the Ad Hoc Committee of the National Conference of Catholic Bishops, which moved in a similar direction with "Restoring Trust, A Pastoral Response to Abuse."[36] The system was not perfect, but the building blocks were being put into place.

2. Approaching Monetary Settlements

While these administrative actions represented the "doing of penance" on a systemic level, the question of monetary compensation to those who had been offended engaged an entirely new set of questions. The turn toward civil litigation for a resolution of the issues surrounding clergy sexual abuse had already been developing across the country. After the Santa Barbara report, the Franciscan friars also experienced a marked switch from the psychological and religious language of pastoral help to the language and culture of legal intervention.[37] Immediately after the public report, civil suits emerged, two being filed within the first three weeks of December, eleven by the middle of February, more than a dozen more before 2001. From the viewpoint of the plaintiffs, the possibility of criminal justice being denied in historic cases, another forum seemed an absolute necessity for holding the Church accountable.[38]

These civil suits brought with them lawyers for both plaintiffs and defendants and a juridical system with established procedures and precise classifications for information and the weighing of evidence. Attorney-client privileges, rights, gag orders, court motions, statutes of limitations, production of evidence, adversarial proceedings, and so on created a thicket of procedures, terms, and relationships bewildering in their initial invocation for both sides of the civil suits.[39] Added to the mix was the perspective of insurance carriers and their corporate cultures. Coverage and its extent were dependent on multiple factors —the definition of "recurrence," interpretations of "malpractice," the wording of policies, proof of coverage, the existence of risk management procedures, the possibility of negligence, a cost-benefit analysis related to legal fees and court appearances, the "time value" of money for the insurance company.[40] From the perspective of Franciscan leadership, the long pastoral culture of a religious order, focused on holding all things in common and personal interdependence, was here confronted with a legal and economic culture developed over many decades of experience, designed within the context of a capitalist society to resolve public disputes and to achieve some semblance of social equity.[41] A new collision of values and perspectives exploded into our awareness, this time surrounding corporate ownership, property, money, liability, and the necessity of justice. Many of us felt that in handling this collision the most important thing to do was to make amends and to keep faith as best we could with the core values of our religious identity as it interfaced with the relationship between justice and economics.[42]

In its long inheritance dating back to Francis of Assisi in the thirteenth century, our medieval religious tradition had undergone many permutations in confrontation with changing economic conditions. Some would say the changes over time had become compromises. Still, the carriers of the tradition had grappled with such questions as the birth of capitalism, the simple use of goods, common ownership, the growth of banking, the culture of private property, the use of contracts, and the acceptability of insurance to safeguard assets.[43] As an ideal that we professed, the commitment of Francis of Assisi to lead a life "without anything of his own" shaped and colored our approach to life, to money, to the sharing of goods, and to our relationships with people. And now these new intersections between Church and society posed for the Franciscans distinct economic challenges of some depth. Were there any guidelines or principles that could help us navigate this new terrain of civil suits? Although later chapters of this book will explore the institutional consequences of a Franciscan approach to American economic culture, it is important that we clarify a few basic principles at this point in our narrative.

Growing up in the emergent profit economy of the thirteenth century, Francis and his early brothers developed a distinctive approach to healing the violence that he believed was caused by the excessive pursuit of personal gain institutionalized in social systems (i.e., the laws protecting the accumulation of wealth and property, the prevalence of litigation over possessions, the proprietary system of the Church, and the social alliances that excluded the poor from citizenship). He named the heart of his social and ecclesial project "poverty," and he directly connected its practice and performance to the purposeful creation of social peace. This high ideal of the practice of poverty became institutionalized in the *Rule* Francis composed for his brothers. Chapter VI began, "The brothers shall not acquire anything as their own, neither a house nor a place nor anything at all. Instead, as pilgrims and strangers in this world who serve the Lord in poverty and humility, let them go begging for alms with full trust. Nor should they feel ashamed since the Lord made himself poor for us in this world."[44] Free from the concerns of owning property, Francis and his companions would be able to encounter everyone with the same greeting: "The Lord give you peace"; they would be forced to open themselves up to dependence on others.

This Franciscan practice of "not acquiring anything as one's own" was meant to give an example of an alternative way to arrive at social concord: To make peace and create a human community people in both Church and society needed to cut the cords binding them to a social world of private gain and to become aware that everyone is their neighbor, to share their goods equitably, to become generous, and to rely on the generosity of others. It was hoped that by incorporating dimensions of this alternate way into their own behavior, those attracted to the vision would help create a society less prone to divisiveness. In fact, Francis believed that this concrete performance of poverty would create a space for gratuity to manifest itself. It would make room in the world for an ethic of sharing that would manifest God's providential liberality toward all human creatures. Today, this orientation of the practice of poverty toward dispossession, generosity, and the mission of peace has been codified in the *Constitutions of the Order of Friars Minor*.[45] It is unique in the Church, no other order making profession to the same ideal as Francis understood it.

At the same time, while calling for the practice of nonpossession, the *Rule* implied and Francis's most famous interpreter, Bonaventure, argued that "poverty" was not the institutionalization of individual and group indigence. The friars were to live by the work of their hands. When necessary, they supplemented this activity by relying on the generosity of others. They were not to practice poverty in such a way as to deny their human dignity. Bonaventure put it this way:

> And it is in this that the proper measure or middle way of poverty consists:
>   In renouncing ownership without rejecting use, while accepting use without claiming ownership;
>   In observing austerity in this use without abstaining from the necessities of life, while providing for our needs without deviating from austerity.[46]

By making the practice of poverty a virtuous mean between the extremes of ownership and complete renunciation, between extreme austerity and superfluity, Bonaventure placed the interpretation and application of poverty in the hands of people's freedom and thoughtfulness. In any given circumstance, virtuous decisions needed to be made, both by the individual and by the group. For the Franciscan, the social choice required by religious profession had changed the approach to political economy: it no longer involved ownership, or appropriation, or acquisition, or the defense of private property as primary values. It had now become, How does one use the goods of this world to create better relationships between people, so as to witness to justice among as many people as possible? The practice of poverty created a social space so that freedom could act for the common good.[47] The practice of poverty was an ongoing discipline that directed economic choices.

In large measure negotiations between plaintiffs' attorneys, our own attorneys, insurance attorneys, and victims occupied much of the time of the Franciscan leadership between January 1994 and 2001. During that period California law governing the statutory limits on civil suits for sexual abuse of a child changed several times.[48] The media focused increasingly on the failure of national episcopal leadership to address the situation and the all too frequent shuffling of offending priests from place to place. Expressing growing frustration with leadership, an increasing number of advocacy groups called general attention to the embedded patterns of resistance and denial in the Church. Emotional reactions of anger, powerlessness, and fear took shape in the use of language, performances of protest, and institutional resistances; the same crevices of good and evil within the human heart as had been observed previously appeared to be opening up.

During this period, just as our penitential tradition had oriented us to perform public penance, so also we tried to make our tradition of poverty guide us in the question of the civil suits. Here I do not mean that we were not acting out of necessity, pressed as we were by the demand for justice now enforced by the legal system. History has its own way of exacting justice and cauterizing institutional resistances; but properly engaged, historical necessity also enables a return to fundamental governing values. Necessity, as we have seen, can open up hidden dimensions of grace and enable a purification of soul and body. Our Franciscan leadership tried as a consequence of our previous experience to embark willingly as much as we could on this path of purification. In the circumstances of civil suits, our tradition of poverty helped guide us in two overarching ways: First, we professed to be peacemakers. Did this not mean that the protection of assets could not become a controlling goal for ourselves or our representatives? The moral imperative of admitting injustice and making peace trumped as much as possible the legal and insurance possibilities of avoiding settlements and maintaining current possessions. We wished to avoid further contentiousness and further hurt on all sides. The strategic value that needed to guide our negotiations, as difficult and prolonged as they might be, was an orientation toward reconciliation, not on our terms but on terms that could be mutually accepted.

Second, while preserving our human dignity, our tradition of poverty required us to make an honest review of what was necessary in terms of money and property for our life and mission and what was superfluous to it. Never before had we so deeply inventoried the relationship between our profession and our actual practice. What was not necessary could be used to make peace, and we tried to weigh carefully the difference between the necessary and the superfluous. At least this is the way in our hearts and in our practice that we attempted within our constraints to approach the situation. The general approach, certainly not always perfect and perhaps not always evident in the eyes of others, was probably shared by many others during the period under consideration. However, it is worth pointing out that subsequent events on a national scene would render all these intentions and practices historically invisible.

On a spiritual level, the practice of poverty as Francis understood it is accompanied by providential care. In fact, for myself and others, when things seemed most bleak, the goodness in lawyers, insurance adjustors, court officers, plaintiffs, and friars came forth to assuage fears and make for justice and peace. Apparently, the power for good hidden in the world awaited only "the right occasion actually to emerge into being."[49] Poverty could in this sense contribute to a more gracious and different kind of exchange between people. I will leave for a later chapter a more elaborate explanation of this social function. Through the choices of plaintiffs, the help of others, and our own choices, the leadership of the province eventually settled dozens of cases without going to court. By the end of 2001 only one or two cases remained. Although we did not know it, we were on the eve of the explosion in Boston. We would need to return to the question of settlements and the Franciscan tradition at an even deeper level.

3. Rebuilding Internal Relationships

The full institutionalization of a "firm purpose of amendment" required not simply appropriate administrative structures, reeducation, and settling monetary claims, but also a rebuilding of the relationships between the friars themselves. I have already spoken about the range of individual emotional reactions. The fact of sexual abuse spread distrust in all directions; dealing with it on an administrative level fed self-doubt; its revelation made those who were associated with the abusers question the ties that bound them to each other. Looking back on it, I would say that the revelation of the abusive activity, the intensity of the events surrounding the Independent Board of Inquiry, the constant media coverage, and the global public exposure engendered by the press conference of November 29 educed a sense of collective shame. It was an experience of systemic trauma. To understand the impact of the crisis in its wider implications this dimension must be considered.

As I have tried to understand this collective level of experience, I would argue that "systemic trauma" occurs when a powerful, even life-threatening, event has a profound impact, both emotionally and cognitively, on the members of a group. It makes them question their fundamental assumptions about other members, their relationship with the public, and their own self-worth. It is an event that lays open people's fragility, vulnerability, poverty, and powerlessness, with the emotional consequences of terror, fear, anxiety, insecurity, confusion, shock, denial, and self-hatred.[50] I believe that this description, although varying in intensity for each person, captures at least part of the group experience that has marked some quarters of the Church during this entire crisis. How a group constructively deals with this experience is central to its own cohesiveness. Failure to deal with it or dismissing it as "unreal" will engender fracturing. The Franciscan friars were not alone in facing the challenge.

Such a situation makes two core demands on a leader: the rebuilding of emotional trust and the reconstruction of a viable intellectual understanding that took account of what had happened.[51] Communication and healing could not be confined to the establishment of administrative structures, education, and the institutionalizing of remedial procedures. What needed to happen was the creation of a space and a framework in which the experience could be shared and openly discussed. Once trust began to be restored, a new framework of interpretation needed to be constructed. This could be done only by building on people's fundamental goodness and their fundamental beliefs. Some of the key questions that the experience raised were: Are we in this together? Whom do I trust and who trusts me? Do we still have a mission? Is the admission of my own sexuality a danger or a blessing? Where is God in all of this? What does it mean to be a Franciscan, a member of the Roman Catholic Church? What is our relationship with the Church? The questions came automatically. No further steps could occur unless the fundamental relationships between people were somehow constructively addressed. Through the help of professionals and our own resources we stumbled into a method for revitalizing our life in community and our life of faith. We called it Fraternity-in-Mission, or FIM for short.[52]

The subtitle of our Fraternity-in-Mission process was "Toward Affective Well-Being and Psychosexual Integration." Narrating and analyzing its details would take this book too far afield. The general framework of meaning that emerged from the experience will form the basis for the theological and spiritual reflections offered in Chapters 5–8. Suffice it to say that after an initial period of planning, the process developed in three phases over a three-year period. It has continued in some measure to the present day. FIM engaged the entire membership in regional meetings, in the training of internal facilitators, in large and small community gatherings, and in days of continuing education. Experts provided packets of reflection materials specifically designed to restore trust and interpret our experience in the light of our faith. Five major themes dominated the first phase of the discussions: friendship, communicating our own story to others, developing skills and rules of discourse among ourselves, living a chaste life, and the difficulties with which we still struggle. The packets of reflection on each theme built the discussions around the fundamental resources of our life: biblical readings, Church teaching, articles from the Franciscan spiritual and theological tradition, articles on the issues in the light of contemporary understandings (sociology, psychology, theology), prayer. Clusters of friars reflected on issues related to affectivity and sexual orientation, affectivity and power, and affectivity from a multicultural perspective. At one stage, the entire group gathered to hear and share their personal stories of how sexuality and affectivity had over time been integrated into religious life in a constructive and peacemaking fashion.

In short, we began to heal the wounds of our trauma by focusing not on what some had done wrong but on what most others had struggled to do right. We learned to tell a public story of goodness, failure, repentance, redemption, and a return to blessing. We were trying simultaneously to engage both our human story full of weakness and our faith story full of our share in God's goodness.

In the three areas of administrative response, monetary compensation, and the rebuilding of internal relationships, not everything was done well or perfectly. All of it was done within its own historical integrity, within the context of a growing consciousness, a search for adequate structures, and a developing awareness of the life of faith. Still, that which was attempted needs to be told. As a result of these actions, which the Franciscan friars were not alone in instituting, when the events of 2002 struck the Church in the United States, friars were affected in a different way.[53] Our own history and the history of many others who developed alternative strategies were swept up into a larger story of mismanagement and ecclesial malfeasance. A new and disturbing question arose: Why do the misactions of some in leadership control the image, goodness, past choices, and future direction of everyone else who belongs to the same body?

Eclipse

THE MOST RECENT PHASE of the intersections between ourselves, the Church, and the society in the area of clergy sexual abuse began in January 2002, with the revelations in the *Boston Globe* concerning activities in the Archdiocese of Boston. Within six months the storm caused by the clouds in Boston flash-flooded into California. The state legislature removed the statutory limits for lapsed civil suits in cases of sexual misconduct with minors for the calendar year 2003. Given the national publicity and the intense public focus on the institutional failures of the Church, at this point in history direct or even indirect work with the victims on the part of our Independent Response Team became difficult. Approximately twenty-three alleged victims came forward in a civil suit. Our provincial administration once again entered extensively into work with lawyers, insurance carriers, and the court system. But this time the public atmosphere was toxic, the news media unrelenting in its coverage of leadership failures in Boston, Los Angeles, Philadelphia, New York, Cincinnati, and Chicago.[54] Other issues in the Church—celibacy, the screening of homosexual candidates to the priesthood, the exercise of authority, seminary education, the role of women, religious life, the lack of orthodoxy—became conflated with the point of crisis of sexual abuse.[55]

In such an atmosphere it was inevitable that the story of the Franciscans on the West Coast would intersect with the national story. News reports in Santa Barbara repeated the original narrations of misconduct, now almost ten years old; local events were now connected with or subsumed into a more national interpretive profile.[56] The conflation was reinforced in May 2002, when one of the Franciscan friars, who had been initially investigated by the Independent Board of Inquiry, evaluated, and disciplined, but who had remained in restricted ministry based on the evidence available at the time, was removed from ministry under new allegations of sexual abuse dating back to the 1970s.[57] The news profile of national administrative failure served as an important template for advocacy groups and cause lawyers.[58] The prominent national cases were shaping every story; the local story, it was claimed, reinforced the national. I was involved in an extensive deposition. On the provincial level, the issue of legal recourse to corporate bankruptcy dominated discussions during this last period. It was, as we have seen, the path already chosen by several dioceses. Chapter 7 pursues this story of bankruptcy in more detail. Eventually, the geographical location where the most extensive abuse took place, the seminary, was sold, the location excised from province identity. In the Spring of 2006, the administration entered into extensive settlement agreements with all of the victims. It was apparent to many of us that the Boston case had been allowed to eclipse fifteen years of careful pastoral and administrative work.

Now, in 2009, a twenty-year process of personal, provincial, ecclesial, and civil conflict appears to be tapering toward its end. There are still things to do and past misdeeds still hang over the present. But time has moved on, to be sure. On the national scene the present situation of the Church in the United States and the profile of its leadership differs tremendously from the decade in which alternative institutional strategies were being developed. The questions now are different; the solutions must be also. Yet, one of the purposes of history is to keep before us the memory of the past so that the future might be shaped by truth. Earlier, in speaking about the experience of systemic abuse, I noted the importance of developing a viable intellectual understanding of the events so as to give coherence and meaning to the group. This involved returning to some basic elements of belief. The same is important for the Church as it continues to discern a more comprehensive understanding of its pilgrimage through history and its experience of the terrible scandal in its midst. Probing the deeper dimensions of the abuse crisis on an institutional, theological, and spiritual level may help constructively to shape a pathway for believers. What has been the illumination that the soul in examining the Church in relation to the times has experienced? That is a question I would like to address in the following chapters from the perspective of the Franciscan tradition and my own experience in leadership as both relate to power, ownership, and the difficult issue of public scandal in the Church.

4. COMMUNITY AND POWER IN THE CHURCH

If, therefore, there be taken away from between us the evil
things which proceed from men,
and if the good which comes from God and belongs to
both parties in common be duly honored,
there will ensure such brotherly concord, such amiable
peace, that the love of Christ
shall gain the victory in men's hearts over the temptation
of the devil.

SAINT AUGUSTINE OF HIPPO
Letter LXI, to Theodorus1

IN AN EARLIER CHAPTER I spoke experientially about the "law of constraints" that bound everyone into a "commonwealth of partial justices." In the unfolding of the crisis different perspectives and interpretations of the data collided. Great tensions marked the interactions between the legal system, the religious culture, the criminal justice authorities, psychological professionals, the insurance business, the hierarchy of the Church, and family life. In many participants a cry for justice arose, accompanied by an impossibility of achieving justice as they saw it. I have also noted how in the intense arguments certain temptations could arise. In the midst of feelings of defensiveness pastoral and professional leaders could be tempted to withdraw or even to dominate the situation through power, authority, expertise, or position. Yet, in many instances, for example in the work of Cardinal Bernardin, who mobilized an alternative pastoral approach and submitted himself to his own established procedures, or in the work between the Independent Board of

Inquiry and the Province of Saint Barbara, or in the daily work accomplished by many legal and insurance professionals, all of the participants tried to persevere at maintaining a constructive relational stance toward one another. Professionals in the Church and the society learned from each other's expertise and worked together to develop some common space marked not by the absence of tension but by threads of collaboration, compassionate outreach, the preservation of personal dignity, adherence to appropriate boundaries, and the establishment of some justice. And in this process, a spiritual vision could be born.

I would like to move now from the level of a local experience to examine once again the national pattern of the crisis. "Power" will be the focus of this and subsequent chapters. It is understood here as the capacity to influence others, "to cause or prevent change" in relationships. Power comes through personal ability, the possession of office, professional knowledge, institutional resources, social status, access to legitimating data, the control of information, or advocacy networking. Power is sometimes connected with "authority," "the right and power to command, enforce laws, exact obedience, determine, or judge."[2] But often those who have authority have diminished power, and those without position have a great deal of power. All of them have some form of relational power. Power can also manifest itself in organizations as "social power" or the patterned relational dynamics expressed in expectations and assumed behaviors that permeate an organization and shape its public message or forms of thinking, feeling, and interacting.[3] Many commentators have identified the issue of power—the capacity to influence others, to shape relationships—as the heart of the crisis.[4]

Certainly, the abuse of power by those who had pastoral authority over children led to some of its most devastating consequences. This personal misuse of power and authority is extremely significant. But as I noted in the introduction, I am primarily trying to discuss the institutional and leadership implications of the sexual abuse crisis. It was on the institutional level that the challenge of handling the scandal coalesced for many the postconciliar tensions that already existed over the possession and use of power in the relationships between the hierarchical and communal dimensions of the Church.[5] The general angry divisions between clergy and laity, bishops and priests, men and women, religious and diocesan members of the Church that surfaced during the 1980s culture wars became focused in the crisis.[6] In the long run, reactions to the misman-agement of the abuse scandal have simply deepened these ten-sions and contributed to the fracturing of community and a less-ening of the bonds of trust between the members of the one Body of Christ. In this chapter, I would like to explain this insti-tutional consequence by first noting the evolution of the sexual abuse crisis as symbolic of the struggles over power. The chap-ter will then conclude by describing the long-term consequences of the scandal as the loss of an ethical space of reciprocal exchange within the Church.

Clergy Sexual Abuse as Symbolic of Struggles over Power

THE OVERVIEW IN CHAPTER I described how the crisis over the sexual abuse of minors by priests shifted over time. What start-ed out as individual cases of sexual misconduct scattered throughout the country was perceived as early as 1985 as a national pattern. Eventually, what began as a problem of per-sonal misconduct ended as a problem of hierarchical misuse of authority and power. Throughout the course of the public crisis disparate elements converged. I have already described how in my own experience on October 28, 1992, a meeting called specifically to discuss misconduct in a Boys Choir surfaced pub-lic concerns about more lay inclusion in the liturgy, the admis-sion of women to the priesthood, and the misuse of pastoral authority in various parochial endeavors. All of these areas involved the question of who possessed power within the Church and how it was employed in any given area of life. By the 1990s, in the public sector the activities of various bishops were being compared against each other. Discussions about how to handle the sexual abuse crisis incorporated beliefs about the role of the laity and the relationship and sharing of power between clerical authority and lay experts. For example, the *Indianapolis Star* unfavorably compared the activities of the Bishop of Lafayette, Indiana, with the more collaborative approach of Archbishop Bernardin. In other ways, newspaper accounts and academic analyses continually framed the crisis in relationship to the celibacy of the clergy, the sexual teachings of the church, and the ordination of gay men. How were power and authority being used in these areas? Some felt that the whole course of events was a product of how the media used its power to feed the society's deep prejudices of anti-Catholicism. In all of these ways the clergy sexual abuse of minors, even while it was occurring, served to carry multiple interpretations. A host of presuppositions about other areas of Church life, initially unrelated to the events themselves, migrated into the discussions about the scandal. While touching profound areas of apostolic authority in the Church, the arguments joined hands with the more general cultural problem of how the power to influence others— relational power—was ordered in the community.

A similar process of combining different strands of opinion in the Church and society has occurred in the subsequent suggestions and courses taken to resolve the scandal. Some persons seem to have become preoccupied, even driven, to preserve a public order of the Church primarily related to the clerical order of the priesthood and its unique sacred power; some to focus on the restoration of a Catholic culture through seminary training, the enforcement of discipline, and the creation of a cadre of chaste and pure clergy. Others have argued for episcopal accountability, transparency, and economic oversight. One commentator has demanded a complete restructuring of the "celibate-sexual system of power relations."[7] Clearly the crisis over the sexual abuse of minors has become a charged social symbol,[8] made to carry the freight in our culture of many different issues, opinions, and solutions to contemporary challenges. Many of us know this symbolic functioning of the scandal from our own experience.

Currently, these arguments over institutional power and authority in the Church appear to be focused in two organizational developments. It is significant, I think, that the Voice of the Faithful originated out of the events in Boston in 2002. The centerpiece of the argument was power. Two sides quickly developed despite the attempts by many to bridge them. On the one hand, some interpreted the crisis as a threat to the basic constitution of the Church; the preservation of the hierarchical ordering between clergy and laity became the focus of attention. On the other hand, clerical abuse and its mismanagement proved the need to assert the community's agency, its economic power, its demand for episcopal accountability and organizational transparency. At times, the divisions have been popularly broken into splits between the laity and the bishops. That division is historically way too simple. The disagreements divide the Church not vertically between bishops and laity but horizontally among groups of bishops, clergy, religious, and laity.[9] It is this horizontal communal sorting that bears examination.

A second organizational example is the current split identified between the priests ordained after the Council and those ordained after 1980. The most recent study of "the new priests" notes a considerable ecclesiological shift and concludes with the following description:

> a specific issue felt with urgency by these priests is in the theology of the priesthood. The young men hold to a sacramental and cultic theology of the priest. They reject a theology defining priesthood as merely a matter of function in church life. They insist that the priest is distinct from the laity, and that emphatically includes

ontological as well as institutional distinctiveness. The priest–lay distinction of the pre–Vatican II era needs to be reconsidered and probably reinstated. The new priests are less enthusiastic than their elders about lay ministers and the possibility of working with lay ministers as equals.[10]

This preexisting trend has been reinforced in the last ten years because of reaction to the sexual abuse scandal. Dimensions of conciliar documents, papal teaching, and curial instructions, which differentiate the clergy from the laity in training, dress, sacramental functions, and governance, have been received by many in the United States as reinforcing ontological difference and the possession of power in the Church. This reaction was understandable within a context that partially attributed the abuse crisis "to a culture of sexual permissiveness and moral relativism."[11] A strong hierarchical authority was needed to right the imbalances in the Church. Still, other passages in the documents that called attention to the role of the laity, coresponsibility, communion, collaboration in mission, the importance of equality, and the significance of service in the configuration to Christ—that is, those areas that touched the priesthood of all believers and the exchange of power that shapes the relationships between people—have slipped into the background.[12]

This emphasis on the differentiation between the clergy and the laity has been indirectly reinforced in the publication of the fifth edition of the *Program of Priestly Formation*. This normative guide for the training of priests makes explicit reference to the need to address the sexual abuse scandal through a clear understanding of clerical identity. The focus on priestly identity is good in itself, but in public speech and action it often seems to have little relationship with the more communal understanding of authority and power expressed in a parallel document on lay ministry.[13] How do the two relate to each other? How can a clear clerical identity be established without a clear lay identity, and how can either be established unless we publicly address the issue of how they are reciprocally ordered one to another in the one priesthood of Christ?[14] In all these instances the sexual abuse scandal has been used as a symbolic carrier of much larger arguments over power, authority, identity, and relationships in the Church. The reassertion of the ontological identity and separation of the priest, his boundary distinctions from the laity, and the reassertion of the laity through the use of economic power or advocacy groups are two sides of the same coin.

Many of these positions that have aligned themselves with the crisis will probably separate out with the passage of time. In terms of the sexual abuse scandal itself we are simply too close to the whole experience to discern its full causes or measure its many ecclesial tentacles and its workable solutions. In this present description, my purpose is not to take issue with these developments or to argue for a programmatic solution. Rather, I simply want to ask if the ferocity of the arguments themselves does not point to the existence of a much deeper issue of how we interpret and use relational power in the Church. At stake is the ability and authority to shape or publicly influence the operating relationships between the clerical and lay, male and female, celibate and married, elite and nonelite, sacred and secular dimensions of the Church. I would like to conclude this section by identifying two particular issues related to power, which were clarified for me in dealing with the sexual abuse scandal. Given that the crisis itself has served as the symbolic carrier of many postconciliar conflicts, I believe that if we can address these underlying issues of power, other areas of division will be influenced for the better.

First, the origins and long-term impact of the sexual abuse scandal cannot be understood simply on an institutional or managerial level. The crisis reveals much deeper and more general struggles touching the affective level, the level of desire, love, and the will. These are the driving forces of our power to relate and to form relationships of trust and mutual respect. We need to appreciate the difficulty in its deepest emotional dimensions in the human person. Seeds of resentment, anger, fear, betrayal, suspicion, powerlessness, and shame cut deeply into people's hearts and affections. This has certainly been true and justifiable on the part of the victims, a reality everyone must acknowledge. But we need also to see how these affective elements emerged in those managing the crisis, those not victims but still caught in the swirl of conflict. We need to discover how these affective elements helped create the general ecclesial atmosphere of mistrust that surrounded the crisis. Experience indicates that anger and resentment at a situation that became increasingly beyond control or at a situation that was a personal threat to identity could cause various reactions: Denial that this was happening, retreat from relationships, the refusal to listen to advice or to acquire information, the dismissal or minimalizing of complaints, or even a drive to dominate the problem through the use of positional authority, advocacy, or appeal to a legal forum.

Additionally, for many of those who did not abuse, the experience of collective shame is felt so strongly that it exposes an individual or a group to various temptations, above all to withdraw into an enclave of self-reference, or to retreat into the interior through institutional apathy, or to become suspicious of any and all relationships. The affective impact of the events on personal and communal identity severely influences the level of group morale. These are all real areas of life that need to be understood if one is adequately to address the overall crisis and especially its aftermath.[15] Our own experience as Franciscan friars indicates that a program of affective renewal that touches both the personal and communal dimensions of identity is absolutely necessary in the wake of the scandal. The issue is, once again, power—not organizational or managerial or positional power, but the power to relate, that power of affective energy to shape the reality and practice of communion between people within the Church. The sexual abuse scandal can be healed only through the cultivation of trust, affection, mutual exchange, and the preservation of people's individual dignity. This type of positive relational power is not the *sacra potestas* of the priest, which is a theological term referring to the distinct powers associated with the ministerial priesthood, nor is it the power of governance in the *Code of Canon Law*.[16] Yet relational power permeates and shapes all others uses of power. If the affections are not ordered toward relationality and trust, power in its manifest expressions can become destructive of community.

Reflecting on these events many years later and turning to tradition for some perspective, I believe that the analysis of Augustine is most appropriate. He lived at a time of extreme polarization in the Church and division in society. The vision that he developed did not confine itself to the externals of Church reform or structural change. Instead, he stressed the centrality of how we use or order our affective energies and power for good or for ill in a social situation.[17] He argued in the following fashion: Called from out of this earthly city, the Church is composed of different types of people, both the good and the not so good. It is like Noah's ark, containing "not only sheep and cattle, that is, holy members both lay and clerical, but, *what is more, beasts of the field, birds of the air, and fishes of the sea, who roam the pathways of the deep.*"[18] The Church is a menagerie of different species; included among its members are lambs and wolves, doves and hawks, tuna and sharks. A parallel mix marks each person. "This is important," Augustine preaches.

> Either you slay iniquity [injustice], or iniquity will slay you. But do not try to slay iniquity as though it were some foe outside yourself. Examine yourself, identify the enemy inside you that fights against you. Make sure that this enemy of yours, this iniquity, does not get the better of you because it has not been killed. Make no

mistake; it originates within yourself; it is your own soul that rebels against you, not some alien thing. With one side of yourself you cling loyally to God, with another side of [yourself] you are pleasurably attached to the world; and the side of you that is attached to the world fights against the mind that cleaves to God.[19]

The bishop ultimately identifies the root problem in himself and in others to be the power within the person that manifests itself either in charity or in its opposite, the drive toward selfishness and domination. And the use of that personal power both shapes and directs and is shaped and directed by the language, customs, habits, and patterns of relating that people choose to create in their social body. Later chapters will explore this analysis more deeply.

In summary, the use of power in the Church is related not simply to the institutional issues at hand, for example, priestly identity or lay authority. The organizational patterns also reflect the underlying struggle between two loves that lie in the depths of everyone's person. Learning that this is a very real and determinative dimension of the issues now confronting the Church may prove beneficial in addressing them. Resolving the struggle in favor of the creation of community will be part of the ethical path that subsequent chapters will try to describe.

Second, in many quarters the long-term consequences of the scandal of sexual abuse have led to a communal sorting of permanent interest groups along polarized lines of power. The institutional focus on the unique "sacred power" of the priest, the arguments over the intentions of the Voice of the Faithful, the recruitment profile of the younger clergy, the divisions over the authority and influence of the National Review Board itself—all of these signs in the wake of the abuse scandal indicate that the underlying disagreements continue. Two years after the crisis in Boston the National Review Board still called attention to the lack of effective "participation of faithful Catholics, whether they be clergy or laity" in the "accountability mechanisms already built into the church's structure."[20] The course of history and the hardening of established separations between the clerical and lay worlds have moved in such a direction that other approaches to the present situation are hard to imagine. Something in the Church has been lost or so occluded as to become institutionally invisible. A language and practice of mediation have disappeared. In many cases, the hierarchical and communal dimensions of the Church—its clerical and lay individuals, its celibate and married vocations, its male and female practitioners, its religious and diocesan members, its secular professionals, and its pastoral professionals—remain sharply disjunctive in public speech, in generational patterns, in educational venues, in institutional structures, in vision, and tactics.

In a way similar to the society at large, perhaps the ecclesial community on local, regional, and national levels has in some sense "sorted" itself by type and commitment.[21] This institutional problem of sorting parallels the personal dimensions that have been identified. On both levels, the sexual abuse crisis, in its reflection of distorted relationships and in its reinforcement of ecclesial divisions, has raised long-term questions of how we can constructively use our power for the creation of a single Body of Christ, a Church of genuine communion. What can be done to help the situation?

Power and the Need for an Ethical Space of Reciprocal Trust

IN ANALYZING THE LONG-TERM impact of changes in institutions and ideas in history, the historian Peter Brown remarks how "each epoch passes on to the next the intellectual and religious vitamin deficiencies created by its own, most distinctive achievements."[22] From this perspective, as we attempt to understand the sexual abuse crisis, we need to become more historically aware. The depths of the scandal and our response to it have damaged some of our most treasured relationships. Bishops, priests, religious, and the laity are affected in one way or another. The financial consequences are most evident; but other issues of the spirit have also been affected. In many cases a veil of suspicion or isolation has descended upon well-meaning people. Our own history has passed on to us some very real "religious vitamin deficiencies" in the area of the use and abuse of power, not only in the realm of how we think about the power that each of us has but also how we use power to shape and form our relationships as members of the same Body. To address the situation, I believe that all of us, particularly those in positions of decision making and/or power, can profit by bringing to the situation not simply the problem of the excising of sexual abuse from the Church but the longer interpretive issue of how we can mine the various religious traditions within the Church so as to give hope and energy. We need, I think, to plumb the depths of our living Tradition.

On an abstract level, my own learning during my time in leadership can be simply stated: The challenge of the sexual abuse scandal as an abuse of power and as paradigmatic of the struggle between the hierarchical and communal structures of our social and ecclesial life demands the creation of a "new ethical space and practice" for relationships within the Church and between the Church and the world.[23] It was clear by the early nineties that the crisis that had lasted for more than ten years touched issues of power and authority. The most fundamental bonds of trust had already been in many cases seriously weakened. The sexual abuse scandal publicly exploded over a fifteen-year period because trust was already tenuous. The worst type of abuse now identified that trust as having been violated in an irreparable way. The underlying issue could be remedied only if people moved through and then beyond the presenting issue of abuse. It could be addressed only by cooperative behavior that restored some degree of reciprocity in relationships of mutual fidelity.

In such a situation, action was needed to create a common

human space between people that bestowed on each person, no matter their status or position, greater human respect and an acknowledgment of the good God did in him or her. This ethical practice oriented to the creation of stronger relational bonds needed to be expressed in patterns of thought and ways of speaking and believing; institutionally it needed to be embodied in concrete behaviors, administrative strategies, policy decisions, education programs, and the formation of cooperative groups. The challenge was not simply to prevent clergy sexual abuse but also to try to order our hierarchical and communal relationships in such a way that there existed between people a better horizontal "exchange of giving and receiving."[24] Only in this way could we arrive at truth and constructively forge a communal way of peace.

Based on my own experience and understanding, having the creation of this ethical space of reciprocity between people as a goal places a demand on those charged with leadership, be they clergy or laity. It means that they cannot limit themselves to working only with their own kind. Nor can they work with those outside their professional group unless they choose to listen to them, receive their advice, view the situation from their perspective, act on their recommendations, and attend to their needs. In this process, this also means that the struggle to stay in relationship involves a struggle to keep one's own integrity, take one's own unique responsibilities seriously, and respect the God-given gifts and position that one has in the Church. It does not mean that there is always mutual agreement between parties or that the legitimate exercise of positional authority and the gift of teaching are undermined. This commitment to create an ethical space of reciprocal exchange acknowledges tension at the heart of reality. Still, if in some way a common exchange can be created, it becomes medicinal in a Body of Christ too often suffering from suspicion, mistrust, and competition for power between enclaves of self-interest.

Looking back on the scandal, I would say that living within this new ethical space demands both an asceticism of humility, obedience, and dispossession and a focused commitment to try to establish trust. After the events in Boston in 2002 spread a public atmosphere of toxic mistrust throughout the society and the Church, the need for this new atmosphere of reciprocal exchange has become simultaneously more urgent and more difficult. Now, with the "sorting" of the Church into significantly divided interest groups, the need to articulate the principles and practices governing this space of mediation between people begs for an even deeper public consideration. It is the purpose of the next three chapters to consider various dimensions of this ethical space and practice as they are illuminated by the Franciscan spiritual and theological tradition.

5. POWER, RELATIONSHIPS, AND THE FRANCISCAN TRADITION I

O how holy and how loving, gratifying, humbling,
    peace-giving,
sweet, worthy of love, and, above all things desirable:
to have such a Brother and such a Son, our Lord Jesus
    Christ,
who laid down His life for His sheep.

SAINT FRANCIS OF ASSISI
"Earlier Exhortation to the
Brothers and Sisters of Penance"[1]

IT TAKES TIME TO discover an interpretive framework that will enable people to deal with systemic trauma. Yet without that framework, people are left to their own devices and a group loses its cohesion. Such has been the experience of many in the Church who have tried to negotiate the last twenty years of the sexual abuse scandal. The crisis, as we have seen, has raised fundamental questions about the restoration of trust, the creation of community, the collision of values, and the resistance of inherited structures to change. It has revealed the problem of relational power between the hierarchical and communal dimensions of the Church. From those whose faith has been severely damaged to those who have been left with only tenuous connections to their community of worship, too many questions remain unresolved for them to move forward toward a better future.

I believe there are many different approaches to these challenges, many distinct and creative frameworks that can help us interpret our experience of the last twenty years. In what fol-

99

lows, I would like to offer one such approach. It stems from my own experience and my membership in one of the Church's well-established spiritual and theological traditions: the spiritual and theological tradition of Francis of Assisi and his thirteenth-century interpreter Bonaventure. Certainly for the Franciscan friars it was this interpretive framework to which we turned in order to navigate the last twenty years of ecclesial life. Some of the spiritual dimensions of this inheritance have already been alluded to, as for example in the reflections in Chapters 2 and 3. The Creation of all things in the Word of God and the centrality of the Incarnation as God-with-us in our experiences of poverty became beliefs central to maintaining an equilibrium of faith in the midst of doubt. At the same time we were also forced to discover on an intellectual level how best to address and to publicly explain other practical questions. For example, what within our Franciscan inheritance made it imperative that we listen to others when they called us to treat them as equal members of the same Body of Christ? What within our tradition, despite our personal reluctance, insisted that we open ourselves to the advice and guidance of people outside of our immediate group? What principles could guide us in the creation of an ethical space of exchange? What Franciscan social values could shape deliberations and choices about how to respond to the economic challenges before us? How could one continue to believe in God's presence in the midst of deep ecclesial scandal? We found that by turning to our own tradition we could at least give a reason for the hope and faith that was within us.

Now, twenty years later, after more reflection and study, I would like to offer in a more systematic way some of the insights from the Franciscan spiritual and intellectual tradition that were learned from the overall experience. In the next two chapters I will elaborate on some of the guiding principles for the creation of what I have referred to as the "ethical space" needed to address the underlying issues of power and mistrust. These insights seem to me all that much more urgent because the course of history itself has made publicly invisible an ecclesial vision that helped shape many people in the Church in the middle stages of the crisis. Our current "vitamin deficiencies" may be balanced by a more constructive recall of some of the riches of our shared tradition. This present chapter will examine the centrality of becoming a brother or a sister in the experience of Francis of Assisi; the next will look at the primacy of the Order of Love in St. Bonaventure. After the systematic exposition, which must necessarily give some exposure to the details of the Franciscan tradition, the two chapters will conclude with some particular references as to how these principles became clarified in the sexual abuse crisis.

I want to acknowledge at the outset that all of these reflections on the Franciscan spiritual and theological inheritance are interpreted in the light of contemporary experience.[2] They are presented as indicators of the richness of one spiritual tradition within the Church. They are not exhaustive, nor are they meant to provide a blueprint for how the challenges that face us must be addressed. They are instead offered as starting points for a broader ecclesial discussion that I believe needs to occur. Perhaps others will find them helpful. Certainly finding an ecclesial way forward must be the work of many.

The Centrality of Becoming a Brother or Sister

FRANCIS OF ASSISI (1181–1226) and his movement began in the midst of great social change and a structural conflict between the hierarchical arrangements of a landed feudal society and the communal arrangements of an emergent urban economic and social world. On the one hand, Francis accepted the inherited vertical hierarchical arrangements; on the other hand, he stressed the new horizontal communal relationships. It is important for our present purposes that we capture both sides of this equation. In Francis's own times the hierarchical and communal poles of life were colliding with great violence.

The world into which Francis was born was a "received Christian world" of social orders arranged in ascending and descending ranks.[3] Inheritors of the Gregorian reform, he and his followers knew a sharp canonical distinction between clergy and laity in spiritual and temporal endeavors, with the world of the clergy "in spiritual things" ultimately judging the world of the laity "in temporal things." The members of the community accepted the teaching of the Church, the authority of the bishops, the distinct power of the priests to consecrate the body and blood and to forgive sins, and the Church's division into the hierarchically arranged duality of clergy and laity. When Francis began his movement, monks and religious themselves were defined as part of the laity; further, it was commonly argued that members of an inferior order in the hierarchy (the laity) could not exercise a public *officium* (office) in the Church, such as preaching and administering the sacraments, since these functions belonged to a superior order (the priests).[4] Obedience and reverence to "our Lord Pope Honorius and his successors," the need for episcopal permission to preach in a diocese, being "submissive and subject at the feet of the same Holy Church and steadfast in the Catholic faith," and "faith in priests who live according to the rite of the holy Roman Church because of their orders" are phrases running throughout the most important writings of Francis of Assisi.[5] He purposely set his own movement over against some of the reforming currents of the day in which both men and women, reclaiming the Gospel for themselves and repulsed by the clerical depravity and ignorance surrounding them, claimed the distinctive powers that had traditionally belonged to the clergy.[6]

In this hierarchical context, Francis placed upon himself a demanding ascetical ethic governing his relationships with those in the clerical order. Pushing for reform was not to fall into an angry rejection of the clergy nor of the hierarchical dimension of the Church. Characteristic of his approach was the following *Admonition,* which he gave to his followers when

they encountered sinful members of the Church who had
received "orders":

> Blessed is the servant who has faith in the clergy who
> live uprightly according to the rite of the Roman
> Church.
>   Woe to those who look down upon them; for even
> though they be sinners, no one should judge them
> because the Lord alone reserves judgment on them to
> Himself. For just as their ministry is greater in its con-
> cerns for the most holy Body and Blood of our Lord
> Jesus Christ, which they receive and they alone admin-
> ister to others, so those who sin against them commit
> more of a sin than [if they had sinned] against all other
> persons in this world.[7]

Bonaventure of Bagnoreggio, a contemporary of Thomas
Aquinas and the finest of Franciscan theological masters, later
affirmed these same distinctions between the clergy and the laity
and these same approaches to reverence in his summary of theology, the *Breviloquium*, and in his commentaries on the
Franciscan life.[8]

This acceptance of hierarchy in Franciscan thought and
spirituality cannot be doubted. Yet, the world of Francis of
Assisi was not simply that of his received Christian world. It
was also one of rapid change in the economic, political, and
educational structures of society. Francis and his companions
belonged to the times and energies of the commune, a distinctive urban movement that emphasized the origin of authority
from below and concentrated power in the newly emergent
class of literate and highly qualified merchants, lawyers, and
professional artisans. Spontaneous movements "from below"
and from within the Church argued for a reform in the inherited Christian world and for greater institutional power and
authority for many faithful believers, for example, in preach-

ing, administration, and evangelizing work. The commune was a government by and of participation.[9] The religious order of the followers of Francis originated in the space between these two different conceptions and practices of how to order power in both the Church and the society, one side pushing for order through the assertion of traditional hierarchies, the other side pushing for order through the assertion of the authority of the people.[10] Social change, a new and direct access among the people to the texts of the Gospel communicated through preaching and the spread of literacy, and an awareness of the sinfulness of the clergy thus birthed dual approaches to ecclesial and social order.[11]

In such a situation where the received Christian world and the emergent Christian world were at violent loggerheads, the Lord revealed to Francis a greeting to be extended to all people: "May the Lord give you peace."[12] This new greeting implied an ethical stance toward the neighbor. It was a new practice not based on the prevalent social and ecclesial arrangements but directly on the Gospel. It was designed to create a space of mediation between people. Francis's task was medicinal, one of soothing the relationships between people so that more peace could reign in the society and the Church. It was a challenge that demanded that each person be granted human and religious dignity and that the society itself learn the laws and disciplines of reciprocal exchange.

Institutionally, Francis's fundamental choice was not a divisive one of either/or, separating the stability of inherited and sacred hierarchical arrangements from the new authority of the commune. He chose instead a relational space of both/and. He chose to live both within the hierarchical structures of the Church and within the participative structures of the commune. He gave that social space that lived in-between an organizational form called *fraternitas*, in English "fraternity."[13]

The name "fraternity" encompassed the men who followed Francis, the women of the Poor Sisters, and the men and women penitents who remained in secular professions—all of whom professed the Catholic faith. Much more than an abstraction, the term connoted a quality of how one turned one's affective powers and position of leadership to others in the act of becoming a "brother" and a "sister." Distinctive for his age, Francis in his own writings used the relational term "*ordo*" seven times; "*religio*" eleven times; and "*frater*" or "brother" 232 times. Ultimately, this term "brother" or "*frater*" had its foundation in the action of Christ, who con-descended to become (i.e., descended so as to-be-with) our Brother in the Incarnation. As the author of Hebrews wrote, "The one who consecrates and those who are consecrated have one and the same Father. Therefore he is not ashamed to call them brothers."[14] The guiding ethical principles for becoming a brother and a sister were reciprocal charity, humility, and mutual obedience.[15] This type of practice had consequences for how people used power.

While respecting hierarchical office and acknowledging the values of communal power, the practice of first identifying everyone as "brother" or "sister" placed each person within the common and shared space of belonging to the same human family. The ethical choice to see and choose this common space as the fundamental reality from which one related to others, the foundation of what it meant to be human, shaped all other relationships within the society and Church. The starting point for Francis of Assisi was not civil or ecclesiastical. When he converted, he took off the robes belonging to an official status within the Church, that of hermit, and put on the clothing of an ordinary human being—a category to which every human being belonged.[16] Within this familial context, the personal gift of hierarchical office and its power and the individual gift of personal power within community were both to be used for other brothers or sisters. Hierarchy and community were meant mutually to check the respective instincts for power over others by the Gospel necessity of acknowledging that one's brothers and sisters also had personally gifted powers different from one's own but equally directed toward the service of oneself and others. We see this fundamental reality of being a "brother" played out in Francis's writings when he classifies the Minister General of the Order, "its lord," as first a "brother," and then identifies even those ordained to orders as "brothers who are priests" or "priest brothers."[17] These were classifications of relationships combining hierarchy and community that were incomprehensible to the society and the Church of the time. Their use by Francis was meant to communicate an ethic of relationships governed by peace and mutual affirmation. It was sorely needed in the Church and society of his time.

"Brother" or "sister" clearly communicated a rigorous biblical social ethic in a violent society and Church: "What I say to you is: everyone who grows angry with his brother shall be liable to judgment; any man who uses abusive language toward his brother shall be answerable to the Sanhedrin, and if he holds him in contempt he risks the fires of Ghenna"; "Why look at the speck in your brother's eye when you miss the plank in your own?"; "Brother will hand over brother to death, and the father his child. . . . But whoever holds out till the end will escape death"; "If your brother should commit some wrong against you, go and point out his fault, but keep it between the two of you. If he listens to you, you have won your brother over"; "'Lord, when my brother wrongs me, how often must I forgive him? Seven times?' 'No,' Jesus replied, 'not seven times; I say seventy times seven times'"; "The other ten, on hearing this, became indignant at the two brothers" (Matt. 5.22, 7.3, 18.15ff., 18.21–22, 20.24). And in the Gospel, it is the sister who is commanded to carry the news to the brothers, placing upon them an ethical demand of listening and responding: "Go and carry the news to my brothers that they are to go to Galilee, where they will see me" (28.10). In addition, reference to Matthew 7.12 occurs eight times in the writings of Francis: "Treat others the way you would have them treat you: This sums up the law and the prophets." Reference to Galatians 6.2, three times: "Help carry one another's burdens; in that way you will fulfill the law of Christ." The ethical center of the life was Mark 12.30 (Matt. 22.39): "You shall love the Lord your God with your whole heart . . . and you shall love your neighbor as yourself." Brother and neighbor were correlative. The single most dominant evangelical text was that of John 17, the prayer for unity. Key for the purposes of the exercise of an office was the Lord's teaching, "I did not come to be served but to serve" (Matt. 10.28).[18] Those placed over others were to assume the "duty of washing the feet of their brothers."[19] These images of both hierarchy and community within a *fraternitas* were largely fraternal, maternal, neighborly, purposely designed in counterpoise to an increasing emphasis on hierarchical arrangements, communal violence, personal objectifications of others as belonging to a particular class or status, and legal separations between people.[20]

At its founding, this vision of a common institutional space where hierarchical and communal dimensions intersected was all the more remarkable in that the *fraternitas* was composed of both clerical and lay members, "learned" and "ignorant" members," members of the society and the church belonging to different economic classes (rich and poor), distinct social categories (serfs, servants, peasants, merchants, nobles), and distinct statuses (contemplatives and actives). As one contemporary historian argues, "The preference expressed by Francis" for the categories of the "unlettered," those "subject to others," and the "poor" (i.e., those without power and possessions) "highlights what were for him the three great evils, the three main poles of repulsion within society: knowledge, power, and wealth."[21] The *fraternitas* consciously set up structures and spaces of exchange stressing not relationships of dominance and subordination in the areas of knowledge, positional power, and wealth, but horizontal relationships of mutual care and promotion. Because of the inherent tensions between its hierarchical and communal dimensions, its clerical and lay membership, its noble and commoner participants, the give and take of *fraternitas* underscored a basic human experience: In the deeper crevices of the human heart there resided not simply the desire to love and be loved, to belong to a *fraternitas* of distinctive equals, but also the drive toward the private possession of power and its use for personal aggrandizement and social domination. Not to know this drive was not to know oneself as a penitent. Choosing to belong to a *fraternitas* in this way created an ethical demand on people that they attempt to resolve conflicts of power through a rigorous practice of self-mastery, mutual humility, and communal engagement. The Gospel texts listed above, especially that of the Great Commandment, were designed in this context to develop a path toward peace.

In terms of their outward mission, those who belonged to this movement of Francis gravitated toward the spaces between people, creating in the society and the Church, for example, con-fraternities where clergy and laity, rich and poor, those over others and those subject to authority, professional and common people could learn self-mastery and constructively intersect their lives and concerns. It is significant that Francis's vision for society included in the same Gospel way of life and mission ordained priests and people, professed religious men, professed religious sisters, and professed men and women among the laity; it was a vision meant for all sectors of the Church. This new ethical space of relationality was meant to witness within a warring society to a better path toward "the tranquility of order."[22] Fundamental to relationality was the doing of penance between people: "Give and it will be given to you. Forgive and you shall be forgiven. If you do not forgive people their sins, the Lord will not forgive you yours."[23]

Among the members of this universe of people within the Church there was meant to be a distinction as to the fundamental uniqueness of each person, a variety of offices, gifts, and functions. Everyone did not occupy the same office, nor did they have the same position, nor did they have the same gift from

God. But out of the multitude, one form or "uni-formity" was created by the quality of the exchange between members of the same family, by their willingness to create a new ethical space, by their conformity to the one Head, Christ, who became a "Brother," obedient and humble in his service to people.[24] Each person in the common space of the following of Christ was a brother or a sister, each both a teacher and a learner, each willing to set an example of virtue for the other and each willing to be edified by his or her neighbor. Another name for the social glue of this powerful reciprocal exchange between the hierarchical and communal dimensions of life was "love." If there was a problem in its execution, the difficulty lay not with the confluence of hierarchical and communal dimensions within the one *fraternitas*, but with the failure to practice penance and humility, to admit in oneself the darker crevices of the human heart's affections where the selfish will to private domination mixed with the generous will to be for others.

Significantly enough, Francis made no reference to one of the most popular scripture texts of the Gregorian reform, Acts 4.33, used to buttress the ordering of the Church by hierarchical grades: "With power the apostles bore witness to the resurrection of the Lord Jesus, and great respect was paid to them all." Nor did he appeal to the egalitarian overtones of Galatians 3.28, popularized in our own time: "There does not exist among you Jew or Greek, slave or freeman, male or female. All are one in Christ Jesus." Instead, he used a text related to those who belonged to the same household: "Extending his hand towards his disciples, he said: There are my mother and my brothers. Whoever does the will of my heavenly Father is brother and sister and mother to me" (Matt. 12.50; cf. Mark 3.31–35). His commentary directed to all disciples, clergy and laity, men and women, reads:

> We are spouses when the faithful soul is joined by the Holy Spirit to our Lord Jesus Christ. We are brothers to

Him when we do *the will of the Father who is in heaven*. We are mothers when we carry Him in our heart and body through a divine love and a pure and sincere conscience and give birth to Him through a holy activity which must shine as an example before others.[25]

These reflections had deep roots in Christian history and fell within the exegetical tradition of Augustine, who eight centuries earlier had interpreted the words of Christ in a similar way.

Whoever does my Father's will, that is my brother and sister and mother. He declares that the people whom he redeemed have all these family relationships with himself, though spiritually; he has holy men and holy women as his brothers and sisters, because they are coheirs with him of the heavenly inheritance. His mother is the whole Church, because through God's grace she certainly gives birth to his members, his faithful. In addition every devout soul that does the will of His father by the fertile power of charity is Christ's mother in those to whom it gives birth, until Christ himself is formed in them.[26]

In a vision such as Francis's there was meant to be a spiritual and material exchange between lay and cleric participants.[27] The charity which bound members of the same body was to take shape in action, in behavior; it was to be seen and felt, to take flesh: "Because the spirit of the flesh very much desires and strives to have the words but cares little for the activity; it does not seek a religion and holiness in an interior spirit, but wants and desires to have a religion and a holiness outwardly apparent to people"; "And let them express the love which they have for one another by their deeds, as the Apostle says, 'Let us not love in word or speech, but in deed and in truth'"; "For he has sent you into the entire world for this reason: that you may bear witness to His voice in word and deed and bring everyone to know that there is no one who is all powerful except Him"; "Whoever envies his brother the good which the Lord says and does in him commits a sin of blasphemy, because he envies the Most High who says and does every good."[28] The *Earlier Rule* (20.3), confirming a tradition present in the Church, even recognized the ritual of confessing one's sins to one's lay brother, a practice meant to be exemplary for the project of social reconstruction among the laity in society.[29] The same was true within the community of sisters who performed a similar act of lay confession. A sister had the power to intercede "to the Lord that He might forgive" her sister, each granting the other mutual pardon.[30] This did not remove the ecclesiastical obligation of confessing one's sins to a priest or detract from the distinctive centrality of sacramental confession; it simply opened up the social path of real forgiveness in a horizontal direction. The tradition of *fraternitas* also emphasized interdependence in the human community in the area of material goods. The administration of things was placed at the service of the whole community; the central maxim was that temporal goods and the labor of one's life existed for others.[31] This aspect will be pursued in Chapter 7, but economically speaking, the friars and sisters among themselves and with the laity were to have a pact of mutual dependence, insuring by the quality of their relationships the continuous circulation of spiritual and material realities. The *fraternitas* institutionalized a social law of reciprocity. It was through this lens of *fraternitas* that Francis saw "the holy, Catholic and Apostolic Church," in which "people in all orders" and "all peoples, races, tribes, and tongues" were called "to persevere in the true faith and in penance."[32]

   In summary, the "ethical space" of the new *fraternitas* and its mission in a Church and society sharply divided begins with the word "brother" or "sister." It then develops into pacts of mutual obedience, sharing, equality of purpose, appreciation of the distinctive gifts of each person, common mission.

Institutionally, while recognizing differences of office and status, it creates mediating spaces of interaction. This ethical space exists where there is a conscious attempt at reciprocity between the clergy and the laity, the sacred and secular dimensions of life. Activity within this ethical space resembles a marketplace of exchanged goods governed by an asceticism of humility and generosity. It is not accidental that the Franciscan movement evolved from the lay world. The evangelizing efforts of the friars remained most vital when they both maintained strong institutional relations with the communal dimensions of the Church and also stayed within its hierarchical structures. Francis's concern was to establish in the Church and society a space where people recognized what they had in common, where they shared among themselves, where they experienced their common membership in the same human family, their coming from the same Father. These realities made them brothers and sisters. Only from within this context could they appreciate their differences. This ordering of relationship within the religious community and the Church was meant to establish a model for the ordering of relationships within society itself. Here was a demanding communal ethic placed at the center of the human project of living with one's neighbor. It was complemented and elaborated on by Bonaventure when, some thirty years after the death of Francis, he turned to the "order of charity" as the principle governing all of reality.

6. POWER, RELATIONSHIPS, AND THE FRANCISCAN TRADITION II

It must be said that the order of love
    that is attained in virtue has this
principally, radically, and essentially in view:
God is preferred to the creature. Every other order is
    connected
and ordered to the divine order as its principal order.
In such ordered love that Augustine describes,
    it is opportune that the Creator becomes sweet to
        the heart
and that the creature diminishes its worth.

SAINT BONAVENTURE
Disputed Questions on Evangelical Perfection[1]

THE MOVEMENT ASSOCIATED WITH Francis of Assisi recognized the vertical and hierarchical ordering of the Church located in *officium*, but its consistently communal focus and insistence on spiritual and material reciprocity between brothers and sisters provided a different fulcrum for action. The difficulty was inserting the values and procedures of the *fraternitas* into the much more pronounced vertical public ordering of Church and society. To outsiders the vision seemed useful but largely incomprehensible and at times threatening.[2] The thinker who grappled most with the institutionalization and theological foundations of this vision was Bonaventure (1217–1274).[3] Trained at the University of Paris where he became a master of theology, his tenure both as a teacher and later as Minister General of the Order of Friars Minor (1257 to his death in 1274) placed him at the intellectual, political, and ecclesiastical center of the battle over how to order relationships in society and the Church.

Major elements of Bonaventure's pastoral thinking emerged during the course of the secular-mendicant dispute at the University of Paris (1252–1269). This intellectual controversy involved far-reaching pastoral questions in the Church: the emergence of new structures of participation, the interpretation of Scripture, the image of God, the relationship between the local (diocesan) and universal (papal) poles of the Church, the application of civil and canon law, and evangelizing activity that met the political and economic challenges of the day.[4] The details of the controversy are beyond the scope of this book. Suffice it to say here that during the most intense period of conflict Bonaventure penned five major works and the vast majority of his spiritual writings.[5] Theological reflections with polemical purpose, the works reveal one major trajectory of Bonaventure's thought that will help us today in our grappling with questions of order and power: In a society riddled with violence, one must live and work in the ethical space created by the order of love. Let me describe how this position developed and then give a few examples of its application.

The Order of Love

There was little doubt that Bonaventure lived in a society and Church full of misbehavior and violence, not all of it external to the Order of Friars Minor. Perhaps his clearest description of the atmosphere occurred in these short lines: "Today there is such great cruelty that a person cannot be satisfied with vengeance. Today impatience and anger rule. People pass evil judgment. Even if a person has not offended me, I will still attribute evil to him. Why is this? Certainly it is because I do not have charity."[6] His writings from 1255 to 1274 were filled with references to the evils manifest in the "one commonwealth of Christians": avarice and cupidity, possessiveness, rash judgment, abuse of authority, the loss of piety and compassion, viciousness, arrogance, false counsel, the defense of falsehood. He wrote in *Collations on the Ten Commandments*: "All incorrect evaluations of creatures come either from a sense of high-mindedness, or from the desire for sufficiency, or from pleasure. The first way is the idolatry of the proud, the second way is the idolatry of the greedy, and the third way is the idolatry of the lascivious."[7] A similar triad had been developed by Augustine in his description of a person's slide into the private zone of self-reference: "What happens is that the soul, loving its own power, slides away from the whole which is common to all into the part which is its own private property."[8]

Bonaventure located these vices in all of the sectors of the Church. "What, then, is a cleric or a priest who fornicates? Certainly an abomination to the Lord." "You are an archbishop or a bishop. So you wish to find grace? Then humble yourself. If we do not humble ourselves, we are robbers. . . . We see certain people raised on high by God who nonetheless rise up against God." When speaking of the grace of piety Bonaventure referred to a Church "poor in merits" and noted: "I believe there was an impediment that kept the Spirit from the people because there was an impediment in the pastor." It was clear that people used their own authority not "discreetly," but rashly: "One who does not have correct zeal cannot judge well. Love and hatred distort judgment. If you hate me, you cannot judge me rightly. And why? Because it seems to you that everything about me is evil." "In the same way, an angry person does not see the truth. Quarrelsome people hinder understanding in themselves and in others. An angry person will stubbornly defend what is false. For this reason the Legislator was the most mild of people. Isaiah 28.19 states: 'Only hardship will give understanding to the person who listens.' A compliant person learns and becomes weak." One of the prevalent problems was the influence of the one who "twists great matters into nothing, good things into evil things, and certitude into doubt."[9] The friars themselves participated in this violence: "Moreover, I shudder at the audacity and insolence of certain brothers, who, contrary to the teachings of our holy Father [Francis], get up in front of lay people and preach against the bishops of the church. By mocking the behavior of prelates in this way they are only sowing the seeds of scandal, ill-will, and strife."[10]

The times were producing upheavals in the inherited vision of ordered relationships. The Church itself appeared to be riddled with sin; every imaginable human vice (Havel again) was emerging as people struggled over the religious, social, and political ordering of their lives. At times the speech turned apocalyptic.[11] In such a situation, where could one turn for an ordering principle? Where could one unite with a secure source of power that provided both meaning and effectiveness while arguing for an institutional openness to a better way. The canonical norms of the time, fixed as they were on the proprietary system of diocesan and local episcopal structures, no longer responded to reality.[12] The battle with the secular masters at Paris indicated the ferocity of the established local system of Church governance and the resistance of its clerical adherents to a different order of things. Bonaventure struggled his whole life against the excessive legalism of this fossilized ecclesiology. A person also could not turn to a civil law or canon law that forbade the development of a new economy of relationships in the society and the Church. The law itself seemed to block the path toward an ethical system of some social reciprocity and equality between people.[13] A person could not rely on clear directives from conflicting papal decrees, some of which granted the mendicant friars privileges and others which removed them.[14] All of these systems of ordering relationships according to hierarchy, law, custom, and inherited tradition were coming into conflict and struggling for dominance. In this vacuum of authority, people were left to impose order by positional power, the shape of the order determined by the culture of their own self-referential communities.

In addition, the Franciscan friars themselves were also afflicted with their own vices and caught in a maelstrom of differing opinions and disordered affections.[15]

Existentially, the issue which arose for Bonaventure was not simply the tense experience occasioned by conflicting demands and motivations of public authorities (in our terminology, the "law of constraints") but also the search for a point of reference that could assimilate the personal and social experience of partial justices, systemic disorder, and the migration of good and evil into the human heart. In the midst of great structural change and its accompanying forces of violent partisanship, he learned the hard way that there was indeed only a tenuous connection between existing ecclesiastical law, civil law, the moral law, and a peaceful social order. The only path toward an increase of social peace that was not reliant on systems complicit in angry dis-order was the ordering of things through the subordination of all things to the primary order of love. This primary order was articulated in Scripture as the Great Commandment. Bonaventure's project would be analogous to the conflicting cultural forces that pushed Martin Luther King Jr. to appeal to a "higher law" to break through and transform from within the social, legal, ecclesiastical, and theological systems of behavior and thought that promoted segregation and inequality.[16] Three examples from Bonaventure's argument with the university masters can be given.[17]

First, the major opponent of Bonaventure in the university disputes argued that their commitment to voluntary poverty made the friars, who were religious and therefore in a higher state, dependent on others, recipients of the free gifts of the laity, who were in a lower state. The practice therefore upset the hierarchical ordering of dominant/subordinate peoples in society and Church. Begging from others was not compatible with a higher status. But this was exactly the point, and Bonaventure justified the activity of the friars by appealing to the evangelical law of friendship as superseding the law of society.

Again, when a friend asks for a gift from his friend, he violates no law; neither the first friend by his asking, nor the second by his giving, nor again the first by his accepting. But the law of charity and divine love involves a greater exchange than the law of society. Therefore, should someone ask that something be given him for the love of God, he commits no offense, nor does he in any way withdraw from the path of perfection.[18]

Second, the Parisian secular master argued that the priest who preached and exercised this office in the Church did so by *power* and possessed therefore a *right* to sustenance. This ordering of things appropriately placed the one who administers the Word of God in a position of superiority and the one who receives under obligation. The argument was positional and reinforced the vertical ordering of hierarchy present in the Church. Satisfaction of this relationship of right and obligation, that is, obedience to the existing order of things, was a question of *justice*.[19] But Bonaventure responded by appealing once again to a higher law, one that did not order the relationships between clergy and laity only in terms of positional power, rights, and obligation. He focused instead on the Great Commandment as embodying a greater order of justice and calling for the priest to act from a different, humbler positioning: "Humility is also the foundation of justice, for justice consists in 'rendering to each one what is his,' whether to God, self, or neighbor. Honor and reverence are owed principally to God. Humility disposes one to do his best, according to what Sirach 3.20 states: 'The Lord alone has great power. He is honored by the humble.' Since the beginning of all justice is the worship and honor of the divine that is shown to God by the humble, humility is the root and foundation of all justice."[20] The mendicant preacher Bonaventure argued, did not place people under the obligation of support but rather begged from them: "But it does accord with the order of charity and dutiful respect, be it of nature, grace, or spirit, for someone to suggest his need to his neighbor and ask his support out of love of God, for every law demands that a neighbor be supported and relieved by a neighbor. Therefore, how is the perversion of order and what follows in that perversion likened to what happens in accord with an order that is right, just and good, charitable and merciful?"[21]

Third, the university master accepted the current juridical ordering as a fixed reality and argued that when "a superior subjects himself to an inferior, then there are disorder and a perversion of order." This humility was not virtuous because "virtue is the order of love." Again, Bonaventure appealed to a higher order than the one currently established by ecclesiastical or civil law.

> To the objection that virtue is the order of love, it must be said that the order of love that is attained in virtue has this principally, radically, and essentially in view: God is preferred to the creature. Every other order is connected and ordered to the divine order as its principal order. In such ordered love Augustine describes, it is opportune that the Creator becomes sweet to the heart and that the creature diminishes its worth. Since the creature that acts most contrary to this order is the individual person with his private good, it is most fitting that a person humble himself to preserve the perfect order of virtue. And this happens when an individual subjects himself to another and places someone else ahead of himself for the sake of God, guarding all the while the dignity of ecclesiastical order which true humility does not pervert, neglect, or relegate to a secondary position. On the contrary, true humility preserves the ecclesiastical order as long as humility is kept interiorly in the heart, while exteriorly the structure of authority remains intact.[22]

The point Bonaventure was making in all three instances was simple: The order of love encapsulated in the Great Commandment was to inform all human relationships in society, in hierarchical situations of superior and inferior, in ordinary exchanges between people, in the relationships between clergy and laity. While the current order of things was good and remained intact, it would be insufficient without the Gospel ordering of people according to the law of charity—a freely given bestowal of gifts and a bond of trust between people. Appeal to this ordering of love, he argued, did not upset the dimensions of hierarchy constitutive of society and the Church, but injected into them values of humility, charity, and reciprocity. Bonaventure, like Francis, was here emphasizing the values associated with *fraternitas*. Loving God above all things ordered love in such a way that a person who loves God loves whom and what God loves: oneself, other people, creation itself. And he or she models the practice of this love on the way in which God loves.

> Also perfect ordering according to the rule of abundant righteousness consists in this that not only the inferior voluntarily subject himself to a superior and an equal to an equal, but also a superior to an inferior according to what is said in Matthew 3:15: "So it becomes us to fulfill all justice." . . . And this humility has three degrees. In the first, one subjects oneself to a greater person, and this is called adequate humility. In the second, one subjects oneself to an equal, and this is called abundant humility. In the third, one subjects oneself to a lesser person. In this lies "all justice." Christ fulfilled this degree of humility. . . . [I]t follows that the obedience that is shown one person by another contributes greatly and collaboratively to the perfection of ordered righteousness as it follows the path that orders dignity and operates according to the law of grace by which a person of great status regards himself as of lesser status.[23]

Bonaventure, following Augustine, ultimately argued that the social and ecclesial ills of the day could not be solved simply by appealing to the standard ordering of society and Church. He lived in an era in which the darker crevices of the human heart had opened up; the prevalent human tendencies toward the use of power for one's private good had become publicly visible in both Church and society. In such a situation, what needed to be addressed and cured were the affections and the disorders of the human will, anger at injustice, and arrogance in the demand for private control. The proper functioning of power was directly related to the trust and human respect that people shared with each other. Without this trust and human respect no power, no matter how legitimate, could effect the betterment of human relationships in obedience to the Gospel. The argument needed to move to a different plane of reality, that of the primary order of love.[24] Appealing to this principle of order challenged people to get to the root of the difficulty by creating a new ethical space where the virtues of humility and reciprocal exchange could begin to circulate between friends or neighbors or members of the same body.

The friar knew in practice what this order looked like because its human dimensions had been revealed in the life, journey, death, and resurrection of Jesus Christ.[25] He Who is the Way, Truth, and Life had sent the Spirit "who makes us to be children of one father [God] and one mother [the Church], and members of one body [the Body of Christ]."[26] Christ had demonstrated the path to peace: He had healed the ills of violence at its roots, curing arrogance by humility, avarice by poverty, the turn to the private by generous service, ambition by the acceptance of humiliation, selfishness by the law of reciprocity, anger by patience, severity by condescending mercy.[27] The following of Christ and the reception of his healing power in the grace of the Holy Spirit made possible the creation of an ethical space, a *fraternitas*, a society of friends, a household of believers, a single body with many members, a Church, a commonwealth. From within this common space people could witness to human dignity, the courage to persevere, and the power to be compassionate with their neighbors.[28] At stake in Bonaventure's apologetic was both the authority of Christ's Gospel and the inculcation of a social behavior that would go contrary to the human vices that cut through everyone: "The disease that corrupts human nature the most," he noted, "is the conceit of pride"; "To demean one's neighbor is to place oneself above him. To demean oneself is to subject oneself to another. The first is characteristic of pride while the second is characteristic of humility and reverence."[29] The errant affections in the Church could be healed only by a willing and deeper embrace of Incarnate Love: "Anyone," he writes in the *Itinerarium*, "who turns fully to face this Mercy Seat with faith, hope, and love, devotion, admiration, joy, appreciation, praise and rejoicing, will behold Christ hanging on the Cross. Such a person celebrates the Pasch, that is, the Passover with Christ."[30] Providentially, the course of his own history opened up for Bonaventure, as it had for Augustine, for the Franciscan Order, and for the Church, conversion to the order of love. It remained a lifelong task.

One other significant element emerged in this turn of Bonaventure's to the order of love in which "God is preferred to the creature." In arguing for the existence of an ethical space of horizontal exchange and for a new institutional space for the followers of Francis, Bonaventure was also making a case for the compatibility of the hierarchical ordering that existed with the communal emergence of a pluriformity of gifts in the Church. Given the need for reform, he argued, sometimes, when the knowledge of Sacred Scripture was weak in the Church's members and its hierarchy, "another radiance is needed, namely that of the knowledge of grace." This was the knowledge "given by the Holy Spirit, I say, moving the soul, inspiring it, and informing it with sanctity."[31] People who were "filled with the Holy Spirit" were needed in order to heal the wounds caused by arguments over power and a failure to acknowledge the primacy of the order of love. What was truly appropriate to the times, the ecclesial leader noted, was the "contemplative soul," "established upon the Church and supported by it," "able to see the whole world" in the light of a God who is love.[32] Of course, Bonaventure was making a case for the existence of the *fraternitas* of brothers (and sisters) in Church and society. He was making a case for the necessity of the charismatic gifts, those given by the Spirit to individual people, in the Body of Christ.[33] And he was making a case that the proper ordering of the Church demanded that mendicant priests be recognized as genuine "co-laborers" with those who possessed the grace of office.[34] In all instances, as he noted in the *Defense of the Mendicants* (XII.8), by approving the Franciscan Order the pope had "adorned the hierarchy of the Church without disorganizing it."

Ultimately Bonaventure's vision of a community unified by the order of love was related to his Trinitarian theology. Its contours need not detain us here except to say that at its center was a concept of God whose generosity and liberality are infinite.[35] He noted in the *Breviloquium,* the Trinity of persons "includes the highest fecundity, love, generosity, equality, relationship, likeness, and inseparability."[36] If one truly loved this God above all things, then one would obey the "order of love" identified in the Great Commandment. Then every relationship would mirror the divine relationality of fecundity, love, generosity, and equality; without this ordering, there really could be no complete order. Obedience to the "order of love" thus included not only loving God but learning to love the wondrous and diverse ways God worked in the world. In the practical realm, for Bonaventure one of these ways was through the sacramental and hierarchical structure of the Church. This was a given, as we have indicated, and in difficult times it was particularly needed to provide stability. Yet this type of order was also circumscribed within the other wondrous ways God worked through people and united himself to them. Hierarchy existed within the larger communion established between diversely gifted people by the one Head Christ and the manifold influence of his love.[37] We can see him working out the reciprocity between these two elements, the hierarchical and communal dimensions, in the following passage.

> Just as a balanced interconnectedness is required for the perfection of a living body, in which all members are conformed and there is a pluriformity of organization in which members are distinguished and ordered and some members are set over others according to various functions, so too is this to be understood about the Mystical Body of Christ. And so the unity of love does not exclude the pluriformity of charisms and the determination of dignities and offices, according to which one member would have to be subjected to another and governed by another in accord with the law of authority and subjection.[38]

In fact, within the Church, everyone had received a "variety of perfections" from the fullness of Christ himself, but this same plenitude did not reside in any single one: "Diverse states, degrees, and orders are derived from him according to the various distributions of the gifts and the various manners in which the Exemplar is to be imitated. To them the manifold perfection of Christ is distributed according to a multiform participation in such a way that it is found at the same time in all things. And yet it does not shine in any one of them in the fullness of its universal plenitude, but each state and degree, according to its measure, receives the influence from such exemplarity and moves forward to imitate it."[39] For Bonaventure, the pluriformity of these interacting gifts made the Church "beautiful": "[T]he Re-creator of the human race not only without favoritism, but also with the great beneficence of his love has bestowed diverse spiritual gifts, has revealed diverse mysterious secrets, has given diverse offices and prelacies, and finally shown different examples of virtues, so that he might propose to one to imitate the other, and to yet another to imitate another according to what the Apostle says about the various levels of continence: 'Each one has his own gift from God.'"[40] In answer to the question whether there was order in the Church, Bonaventure responded that order was necessary for two reasons: "beauty and rightness." In the Church God had brought forth many things in a beautiful arrangement and had also provided a regime of ecclesiastical offices and powers "so that the Church may be ruled and guided without error."[41] Anyone accepting the "order of love" would need to accept God's providential guidance through both dimensions of the Church. This too was part of the new ethical space of reciprocity.

Learning a Path Forward

IN THE LONG COURSE of the crisis over sexual abuse, while some of the contours of this Franciscan tradition became clearer, its challenge became more pressing and difficult. In the centrality of becoming a brother or sister and the primacy of the order of love I have tried to identify two of the key elements that appear to me now, some fifteen years later, as central to the whole endeavor. It is not that these values and guiding principles always took first place; at times they disappeared both in thought and action in the heat of controversy. Yet the centrality of becoming a brother and the primacy of the order of love did emerge as necessary components of this new ethical space. I have tried to give these values intellectual support from the Franciscan spiritual inheritance so that we might see how the broad Tradition of the past may be brought to bear on a contemporary problem in the life of the Church and society.

I have argued that the whole crisis of sexual abuse is emblematic of larger ecclesial and societal problems related to power and the relationship between hierarchical and communal dimensions of life. If the ultimate roots of the crisis lie within the depths of the human heart, in its will and its affections, then the creation of a new ethical space of human dignity and trust, reciprocity and exchange become central to developing a better Church and society. The primacy of the Great Commandment needs to become a key foundational emphasis in preaching and acting. In many sectors the scandal has left in its wake an atmosphere of suspicion or separation and a hardening of boundaries between bishops and priests, clergy and laity, celibate and married, men and women in the Church. In some quarters it has occasioned argumentation for a sharp divide between the Church and the society around it. In this atmosphere the two elements that have been identified seem to point toward a way of breaking the impasse that has now been created. History is the teacher of truth. By way of summarizing the centrality of becoming a brother or sister and the primacy of the order of love, let me enumerate several areas where I think the attempt to create an ethical space of reciprocity shaped the Franciscan response to the sexual abuse crisis. Reflecting on these elements also gives some indication of a path to the future.

First, if we place as a starting point in the middle of our discussion and actions a primary category of human relationships such as brother or sister, then the ethical demands that come from such a relationship need to permeate without subverting the other types of relationships that we have in Church and society, be they pastoral, positional, hierarchical, or professional. We are first creatures of the same God, Father, Son, and Holy Spirit, and members of the same human family. For example, in the course of the abuse scandal we discovered that the ethical demand of treating everyone with dignity and witnessing to the law of reciprocal exchange needed to include in its extensiveness brother and sister lay people who were members of the same ecclesial family and therefore brought their truthful teaching and their demand for justice to the situation. The family that originally came to the friars and the Church and cited 1 Corinthians 12.20–21 was expressing the same underlying reality: "As it is there are many members, yet one body. The eye cannot say to the hand, 'I have no need of you,' nor again, the head to the feet, 'I have no need of you.'" From a Franciscan point of view there was no choice but to try to respond to the lay people in some reciprocal fashion, even if the learning was slow and at times not done very well. It required and still requires the learning of humility.

The creation of this ethical space of exchange also included the demand to make alliances with professional people in the world of law, psychology, insurance, media, and the court system. These people, believers and unbelievers of good will, were first members of the same human family, brothers and sisters who could not be dismissed as "outsiders." By their disagreement with one's own understanding they served at times to cauterize the darker forces of privatization or avoidance within the ecclesial and social body. In the course of our experience we discovered that unless these types of relationships were maintained, however painfully, then the deeper roots of the institutional crisis in the affections would remain hidden, unknown actually to both sides. So strong is the force of custom and inheritance, Augustine would say, that the human heart knows not its own complicities in the drive toward private power unless history and others outside one's own group become the surgeons who excise the disease. Of course, the cauterizing function worked both ways. The interchange itself brought balance.

It can be more important and more healing in the long run to maintain a relationship with a sometimes contentious Independent Board of Inquiry than to break the bonds of exchange. The same truth emerged when the brothers who were offending priests were sent not to church-run treatment programs but to secular sexual offender programs. Contact with secularity deepened, not weakened, maturation and growth in the fullness of Gospel truth. In the midst of the conflicts, it made us turn to the order of love and enabled us to practice penance. The establishment of a permanent Independent Response Team composed of both lay and religious membership moved in a similar direction. In some ways we had to incorporate this wider community of peoples into the internal life of the fraternity and the Church without damaging the integrity of a distinctly religious identity. This same pathway of reciprocal exchange might be helpful to the Church today lest it fall prey to an institutional pattern formed by the vitamin deficiencies that the explosion in 2002 has bequeathed to everyone. Without a forum where those outside one's own group are allowed to cauterize the inherent institutional drive toward the private, evangelical freedom cannot emerge in all of its fullness.

Second, if we place obedience to the "order of love" in the center of our discussions and actions, then the ethical demand that flows from such obedience begins to take expression in attitudes and structures that make a conscious attempt at mediation and peace. Confronted with the "law of constraints" on almost all sides, we discovered in the course of the sexual abuse scandal that there was very little anyone could do to shape the outcome when various perspectives and jurisdictions collided. Defending one's own turf on one's own terms became a non-option; in fact, the lack of equity, as has been mentioned, became palpable. A difficult lesson, to be sure, but the experience opened up a new perspective. On the level of attitude, over time it became evident that if any single order that could produce peace could not be established, then at least in all circumstances a personal choice could be made to witness to a greater order of love, in fact, a greater order of justice. The intention to remain rooted in this order and to make choices from within it, as Augustine indicated in the *Confessions* and Francis discovered when the Lord revealed the greeting of peace, needed to take root in the will and find expression in small actions of nonviolence, forgiveness, humility, and an openness to reconciliation.

Structurally, the Franciscan friars discovered that throughout the entire process choices had to be made to "operationalize" the order of love so as to mediate some peace through legal strategies of reconciliation and settlement. For example, when we entered into agreements after the 2002 revelations in Boston, creation of this ethical space required leadership to meet personally with individual victims within the context of a civil court proceeding. None of these attitudes and approaches could be developed without the aid of supportive brothers and sisters, both in the Church and outside of it. In actual fact, the course of history itself, the law of constraints, and people's reluctance challenged our attitudes, closed some administrative doors, and opened others. But this path of justice in the order of love was a better way toward peace.

Third, the centrality of becoming a brother or sister and the primacy of the order of love points to the existence of a multiplicity of gifts at the heart of what it means to be Church and society. We have seen this clearly in the thinking of Bonaventure. At stake in the controversy is not simply one structure or another but our image of God, God's presence in history, and God's providential call to life-in-communion with each other for the sake of the world. As Bonaventure would argue, "It is likewise evident how wide is the illuminative way and how in everything which is perceived or known God Himself lies hidden within."[42] We discovered in the course of the abuse scandal that in fact God's gifts were manifest in multiple directions: In the *officium* that went with hierarchical position, in the gift of the priesthood and religious life, in the expertise that went with our lay collaborators, in the call for truthfulness that was manifest in victims and family members, in the drive toward repentance hidden in those who had offended, in the fraternal love manifested in the friars, in the law of reciprocity manifested by a global Church. The great spiritual exchange that took place after the "contemporary last supper" indicated that God's presence operated in the hearts of a believing com-

munity and in the hearts of people of good will spread throughout the world. As was noted earlier, what was needed was both
the occasion and the practice of repentance to allow this goodness to "emerge into being."[43] When we were tempted to withdraw into our own protected enclaves of partisanship, or when
we assented even partially to the private possession of our own
good and ignored the good of others, this overwhelming liberality and generosity of God, so consoling and so helpful, so revelatory of "glory" present in the world, hid itself and we were
left alone.

Fourth, if the crisis over the sexual abuse of minors in the
Church has indeed reflected a much wider issue of the disordered affections that often drive relational power in the Church,
then any long-term administrative procedure, legal solution, or
intellectual explanation that does not acknowledge and address
the root cause will simply hide the disease. The challenge of
relational power continues. Unless the hidden cancer of disordered affections is attended to, it will mutate, take a different
form in some other part of the social body, or publicly withdraw, lie dormant, and await a future blossoming. A much more
profound conversion is needed, one that is ascetically exacting.
In Chapter 3 I tried to describe the long-term importance of a
structure of conversation that supported affective conversion;
we called it Fraternity-in-Mission. Others may call their own
programs by a different name. The necessity of such a program
cannot be doubted. However, with respect to what we have discussed in this chapter, the social virtue correlative with the reconciliation of hierarchy and community in their relationships of
power is humility.

Practically, as we have seen from our Franciscan teachers,
humility means choosing to "become subject to every human
creature," learning to appreciate and foster the grace of another, learning to give and receive truth and bread from others
while not abandoning one's own identity, learning publicly to
admit complicity in sin and therefore the need for correction

and repentance. Bonaventure's technical name for true humility was "condescension," and he noted that its liberating power came from the person of Jesus Christ:

> But who will liberate us from these plagues? There is indeed only one who comes in order that he might liberate us, namely Christ, who accepted ten condescensions atoning for the ten plagues. This is symbolized in the book of *Kings*, where it says that the sun receded ten degrees. [2 Kings 20.8–11.] By that is signified the ten acts of condescension which the Lord accepted for the sake of human beings.
>
> [1] The first condescension was the taking on of our flesh.
>
> [2] The second was the taking on of our mortal nature.
>
> [3] The third was the acceptance of our needs, because he suffered hunger, thirst and cold.
>
> [4] The fourth was the acceptance of our poverty, because he was made needy, not having a place in which to rest.
>
> [5] The fifth was the acceptance of our temptations, when he permitted himself to be tempted; and in this he bore our infirmity. The Apostle says: "We do not have a high priest who cannot have compassion on our infirmities, but one having been tempted in all things." [Heb. 4.15]
>
> [6] The sixth was the acceptance of our bodily weariness and our labor.
>
> [7] The seventh was the acceptance of our anxiety. So it says: "Jesus began to fear and to be weary and he said, 'My soul is sad even unto death.'" [Mark 14.33–34]
>
> [8] The eighth was the acceptance of the cross, and that was amazing.

[9] The ninth was the acceptance of death.
[10] The tenth was by descending to the prison of the underworld.[44] [7.16]

For the future, negotiating the path that Jesus himself did not reject will require obedience to the Order of Love, the grace of the Holy Spirit, and, as we have seen in Bonaventure, a deeper following of the redemptive and loving human path of the Way, the Truth, and the Life. This asceticism of humility that touches the mind, the heart, and the will, and takes concrete shape in prayer and conversation with others will not subvert either hierarchy or community. The asceticism of humility will give both hierarchy and community a different center of gravity in service to the neighbor and in the openness to receive from others.

In the long run, as we recognize the scandal of sexual abuse and note its deeper connections with problems of power, perhaps the comment of Augustine, repeated by Bonaventure and known so well on an experiential level by Francis of Assisi, needs to be demonstrated in the life of the Church for the sake of the world: "The saying comes true in us, that *anyone who increases knowledge increases sorrow* (Eccles. 1.18). As charity grows strong in you, you will suffer all the more over a sinner. The greater your charity, the more agonizing will your pain be over the sinner you must tolerate, though he will provoke you not to anger, but to pity for him."[45]

7. OWNERSHIP AND FREEDOM

As imperfection is not necessarily sinful—
so perfection is not merely the rectitude of justice, but also
liberation.
Riches, being alluring and dangerous, prevent this
        liberation.

SAINT BONAVENTURE
Defense of the Mendicants[1]

UP TO THE PRESENT I have argued that one of the casualties of the sexual abuse crisis has been disappearance from our historical memory of alternative approaches that developed in the course of the events. In the wake of Boston, opposing sides have hardened in their divisions, and the development of an ethics of reciprocity between people has become occluded. A space of mediation has been lost in the Church. Using the Franciscan tradition as an example, I have tried to identify two of the guiding principles for developing this space of reciprocal exchange in the future. First, the primary belief that all human beings share the common human bond of brother and sister needs to be expressed in word and action. This first point of entry needs to permeate all other definitions of identity. Second, the choice to live subject to the Order of Love expressed in the Great Commandment needs to become the focus of preaching and performance. These two principles, which could shape relationships in the Church and society, have as one of their foundational virtues humility, described by Bonaventure as "the gate of wisdom," the "foundation of justice," and the "dwelling place of grace."[2]

To clarify the depths of this vision and its confrontation with other difficulties in our society and Church, I would now like to explore the crisis as it related to the questions of institutional ownership and freedom. Although the topic of corporate bankruptcy has already been alluded to, it is now appropriate to describe its wider significance. Again using the Franciscan friars as a case study, the chapter will first address some of the questions that may have confronted many leaders as they dealt with the issue of financial reparation. In the course of this description, I will try to indicate why I found the Franciscan inheritance of dispossession helpful in creating an ethical space where reparation could occur. That explanation will be followed by more systematic comments that articulate this spiritual and theological tradition in Francis and Bonaventure. The chapter will conclude by indicating why this tradition of dispossession might prove beneficial for the creation of the communal space of reciprocity that is needed to move forward.

Bankruptcy and Dispossession: A Case Study

As we have seen in Chapter 1, the sexual abuse scandal from 1984 to 2006 gradually migrated from the realm of the Church's pastoral action to venues associated with the adversarial realm of the legal system and court proceedings. Much of this movement was in reaction to the refusal of some Church leaders to respond adequately to the multiple dimensions of the problem. The difficulties of the Church in Boston illustrated the major developments. Based on extensive interviews, documentation, and "civil disposition transcripts," the National Review Board concluded: "The picture that emerged was that of a diocese with a cadre of predator priests and a hierarchy that simply refused to confront them and stop them."[3] This pattern and parallel developments in other large archdioceses began to dominate the interpretation of the national picture. The documentation surfaced that rights were violated, power abused, and justice delayed in many sectors of the Church.[4]

Out of such a tragic failure to deal with abusive activity it was inevitable that people sought justice in a civil forum. Those involved in the cases witnessed at first hand a drama including not just the sexual abuse of a minor by a clergyman but other allied encounters where values collided. In the civil court system defendants, insurance carriers, and plaintiffs' attorneys argued over culpability and monetary amounts. In more private venues, others negotiated who was responsible for payments to therapists and treatment centers. In some instances, priest offenders confronted superiors and dioceses over the obligations of financial support. In numerous Church communities discussions took place as to who was responsible and how to pay the reparations. The threat of long court proceedings, public disclosures, punitive damages, and the loss of significant resources for ministerial and charitable works served as a backdrop to protracted negotiations. By 2006 many dioceses had declared bankruptcy.

At some level these various confrontations involved questions of ownership, property, and money: Who controlled Church property? To whom did it really belong? Who had how much, and how much would be enough? Why should the people pay for the misdeeds of the leaders? Given the varying amounts for settlements paid out in different states, the increasing cost of cases, and the positioning the different sides took throughout the more recent phases of the crisis, there can be little doubt that the question of clerical sexual abuse had now become mixed up with the economic forces, institutions, and culture of a predominantly free market society.[5] I have already highlighted, in Chapter 3, some of these areas of confluence in the description of the early monetary settlements. Most of us are still too close to these events in time to sort out all the issues and their complex interaction. What I can present here is one perspective that emerged from my own experience and tradition while confronting another collision of values. It seems to me a valuable one in analyzing both interior dimensions of the crisis and in discerning a path for the future.

Early in 2006 a group of about twenty Franciscans gathered

at our friary in Oakland, California. We had before us a very important question and decision to make: In the wake of the new civil suits filed against the province because of the "window legislation" adopted by the California state legislature (i.e., the lifting of all statutory limits during the calendar year of 2003 for civil suits in cases of the abuse of a minor), would the province as a corporation be willing to declare bankruptcy? Or, following its previous policies, would the province settle with the plaintiffs and thus open itself to a state of financial fragility? We had committed ourselves to the establishment of just reparation for the terrible misdeeds of our brothers. This had been our commitment since the early beginnings of the crisis. But these newly filed civil suits brought new challenges. The Franciscan Friars of California did not have a great amount of money; we owned only a few properties not directly aligned with our ministerial works. In July 2005 we had sold for $21 million the only substantial piece of property not directly connected with work in the Church, the former Saint Anthony Seminary where most of the abuse had taken place. But settlement demands could easily move both beyond this amount and the other monies we did have.

This institutional question had no precedent in our experience. Confronted with the legitimate demands for reparation, our need and desire to do penance and create some justice, and the disparity between our resources and what might be needed to amend the harm our brothers had caused, we faced various questions: Which course of action would establish the most equity for everyone concerned? If we settled for an amount that went beyond our capacities, how could we continue even at a minimal level our daily operations, our mission of preaching, parish Church ministry, help for the poor, and education? How could we continue to support the elderly or pay for the education of future recruits? How did this do justice to the people whose contributions had supported and continued to support all of our services? What was the common good? If we declared bankruptcy, how would that happen? What types of complicated and protracted litigation issues would arise with the plaintiffs? What did it mean to have a court appointed overseer with jurisdiction over any transactions beyond the ordinary course of business? What would be the legal fees? Would this avenue establish an equitable settlement among all those concerned? In short, we considered in some detail the impact our decisions would have on plaintiffs, on our own morale, on our relationships of interdependence, on the group solidarity that had emerged in the course of the renewal program, on the future course of our life and work, on the lay people who were served in parishes, retreat centers, formation programs, and outreach efforts with the poor.

Discussing our options made us very aware of our own unique tradition as professed followers of Francis of Assisi. This was a challenge. It meant that the interior renunciation of ownership on both a personal and a corporate level (what I call "dispossession") needed to guide our intentions. Materially, while engaging in apostolic works of ministry and charity and having enough to preserve our human dignity, it also meant that we needed to make a concerted communal effort to distinguish that which was needed from that which was superfluous. Our own Rule reminded us: "Let the brothers not make anything their own, neither house, nor place, nor anything at all. As pilgrims and strangers in this world, serving the Lord in poverty and humility, let them go seeking alms with confidence, and they should not be ashamed because, for our sakes, our Lord made himself poor in this world."[6] The issue of bankruptcy had now brought us to a much deeper consideration of how this tradition interfaced with the workings of American society.

Two economic realities with great consequences for public presence and witness became clear. First, the civil bankruptcy law, framed as it was within an economic system that privileged entrepreneurship and protected individual private property, made a distinction between corporate and personal bankruptcy.

When a corporation declared bankruptcy, the declaration did not necessarily place the personal assets of individuals at risk. The distinction allowed persons to move forward on an individual level while losing assets on an organizational level. The difficulty was that while the corporate structure of the Franciscan Friars fell within the purview of the law, our Franciscan religious tradition of both corporate and personal dispossession did not. We made no distinction between personal and corporate ownership; all property and money were shared in common. For us, corporate and personal bankruptcy would be the same. Although many of the questions were the same, our situation was not quite comparable to that of the diocesan Church in which both the priests and the people kept their own personal assets and property and where the bishops for the most part were corporate owners. In declaring bankruptcy, we would choose to make the court itself the arbiter not only of our corporate goods but also of our personal choices to share everything in common. A declaration of bankruptcy could jeopardize our core values, our freedom to choose to be communally interdependent, and ultimately our distinctive witness and mission. It might fracture our fraternity on both a material and spiritual level. Here was a clear confrontation between a medieval system that inclined toward socialism and the modern system of American market capitalism

Second, and equally as important to us, declaring bankruptcy was a legitimate social means of self-protection in establishing a broader equity in the community. But this path did not immediately accord with our commitments to make reparations in as much as we could. Choosing such a course would lead both sides of the disputes to engage in protracted litigation. We had seen before the impact of these types of legal and insurance procedures, which could easily move beyond the direct control of the litigants into the hands of others with different economic values and purposes. How did this fit with our tradition of making peace? This was not the experience of everyone, but we believed that the personal and systemic traumas of sexual abuse once exposed to the structures of civil adjudication might only be compounded.[7]

From these converging internal perspectives, declaring bankruptcy became a non-option, not only on the level of tactics but also and primarily on the level of principle. The decision was made to try to settle the cases and negotiate as far as we were able with the claimants. In God's Providence, I believe, the new claims were eventually settled for $28 million. To be sure, it was an institutional and corporate stretch. But professing the central values of living without anything of our own, the doing of penance, and the making of peace had acted like a force field in our decision-making process, moving us in a direction that we had never taken before. Our choice was not compatible with the governing values of American society; it was, however, compatible with our spiritual and theological tradition.

What did we learn from all of this that might be helpful today? Primarily, as I look back on it, I think many of us learned how the proprietary forces of our own culture penetrate into the depths of the human heart. Residing there they can affect the actions we take toward others in numerous areas. Experientially, the challenge of bankruptcy raised to a conscious level the hidden personal and corporate ambiguities culturally associated with questions of money, property, and corporate security: possessiveness, fear for the future, mistrust, resentment at material loss. These human drives pushed in the direction of defensiveness, the total protection of one's own power and property, the pursuit of private gain, and the objectification of the opponent. The entire situation provided multiple opportunities for wrangling and tactical maneuvers to protect the boundaries between "what was mine" and "what could be yours." From my own perspective, the "insane warfare of the courts"[8] appeared riddled with questions related to money, property, and public power. This is not to deny that the pursuit of justice was at work, nor that there were great wrongs that people needed to put right. Those elements were uppermost. Yet, as we have seen earlier, profound questions of equity arose, equity between the litigants and equity for all the members of the Church.

In such a situation, in order to discover some framework of meaning that could assimilate the new and painful learning, we Franciscans turned to our own spiritual and intellectual tradition. We reread the past so as to take hope for the future. In our understanding, Francis's message appeared timely because he and his brothers had seen similar dimensions of the human heart operative in the "cares and concerns" that dominated the life of his merchant father and entered deeply into his own heart. Acquisitiveness was not an isolated vice. He had discovered these same "cares and concerns" in the civil and communal wars over geographical expansion and commercial influence. He had experienced them legally in the inequitable arrangements between the different classes in Assisi so as to exclude the truly poor from the social contract. He knew from his own experience the types of relationships created in a monetary economy, which denied to many their human dignity and placed social structures and law at the service of private gain. Lastly, Francis and his early brothers had witnessed these same forces in the human hearts of the ecclesiastics of his day in their political battles over social image, property, and power.[9] And in the midst of this combination of forces, which derived from the shared culture of his day, Francis had chosen to renounce all forms of ownership. The inner drive toward private ownership and control was one cause of the violence in society. He had committed himself to the virtue and performance of dispossession so as to become free to practice peace, to create an ethical space of reciprocal charity. His point of entry into contentious situations was not the protection of his own property but the drive to establish human community. For myself, clarifying the challenges and ultimate meaning of this path of dispossession and its relationship to the freedom to make peace was one of the great benefits of the crisis.

"Dispossession"—the way the Franciscan tradition under-
stands it sheds light on our human condition and how within
the structures of a market society the Church itself can be called
through its experience to establish "forms of economic activity
marked by quotas of gratuitousness and communion."[10] Its contemporary pertinence can be seen when it is read as a commentary on the insights so well expressed by Václav Havel earlier in
this book. He referred to "the ambiguous moral tendencies"
that emerged from dormancy as people tried to build a new
order of things. We have seen these "ambiguous moral tendencies" manifest themselves in intense and sometimes violent
struggles over power, in the hardening of positions by the "sorting" of the Church into interest groups, in the long and protracted financial negotiations to settle the cases of sexual abuse.
Our analysis of the sexual abuse crisis as manifesting a larger
problem of "disordered affections" (Chapter 5) pointed in a
similar direction. The question was not simply one of clear
thinking and correct management; it was also one of a purification of the affections. Commitment to dispossession helped cauterize those hidden affections. The next two sections of this
chapter will elaborate upon these learnings using key Franciscan
sources. Once again I simply wish to illustrate how the recover-
ing of a living spiritual and theological tradition might help the
Church in its current travails.

Francis, Dispossession, and the Human Heart

IN THE DECADES OF the 1240s and 1250s, the Franciscan friars
were grappling with their tradition of poverty and living "without anything of their own." By this time they had become firmly entangled with the civil and ecclesiastical world of a proprietary society.[11] As a corrective, two stories from the early days
began to circulate, one dealing with their relationship to society and the Church, the other dealing with the possessions
entrusted to them. First, "When they were begging alms

throughout the city," the oral tradition recalled, "hardly anyone would give to them; instead they denounced them for disposing of their possessions so that they could live off others, and therefore they suffered extreme want." The Church also, more solicitous for the welfare of the brothers, confronted the situation in the person of the local bishop.

The bishop of the city of Assisi, to whom the man of God [Francis] would frequently go for counsel, receiving him kindly, told him: "It seems to me that your life is very rough and hard, especially, in not possessing anything in this world." To which the saint said: "Lord, if we had possessions, we would need arms for our protection. For disputes and lawsuits *usually* arise out of them, and, because of this, love of God and neighbor are greatly impeded. Therefore, we do not want to possess anything in this world." The man of God's response greatly pleased the bishop. For Francis scorned all worldly goods, but money most of all; so much so, that in all his rules he most forcefully commended poverty and repeated that the brothers be eager to avoid money.[12]

A second story was also called to mind. This one considered how the friars were to use the goods of the churches entrusted to them. One day,

Brother Peter of Catanio, the saint's vicar, saw that great crowds of brothers from other places visited Saint Mary of the Portiuncula, and that the alms received were not sufficient to provide for their needs. He told Saint Francis: "Brother, *I don't know what to do*; I don't have enough to provide for all the crowds of brothers pouring in from all over. I beg you, please allow some of the goods of those entering as novices to be kept so that we

can have recourse to these for expenses *in due season*."
But the saint replied: "May that piety be elsewhere, my
dear brother, which treats the *Rule* with impiety for the
sake of anyone." "Then, what should I do?" asked
Peter. "Strip the Virgin's altar and take its adornments
when you can't care for the needy in any other way.
Believe me, she would be happier to have her altar
stripped and the Gospel of her Son kept than have her
altar decorated and her Son despised. The Lord will
send someone to return to his Mother what He has
loaned to us."[13]

On a very simple level, the stories captured the connection
that Francis saw, and the brothers were currently experiencing,
between ownership and the adjudication of what was "mine"
and what was "yours" through civil disputes and public litigation. From the viewpoint of Francis of Assisi the ownership of
property was not only a means of economic exchange but also
a carrier of the divisions between people. He chose the way of
renunciation of ownership, money, and goods not because ownership and money and goods were evil, but because, on an experiential level, the ownership of property and the felt need to
secure the future would probably become entangled with violence and social discord. Put another way, his choice of "poverty" emerged out of a searing and astute experience of the deeper "crevices of the human heart," which subtly turned
ownership, money, property, and goods—the material things of
life—toward private gain and the use of power to secure positions and alleviate fear. This could happen equally in the civil or
ecclesiastical arenas because in both areas the complexities of
the human heart were the same.

Francis used the intellectual tools available to him, his spiritual inheritance in the desert fathers and monasticism, to interpret the situation. These spiritual sources taught him to address
problems at their root cause in the disordered affections of the

human heart.[14] In his *Earlier Rule* he referred to these deeper dimensions of human life by citing the Gospel: "From the heart proceeds and come evil thoughts, adultery, fornication, murder, theft, greed, malice, deceit, licentiousness, envy, false witness, blasphemy, foolishness. All these evils come from within, from a person's heart, and these are what defile a person."[15] This was the situation from which no human being was immune. "Let us beware of the malice and craftiness of Satan," he wrote, "who does not want anyone to turn his mind and heart to God. And prowling around he wants to ensnare a person's heart under the guise of some reward or assistance, to choke out the word and precepts of the Lord from our memory, and, desiring a person's heart, [he wants] to blind it through worldly affairs and concerns."[16] Given this spiritual diagnosis for the disease of violence, the renunciation of things, living "without anything of one's own," acted like an intellectual and practical brake on the anger, resentment, defensiveness, and search for a total justice in one's own favor that seemed to emerge when property was threatened. As a "therapy for the soul" or "discipline of life" the profession of dispossession became a magnet that rearranged the selfish filings in the human heart. It directed the person in a contentious society away from the use of his or her affective energies to accumulate things toward the use of these same energies to love God above all things and love the neighbor as oneself.

Socially, "living without anything of one's own" broke from the ordinary economic ways of doing things. It forced people to engage not just the possibilities but also the problems at the heart of the emerging market society. While supporting the pursuit of justice, it directed justice toward its higher goal, charity. Within the Church, this choice for dispossession provided a "prick of conscience" for those members of the Body of Christ entangled with the interests of social influence, property, and power. It argued for the importance of a different type of Christian presence in the world. As Francis understood it, his choice for dispossession was meant to foster in others an insight into the concrete priority of the Great Commandment and a practice of extending to everyone, friend and foe alike, the greeting that had been revealed to him: "The Lord give you peace." Unique in its contours, this calling possessed a public purpose in both Church and society.

Bonaventure and the Insertion of Dispossession into Public Life

AS WE HAVE SEEN previously, it was left to Bonaventure, the Paris theologian and the Minister General of the Order, to create a public apologia for Francis's vision in the Church and society. Where Francis had spiritually and intuitively felt his way toward the value of dispossession, Bonaventure was able to relate the embrace of poverty to a much more developed theological tradition. His view of the human person relied on Augustine. Some in the Church found this vision useful; others "admirable" but "not exemplary" (i.e., not to be emulated or followed); and many others, only destructive to the commercial order.[17] It was meant to be illuminating, consoling, and socially productive of peace.

From Bonaventure's perspective concrete difficulties within the Church and society revealed the disordered affections of the human heart. People chose to turn what God had given for the common good toward what they could own for private gain. Throughout his writings, Bonaventure relied on the teaching provided by 1 Timothy 6.10, "Avarice is the root of all evils, and some in their pursuit of it have strayed from the faith."[18] "Since the vice of covetousness and its disorder," he wrote, "find their root in a disposition of the mind and their occasion and fuel in things possessed externally, perfect extirpation of this root must apply to both in order that the damaging passion of avarice and the alluring possession of earthly wealth may be abandoned both spiritually and materially." The theologian's use of "disposition of the mind" (i.e., heart, affections, will) should be noted. He placed his analysis of the complexities of human behavior, as had Augustine before him, on the level of their source in the human being's inner self, his or her affections, desires, and emotional energies associated with the will.[19]

This teaching on the centrality of desire and will in shaping the relationships with people and with things was not an abstraction but an experiential description. It occurred against the backdrop of Bonaventure's knowledge of the forces of greed in himself, the Franciscan friars, the members of the Church, and the society at large.[20] He was a good observer of human life: "Today," he noted, "there is more concern for possessing temporal things than for distributing them"; avarice "reigns above all at the end of the world."[21]

The real problem of human sociability lay within each person, even though it was aided and abetted by the internalized patterns of familial, political, economic, and commercial life. One reason people acted the way they acted was because custom, habit, and established pathways of relating too often reinforced the weak "weight" of the will and its desires or loves: "In my case," Augustine had written, "love is the weight by which I act. To whatever place I go, I am drawn to it by love."[22] And Bonaventure concurred: "A stone tends downward; fire tends upward; rivers run to the sea; the tree is joined to its root, and other things are joined to their root. The rational creature is God-like. It can turn back to its sources by means of memory, intelligence and will. But unless it turns itself back to its source, it is not pious."[23] The difficulty was that people's affections and love, the creative powers of their will, became attached to things in an inordinate way: "By its lack of harmony with the highest goodness, the will is rendered needy and becomes involved in an infinite quest through disordered desire (*concupiscentia*) and cupidity, as is related in Proverbs: *Fire never says 'enough.' The covetous person will not be filled with money*, as we read in Ecclesiastes. Thus humankind is always seeking and begging."[24]

For Bonaventure, as for Francis, the choice to "live without anything of one's own" was designed to force awareness of this human propensity to ownership and use of things shaped by greed, to cauterize it, and then produce an action based on charity, an action that would create a new pattern in human relationships. The renunciation of things in private and in common, a social act visible to all, disposed a person "for the mortification of the flesh and to the perfect abnegation of one's own will, since a person retains nothing for himself, neither house nor place nor anything."[25] "Again," he wrote from his experience, "riches are an incentive to cupidity, since it is difficult to have them without loving them. But the more anyone distances himself from the incentive to sin, the more perfectly he acts. But the person who renounces everything in common and in private does this."[26] He cited Augustine: "The poison of love is the hope of getting or holding onto temporal goods. The nourishment of love is the lessening of cupidity. The perfection of love is no cupidity. The sign of its progress is the lessening of fear."[27] Through the profession of the following of the poor Christ and the refusal of ownership in all its forms, the person committed himself or herself as much as possible to separating out the human drive to love God, self, neighbor, and the good things of the earth from the human tendencies to possess these things on one's own terms.

Applying this way of renunciation required self-reflection, the acceptance of challenges from outside one's own world, and the providential care of brothers and sisters. As experience showed, the promise itself to live "without anything of one's own" was deepened and made operative by the course of life itself. Real life brought with it a sense of exposure, fragility, humiliation—a knowledge that indeed the customs and patterns of the world cut through one's own heart. Augustine had narrated his own pilgrim journey in his *Confessions*: "When my mind speculates upon its own capabilities, it realizes that it cannot safely trust its own judgement, because its inner workings are generally so obscure that they are only revealed in the light of experience."[28] And yet, along with its difficulties, this human journey toward love was not a way foreign to God himself, who had accomplished it without sin so that we might be accompanied, forgiven, and follow in his footsteps: "Christ was poor at his birth, poor during the course of his life, and poor at his death. In order to make poverty lovable to the world, he chose a most poor Mother. He willingly suffered the pains of poverty, and went about unshod as a poor and destitute person."[29]

Positively put, the choice for voluntary poverty, inspired by the Holy Spirit, was really an invitation to enter the kingdom of God. As a human task, it challenged its adherents to make citizenship in that kingdom of God more visible on earth. Moved to place the Order of Love (the Trinitarian communion of goods) at the center of life, a person committed himself or herself to the reconstruction of the "giving and receiving" in human relationships that existed at the very beginning of creation. Such a practice showed oneself and others to be made in God's image; here sociability was achieved not through the "modality of possessions" but through the "modality of a communion of love."[30] In such a world, the "affection of perfect charity" produced its own obligations, ones not arising from the debt of sin: "Owe no one anything except to love one another."[31] In this world a person tried as much as possible to anticipate this kingdom of God by marking relationships with personal dignity, mutual affirmation, the sharing of goods. "And it pertains to the perfection of the mystical body of Christ that its members share with one another 'in giving and receiving,' so that they together might supply for one another's indigence."[32]

It should be noted that for Bonaventure this profession of voluntary poverty did not denigrate ownership or possessions in themselves. As with many of the mendicant theologians, he did not condemn the life of the merchant or those who possessed private property. The Church itself had a rightful claim to dominion, property, and rights; certainly individuals and communities could also claim ownership.[33] He argued strong-

ly against a pessimistic position that would see the things that
mark our economic and material relationships as evil: "For if
anyone believes that sin exists in wealth, either causally or for-
mally, he is erring with the Manichaeans. . . . Wealth, in fact,
offers no difficult obstacle to those who desire to enter the
kingdom of God, except by being an occasion of propensity
toward evil or of distraction from the good." Bonaventure
cited Bernard, "[T]he principal reason why people should flee
from riches is that they can scarcely or never be possessed
without falling in love with them."[34] The root difficulty was
the relationship between the profound human disposition to
attach itself in a proprietary way to the goods of this world
and the goods themselves; to say to the neighbor, this is for my
exclusive use and my exclusive gain, not at all for you and
your benefit.

Because of the human disposition toward cupidity, the
things of this world became "alluring," awakening, if you like,
the passion of covetousness: "The cravings and senses of almost
every person may easily lead to 'the lust of the eyes' and to being
dazzled by riches";[35] personal property "carries with it some
consequences that may occasionally become obstacles to good
and enticements to evil."[36] This drive toward the private possession of things could shape people's relationships to almost anything: positions, social honor, prestige, possessions, ideas,
power, status, and people: "[N]o sin is more abominable than
the covetousness and desire for honor of ecclesiastical persons,
for in these two sins the Holy Spirit is either bought or sold with
the result that the house of God becomes 'a den of thieves.'"[37]

From my perspective and experience with the sexual abuse
scandal, Bonaventure's locating social and ecclesial problems in
the complexities of the human heart was important in two significant ways. First, in his defense of the Franciscan way of life,
Bonaventure acknowledged that from both the civil and ecclesiastical perspectives this renunciation of ownership seemed useless. It was not God's calling for everyone; it was certainly diffi-

cult; and in the real order of life some who owned property were not affected by greed, and those who practiced renunciation could often be carriers of greed.[38] So, why pursue it? On the one hand, Bonaventure's whole point was that an articulated and publicly accepted tradition of dispossession was necessary as a corrective to the established economic patterns in society. It broke through them, as we have seen, to argue for a "practice of communion." On the other hand, this asceticism of dispossession served to cut through the entrenched public pathways of defensiveness that often shaped the Church in its pastoral structures and its institutional choices.

Second, by focusing on the struggle within the human heart, Bonaventure proved insightful about the relationship between the hierarchical and communal elements in the Church and society. He recognized the hierarchical differences created by office and authority; he did not compare people in different states of life with each other; nor did he wish to reduce everyone to the same way of life.[39] "These orders," he wrote, "are distinguished in relation to their greater or lesser perfection."[40] The vocation of the prelates, the monks, and the friars; married couples, singles, and virgins; those living without anything of their own, those who held common property, the priests who owned private property, and the laity who possessed a multitude of things—all could be legitimate and holy callings within the diverse world God had made. Yet, in such an ordered world, people needed to be watchful lest through the vices of arrogance and avarice they divide good and evil into discernible social groups, chosen professions, or material locations. Possessiveness cut through the relationships with everything and was especially dangerous when a person clung to position, office, or clerical identity as if it were his own. In reality, the complexities of the human heart belonged equally to a public official, a judge, a lawyer, a professional person, a Franciscan friar, a priest, a prelate of the Church, any man or any woman. That person might be a citizen of the city or a vassal of the pope.

In effect, Bonaventure's understanding of human life "dematerialized evil" by breaking it out of the human tendency to locate it in a world external to the self or external to one's own group of confidants. Neither the Church, nor any particular way of life, nor the world had a monopoly on goodness, truth, or beauty. People were different, called to follow Christ in distinct ways, "out of the highest dispensation of the wisdom of God 'who allots his gifts to everyone as he will.'"[41] But everyone was called equally to a life of penance and conversion.[42] In such a world, one could not cover over the complexities of the human heart by an appeal to a purified ideology, or by the status one held in the Church, or by a claim to a special religious calling; one could not hide the struggle behind a sociological, professional, or religious façade of knowledge or removal from worldly affairs. Good and evil could not be separated out by gender or by comparisons between classes and statuses in the Church. It all depended on the quality of a person's love: "Sometimes a lay person may be more perfect than a religious."[43] In fact, people needed each other in order to give full witness to the overwhelming plenitude of Christ's grace.

> Now since the perfection of state that derives either from a vow or from an office is of little worth without the perfection of merit and since perfection of merit cannot be obtained without love, which is a gift of the Holy Spirit and since no one knows whether one person is more highly favored than another, for even the favored one is unaware of any particular gift, it follows that no one should esteem himself more perfect than another. Rather, in accordance with the teaching of the Apostle, if a comparison is to be made between two persons with regard to their perfection, every person, however perfect he may be, should "regard others superior to himself."[44]

In all instances, the virtues of humility and poverty externalized in deed were needed to heal organizational wounds and social divisions caused by the private ownership of God's goodness. Everyone was subject to God's free gift of grace.

Once again, living in a world in which the hierarchical and communal dimensions of the Church were in conflict, in which clergy and laity, men and women, struggled among themselves, Bonaventure had leveled the playing field, carving out an ethical space where each was called to the practice of the Great Commandment. The approach went back to Saint Augustine. In one of his sharpest passages pertinent to the present circumstances, the doctor of Grace had written:

> These two loves—of which one is holy, the other unclean, one social the other private, one taking thought for the common good because of the companionship in the upper regions, the other putting even what is common at its own personal disposal because of its lordly arrogance; one of them God's subject, the other his rival, one of them calm, the other turbulent, one peaceable, the other rebellious; one of them setting more store by the truth than by the praises of those who stray from it, the other greedy for praise by whatever means, one friendly, the other jealous, one of them wanting for its neighbor what it wants for itself, the other wanting to subject its neighbor to itself; one of them exercising authority over its neighbor for its neighbor's good, the other for its own— these two loves were first manifested in the angels, one in the good, the other in the bad, and then distinguished the two cities, one of the just, the other of the wicked, founded in the human race under the wonderful and inexpressible providence of God as he administers and directs everything he has created. These two cities are mixed up together in the world while time runs its course, until they are sorted out by the last judgment.[45]

In summary, the spiritual and theological tradition of Francis and Bonaventure links together humility, the practice of peace between people, and the necessity of "dispossession," or living "without anything of one's own." It tries to address the ecclesial ills of its day by pointing to the disordered affections of the human heart and the reinforcement of these patterns within the body of believers by the unconscious acceptance of the values of a proprietary world. These patterns run through everyone. As a remedy, both Francis and Bonaventure argue by word and example for the public acceptance of some key social virtues. In his writings, Francis describes how "humility" and "poverty" are sisters and how both counteract two dominant vices, arrogance and greed: "Lady holy Poverty, may the Lord protect You, with Your Sister, holy Humility. . . . Holy Poverty confounds the desire for riches, greed, and the cares of this world. Holy Humility confounds pride, all people who are in the world, and all that is in the world."[46] And Bonaventure, even more pointed in his argument, notes, "So if the foundation and perfection of the city of God consists principally in love and love is especially perfect when every trace of cupidity is excluded, because cupidity poisons love, then a person who entirely banishes this cupidity is the one who absolutely renounces all things in deed and in will. Just as 'the root of all evils is cupidity,' so too is the highest poverty the root and beginning of perfection."[47] If humility is designed to purify how people exercise with others their God-given dominion over themselves, so dispossession is designed to purify how they use for others their God-given dominion over things. Both virtues remain a challenge for today.

Toward an Ethical Space of Reciprocal Dispossession

IN CONCLUSION, I WOULD like to enumerate just three ways in which the public recovery of this tradition of dispossession might serve us in today's Church and society.

First, property in the Franciscan perspective, even when it is the property of the Church, is not an absolute; nor should the fear of what could happen and the need to secure the future drive our attitudes. In fact, in many cases our possessions and our insurances, the cupidity hidden in the crevices of our own hearts, may prevent our witness to the Gospel imperative of love. The higher standard of dispossession needs to be put within the horizon of our ethical decisions, even if it cannot always be performed. Guided by this commitment in both intention and action, a person freely chooses to affirm each person's human dignity, the inclusion of all in the community of goods, and the creation of solidarity. A different kind of freedom develops when freedom is divorced from the possession of property and money.

Second, this spiritual and theological tradition of dispossession calls explicit attention to the free choice we must make as members of the human community to balance our needs against the needs of our neighbor. Bonaventure argued centuries ago that not everyone need see their responsibilities in terms of living without anything of their own. People are given different callings. The hierarchy of the Church has different responsibilities and may make different decisions with respect to property and possessions.[48] The laity concerned with family life and the future of their children in society may choose to emphasize more the importance of economic security. The survivors of clergy sexual abuse may closely link justice with economic remuneration. These are legitimate ethical choices that are compatible with Gospel values. Sometimes they place members of the same community on course for a collision of values. Still, the deepest ethical issue is how we use the goods we have on loan from the Creator to fashion a truly human community. The "logic of the market" and the "logic of the State" must not be allowed to become the sole unconscious norms of our communal actions.[49] Embedded in the Franciscan vision is the hope of calling attention to other significant dimensions of our decisions: How are our economic practices and our life of faith connected? Do we allow the assertion of one ethical value as primary in a decision-making process to compromise unduly other significant human values? How much do the complexities hidden in the depth of the human heart drive our decisions? The insertion into the public discussion of the Church and the society of the tradition of the relativity of ownership, the traditional ideal of "all things in common," the diversity of gifts, and the struggle to create harmony when values collide is at least a modest proposal but a large intellectual and practical task.

Third, within the Church, I believe that the hierarchical and communal divisions of which we are all a part and the institutional sorting that has occurred no longer publicly foster the formation of an ethical space of reciprocal exchange as much as they could. Yet, unless the various gifts of different Church members, prelates, priests, vowed religious men and women, and married and single people create and establish new institutions and conversations where the gifts and values of each are not only treasured and affirmed but become the common currency of exchange, the plenitude of grace that Christ has given the Church will be restricted and the poor excluded—especially those made poor by the misdeeds of pastoral leaders and the members of the Church. The fullness of the Body of Christ will be lost from view. In many situations I have to agree with Augustine and Bonaventure: So deep is the drive toward the private that without the active engagement of various traditions in the Church and the views of others outside our group, even the laudable actions of leadership can mask a partial penchant to create a private world of self-aggrandizement. We have seen this force of custom with its established pathways operative in the divisions that led to the sexual abuse crisis; we have seen it operative in the crisis itself; it has reappeared again in the sorting that followed the wake of the scandal, even though the presenting misconduct has almost disappeared. Today, mediating spaces where relational power is exchanged beg for creation. As paradoxical as it may sound, Francis and Bonaventure both demonstrated a simple Gospel truth: Placing the values of humility and dispossession in the midst of our ethical spaces of responsible leadership, be that leadership given to us as members of the hierarchical or communal dimensions of the Church, may open us to the reception and enjoyment of a world of goods that is beyond our institutional imagination. Fortunately, God has given us each other on our relational path to salvation.

8. SCANDAL AND THE CHURCH

Now in this body, which is the Church, there are many
    and diverse people.
There are wayfarers and infirm people.
There are also folks beset by daily sins.

SAINT BONAVENTURE
Commentary on the Sentences IV[1]

UP TO NOW WE have considered power and ownership as two wider public dimensions of the crisis that has plagued the Church in the last twenty-five years. There is a third member of the triad of public issues that emerged in the course of the clergy sexual abuse experience: The reality of prestige or institutional credibility and its loss on a social and personal level in the experience of public scandal. As a social institution, the Church claims moral authority; as a religious institution, it claims truth and "holiness." Such has been its self-presentation in America since the early years of the immigrant Church, a public posture only strengthened during the era of the Cold War. As the *Baltimore Catechism* phrased it, "*Holy*" was a central mark of the Church; it was a social body "always teaching *holy* truths and making people *holy.*"[2] The public institutional carriers of that "holiness" were the priests and the bishops who had received the sacrament of "*Holy* Orders, and who administered the *holy* sacraments." Yet, from the very beginning of the present crisis, as early as 1985, many people had become aware that something that had been institutionally invisible was now beginning to emerge into open view; that which had been veiled from the public's perception was now being unmasked for all to see. What was coming into full view was not good; it was not "holy." It was sinful, and this problem of sinfulness was located precisely among those persons who claimed to be acting *in persona Christi* and to be mediating the holiness of God to people: the priests and the bishops.

The sexual abuse crisis involved not simply the complications of power and the drive toward private ownership but also the discovery of deeply embedded moral disorders that damaged the perceived identity of the Church, its public credibility as a teacher of truth, and its moral witness to holiness and justice. Throughout the crisis, victims noted how the personal experience of abuse had severely affected their belief in God and in the Church. They were "scandalized" in the deepest sense of the term. A "stumbling block," a *scandalon*, had been placed in the way of their faith. Others faced not a comparable but certainly an analogous challenge. Priests felt betrayed by fellow priests; religious by their brothers; bishops by their clergy. How could such behavior occur among ourselves? Eventually, as the crisis progressed, many in the Church felt scandalized by the behavior of their own leadership. How could those who claimed to teach "holy truths" and argued for the Church's moral superiority minimize a moral disorder of this magnitude, in some cases deny it, or, knowing it, ignore that it was happening? What did this prevalence of sexual abuse and its mismanagement say about the Church, about one's own belief, about the community of believers to which one belonged, about the priests and bishops, about how God is present in this world? How could such sinfulness exist in a "holy" Church?

The challenge for many believers in this situation became not simply how to solve the problem of sexual abuse. Once the Dallas Charter and Norms had been adopted in 2002, the question shifted: For those who had experienced scandal, how could one continue to believe? One modern commentator defined the experience of discovering the "scandalous" in these words: "We speak of scandal when people (or an individual) are so moved, wounded, and threatened in their personal attitudes and beliefs that their existence is seriously jeopardized, and they adopt an emotional and defensive attitude towards this disruption of their normal life and thought."[3] If the crisis of sexual abuse did anything, it disrupted the ordinary course of believing. It is this experience of disruption by way of scandal that has contributed as much as anything else to the loss of an ethical space of reciprocal trust in the Church. In times of disorientation, the retreat into enclaves of moral and ritual perfectionism has been a typical temptation within the long course of American cultural history.[4] For survival's sake, it seems to me, many have withdrawn in one way or another the relational energies needed to create mediating structures of exchange and power in the Church.

In this present chapter, I would like to explore a few of these issues by first describing the crisis over the sexual abuse of minors as a "scandal." This was such a central component of the experience of some of the Franciscan friars and many others in the Church that it can hardly be ignored. Conversations, personal observations, and study provide the deeper background. I am particularly interested here in how the fear of scandal shaped the earlier responses to the sexual abuse crisis, how the definition of "scandal" changed in the course of the crisis, and how the challenge of scandal touched the consciences of those in leadership positions. Since I am arguing for a retrieval of some mediating spaces in the Church, the central question becomes: How can this awareness of sin in the Church be integrated into the continuing life of faith and action? In a second section, following our method, the chapter will offer some insights on how these challenges to our faith might be approached from within the Franciscan spiritual and theological inheritance.

Scandal and the Awareness of Sin in the Church

THE STUDY OF THE National Review Board established by the bishops indicates that initially the need to preserve a public image through the avoidance of visible flaws was one of the primary blockages to priests and bishops dealing openly with complaints about the conduct of their peers: "Faced with serious and potentially inflammatory abuses, church leaders placed too great an emphasis on the avoidance of scandal in order to protect the reputation of the church, which ultimately bred far greater scandal and reputational injury."[5] The leadership's desire to "keep problems 'within the family' also may have come from a shortsighted concern that the faith of the laity would be shaken by their exposure."[6] No one had been catechized to accept the prevalence of sin in the ministers of the Church. With scandal came public shame, and shame destroyed personal prestige. For anyone in a position of status in the Church this was a difficult pill to swallow. It carried with it public humiliation.

These drives to maintain the Church's public image by avoiding revelations of scandalous behavior and to avoid disrupting people's trust and belief in the Church by keeping scandalous behavior private shaped many different actions throughout the crisis. The blockage of scandal issued in the denial that the misconduct could even occur, the withholding of information, the pressure placed on victims not to "go public," the secret removal of priests without informing anyone of the reasons, the failure to report to civil authorities, the hiding of personnel records. Sensitivity to scandal opened leadership up to blackmail by offending priests, facilitated hidden settlements, kept the local parish communities uninformed, and helped feed the cultural tendency toward sensationalism. All of these tendencies were aided by the peculiar experience of the Catholic community in the United States: The sense of being a minority faith in a hostile Protestant or secular culture. Defensiveness about one's frailty and sinfulness came naturally.

In June 1993, John Paul II wrote to the United States bishops in his first attempt to address the emerging crisis. His letter began with the biblical quote: "Woe to the world because of scandals" (Matt. 18.7). The pope insisted on the application of the canonical penalties for those who had "sinned against the little ones": "These [penalties] help to maintain a clear distinction between good and evil, and contribute to moral behavior as well as to creating a proper awareness of the gravity of the evil involved." He also called attention to another type of scandal.

> While acknowledging the right to due freedom of information, one cannot acquiesce in treating moral evil as an occasion for sensationalism. Public opinion often feeds on sensationalism and the mass media play a particular role therein. In fact, the search for sensationalism leads to the loss of something which is essential to the morality of society. Harm is done to the fundamental right of individuals not to be easily exposed to the ridicule of public opinion; even more a distorted image of human life is created. Moreover, by making a moral offense the object of sensationalism, without reference to the dignity of human conscience, one acts in a direction which is in fact opposed to the pursuit of the moral good.

The bishops, the pope believed, were caught between two imperatives. They needed to deal with the clergy through whom scandal had occurred. This could be done through the imposition of the appropriate canonical penalties. They also had a responsibility to the "whole of society systematically threatened by scandal and responsible for it. A great effort is needed to halt the trivializing of the great things of God and man."[7] In a context of what was perceived as militant secularism and a thirst for sensationalism, Church leaders felt some pressure to avoid feeding sensationalism by exposing the Church's faults.

While fear of scandal shaped the course of action, the growing awareness of the crime of sexual abuse also pushed the national Church response in another direction. Multiple responses were possible. On the one hand, there was reaction to the severe public exposure caused by the revelations about

Father James Porter in the summer of 1992. Was this happening because of a hostile press or the emergence of a latent anti-Catholicism? These types of revelations and interpretations, as accurate as they might have been, reinforced institutional patterns that were already shaped by fear of scandal and already predisposed to secrecy and defensiveness. On the other hand, public exposure and the need to establish credibility also contributed to the very open disciplining and removing of priests in the procedures initiated by Cardinal Bernardin in September of the same year. No single approach seemed adequate. There were different ways of dealing with scandal.

As we have seen, the November 29, 1993, press conference that the Franciscan Friars held in Santa Barbara, California, received a mixed response. Some interpreted the actions as prophetic, public truth telling; others saw the revelations as aiding and abetting "scandal" among the faithful and therefore worthy of condemnation. Many individuals with whom I spoke retreated into silence or simply denial. The "scandal" was simply too much to handle. One prominent bishop, who spoke for other ecclesiastics, noted: "We respect what the Franciscans have done; we do not admire them." From my experience, I would say that the responses depended on where people were standing, the responsibilities they held, the pressures they felt, their personal convictions, their own interpretation of the situation, their own understanding of the Church. "Scandal," like "justice," seemed to be a relative term. The pope's words easily indicated the complexity of the problem. When dealing with the cultural issue of prestige, the necessity of honesty, and the problem of scandal, who fashioned the interpretive lens? What forces were at work in the need for public exposure? What drove the ethical decisions touching public image? Was a choice to confess in public actually a choice to aid sensationalism? Was the revelation of the abuse a scandal, or was the failure to admit the abuses the real scandal? Initially, some leaders were confronted with a host of colliding opinions and values.

As the crisis played itself out, the intensity of the difficulties and the location of what was truly "scandalous" became increasingly clearer. Scandal attached itself to the depth with which many in positions of national prominence clung to the protection of an inherited vision of the Church's public presence: The Church was holy and needed to appear holy, its standing in society and the faith of the people protected. Public scandal that damaged the prestige of the Church and fed society's thirst for sensationalism needed to be avoided at all costs. The more demand for public disclosure by protest groups and media investigation, the greater grew the need to manage the risk. And inasmuch as this avoidance of scandal determined the course of action, more scandal occurred. Patterns of denial, mistrust, blaming, suspicion, anger, and shame developed in all directions. Eventually a feeling of nakedness in the face of unremitting media exposure surfaced. I believe that in some instances this social experience has induced a shared sense of shame, as the classification of the many has been determined by the failures of the few.

"Scandal" had now geometrically multiplied, moving from reaction to specific clerical misconduct to a general disgust at leadership malfeasance. The community of the Church in its relationships, its management, and its structures of accountability appeared in all of its frail humanity as riddled with sin. This was a situation of enormous "scandal." The Review Board of the bishops summarized its conclusion in the following terms: "[T]he board believes that the overriding paradigm that characterizes the crisis is one of sinfulness. The actions of priests who sexually abused minors were grievously sinful. The inaction of those bishops who failed to protect their people from predators was also grievously sinful. Somehow, the 'smoke of Satan' was allowed to enter the church, and as a result the church itself has been deeply wounded. Its ability to speak clearly and credibly on moral issues has been seriously impaired."[8]

It is difficult to plumb the depths of the crisis without

attending to the human dilemmas of conscience, faith, and communal identity that were involved in the question of scandal. Here I will appeal directly to my personal experience and conversations with many others in the Church. I would say that scandal could plague a person on the level of leadership, on the level of personal belief, and on the level of institutional allegiance. Initially, on the level of leadership, the fear of causing scandal appeared to be an appropriate biblical and moral category for those in responsible positions of faith leadership. The traditional guidelines touching detraction or the revelation of truths were misapplied through the lens of a culture of secrecy.[9] But to hide patterned wrongdoing under the guise of avoiding scandal in a society that valued openness, pluralism, and a free press was quickly perceived as a choice to cover up criminal activity. What was initially understood as a choice between bad alternatives had within a few years become a clear need to admit public wrongdoing. The avoidance of scandal was itself a scandal. A recurrent dilemma thus ran through the years of the crisis: When was the avoidance of scandal a greater evil than the causing of scandal by the exposure of scandal?

This collision of values on the level of leadership became even more complicated as it intersected with the level of personal belief. The admission that a significant number of clergymen had committed crimes against minors and so betrayed their fellow priests dissolved the inherited interpretation of how holiness and sin worked in the Church and in the world. Things were not what they appeared to be, nor what they claimed to be. The implicit connection between priestly status and holiness had been part of the Church's public identity and certainly part of the unconscious self-identity of the priests and bishops; this truth was implicit in the faith of many believers. The connection was now severed. Some leaders denied the situation or remained indifferent. The most tempting thing to do was to isolate the scandalous behavior to single individuals, but this became increasingly impossible as the crisis evolved. The reality of the abuse and then the mismanagement, for those who did not have the luxury of avoiding it, was undeniable. Events were subsumed into the totality of a single dark image. I would say from my experience that the reaction could be one of fear and anger, eventually disappointment, betrayal, and self-doubt. What followed was shock, affective alienation from leaders, and intellectual obscurity. How much in the Church was hidden? These were the new personal questions engendered by the experience of scandal. The whole event was "un-believable." In such an alienating situation, the preferred prayer became that of lamentation: "My God, my God, why have you forsaken me?" (Ps. 22.1).

Finally, as the crisis evolved and the mismanagement of some leaders began to dominate awareness, parallel questions of institutional allegiance arose. Scandal became related to the perception of hypocrisy: How could the Church claim holiness while marked with such a pervasive pattern of leadership wrongdoing? Were leaders such as these actual carriers of "holy" teaching? Could they speak about a "moral life"? Did those who claimed to teach have concern for the impact their actions made on others? How much did the politics of the Church shape the decisions that were being made? In the midst of such questions, it became increasingly difficult to integrate the knowledge of such "scandal" with faith in God and God's covenantal relationship with the Church. On the one hand, the experience of faith and the presence of so much truth and sacramental goodness in the Church continued to answer "Yes." On the other hand, another experience of life asked, "Really?" "How?" Hypocrisy, real or imagined, bred incredulity. And who talked about it? The search for a different vision that could assimilate all of this experience plagued the consciences of those who grappled with such challenges.

This scandal, at its depth, I believe, has raised some profound spiritual questions. It marks a watershed in the history of American Catholicism. The Review Board in its final assessment indicated that the crisis was "fundamentally, the age-old issue of good and evil. The church must be holy; her ministers must be holy; her people must be holy."[10] This is undoubtedly true, but from my experience I would say that for myself and probably for some others the issue was more far-reaching than that. The problems of knowledge and faith that I have identified cannot be solved by isolating the misbehavior, expelling it, and then having everyone pursue holiness. Ridding the Church of the evil of sexual abuse must be the first priority; but there is more than that. As we have seen repeatedly throughout this exposition, the sexual abuse of minors was not only a question of clerical misconduct and sin or leadership mismanagement. The convergence of events indicated the connection between this crisis, the patterns of power in society, and the inherited tensions between the hierarchical and communal dimensions of the Church. The crisis revealed a Church and society whose institutional pathways of relationality and action could be yeasted on all levels with well-known vices: arrogance, anger, greed, possessiveness, abuses of power, manipulation, and pretensions to absolute knowledge. The Gospel illuminated the situation. The deeper crevices of the human heart had been opened, and the battle between Augustine's "two loves" made visible. In the end, a sense of communal reciprocity disappeared. These social and political dimensions of the scandal could not be handled by surgical excision. Rather, as I have argued, on the institutional level they raised the challenge of the creation of mediating spaces where the virtues of one could balance the vices of another and vice-versa. On a spiritual level they demanded conversion to the Gospel. And on the level of faith seeking understanding, they raised the disturbing question of how to believe in a world and a Church where holiness, human limitation, and a propensity to sin dwelled together in the same house. Such knowledge "engenders affliction."[11]

What can be done in such a situation? People will certainly have different solutions. Not everyone need ask the same questions. Not every one is "scandalized." Here I can only offer some insights that occurred to me and some of the Franciscan friars as we turned to our own spiritual and theological tradition to help guide us through our difficulties. During the abuse scandal, I was struck with how many times questions related to sin, public shame, and scandal arose in our own historic sources. It seemed to me that Francis and the early fraternity, while recognizing these elements as part of human life, wanted to go beyond them. They wanted to know and believe something much more profound about the human condition of the Church and of the people around them. In addition, as I began to explore this theme in the theology of Bonaventure, I realized that he too knew at first hand the disjunctions between what the Church claimed and how the Church acted; he too knew the social problems that destroyed human dignity. For Francis and for Bonaventure, the human condition in its glory and its sin was a place where God could be found. The Church with all its flaws still remained the holy place, the Body of Christ, where God chose to accompany the people. In what follows I offer three themes that emerged from our tradition and helped interpret this experience of scandal: Francis of Assisi's conversion story and his experience of God's condescending love; the tradition's understanding of the mix of the good and the not-so-good in the Church; the practice and prayer of the Body of Christ. Perhaps some may find these reflections helpful or at least encouraging. Once again, a complete vision needs to be the work of the whole Church.[12]

The Disfigured Body of Christ

Conversion and the Experience of God's Condescending Love

Some of us discovered during the sexual abuse crisis that dealing constructively with places of "scandal" was a part of our Franciscan religious identity. The starting point for conversion was all-important. Francis of Assisi's project involved engagement with himself, the world, and the Church the way they appeared in history. He did not pretend that he was an out-sider sent to do good, charged from above to separate out the pure from the impure, the perfect from the imperfect. Rather, his first choice was the choice to admit his own citizenship in a society and Church where good and evil were mixed together. And from within that place, as an insider, he wanted to exemplify a universal call to repentance and to reveal for others a God Who "is the fullness of good, all good, every good, the true and supreme good, Who alone is good, merciful, gentle, delightful, and sweet."[13] At this time in the Church, with so many suffering from genuine "scandal," his is a story worth sharing.

In his final *Testament* Francis of Assisi presented the starting point for his own conversion. The few lines he wrote were an *exemplum*, a short story of the personal encounter with his neighbor that moved him to change.

> The Lord gave me, Brother Francis, thus to begin doing penance in this way: for when I was in sin, it seemed too bitter for me to see lepers. And the Lord Himself led me among them and I showed mercy to them. And when I left them, what had seemed bitter to me was turned into sweetness of soul and body.[14]

To comprehend this little story we need to understand the symbols and how the turn from bitterness to sweetness was negotiated by its incorporation into the much larger story of God's creative embrace of human history.[15]

In the thirteenth century, lepers were those in the Church and society considered the most putrid and foul-smelling, heretical or infirm, the most morally weak. Physically disfigured, they were also individuals full of unruly emotional disorders: anger, craftiness, sexual lust, greed, deception, perversion, manipulation, evil intentions.[16] Their disfigurement symbolized all the evils associated with the human condition of being poor in health, poor in virtue, poor in resources. The deformity of leprosy represented a threat to a stable and prosperous society. It was a condition that eluded control, signifying human abandonment. Lepers needed to be removed from the life of the city, hidden from the eyes of the ordinary believer. The archives of Assisi possess for the period of Francis of Assisi a ritual in which the Church tried to care for lepers spiritually while affirming their bodily separation from the city.[17] The ordering of ordinary life did not include them. They were not easy companions, and association with them brought social shame. Initially, the sight and touch of lepers nauseated Francis of Assisi.

In "show[ing] mercy" in that very poor and sinful place of other human beings, Francis himself discovered God's goodness. As he looked back on the experience toward the end of his life, he identified the chief agent of the change: God, the one who created him, was the primary mover in his human journey: "the Lord gave me . . . the Lord led me," he noted in the *Testament*. Here in the course of his own history God invited him to follow in the footprints of the Lord himself, to take on the yoke of his humanity and learn from him (Mark 1.12–13; Matt. 4.1–11; Luke 4.1–13; Matt. 11.28–30).The Spirit had led Jesus into the desert of life where he would be tempted and in the midst of temptation proclaim the overwhelming gratuity of a divine love that conquered death. So also the Lord led Francis to that place of being among lepers. He showed mercy to them. He lived with them, washing their sores, kissing their hands, suffering their shame. He visited their hospitals and urged his followers to do the same. He worked and labored to make their lot better, to heal their wounds. He called the lepers "Christian brothers."[18]

While he was engaged with the lepers, something happened to Francis of Assisi. In his *Testament* to his followers he coded this experience of his conversion in the biblical terms of a movement from "bitterness" to "*sweetness*." As narrated in the story of Exodus, "bitter" was the experience of the pilgrim people of Israel when, hungry and thirsty, they tried to drink the waters at Marah. Their journey, supposedly one of liberation, had led them into a place of great distaste. Why had the God of the covenant led them to that place? (Exod. 15.22–25). "Bitter" with all of its resonances communicated for Francis the difficulties of engaging with lepers, the humiliation of being associated with them, the daily struggle to practice compassion, to do penance. It was accompanied by the human experience of social shame. Is this where God had led him?

Francis, through the Scriptures, could interpret his difficult experience in a liberating way. The bitter waters of Marah turned sweet when Moses at the indication of the Lord threw the piece of wood into them. What could this mean? What would make the bitter water of doing penance with lepers "sweet"? The word "leper" occurred in the Vulgate scripture in numerous places, but above all in the Song of the Suffering Servant: "Yet it was our infirmities that he bore, our sufferings that he endured, while we thought of him as stricken [that is, in Latin, *quasi leprosus*, in English, "as if a *leper*"], as one smitten by God and afflicted. But he was pierced for our offenses, crushed for our sins" (Isa. 53.4). Through the encounter with his poor lepers, Francis seems to have been learning something new: Christ, the Word become flesh, took on human disfigurement, appearing among people "as if a leper." The Son of God himself had not disdained to enter the human condition, to become a brother (Heb. 2.11–12). In the encounter with lepers Christ could be found. "For our sake God made him who did not know sin to be sin, so that in him we might become the very holiness of God" (2 Cor. 5.21; Rom. 8.3).

Francis connected his own life with the Gospel message of God's presence: "Taste and see how good (i.e., *sweet*) the Lord is"; "*sweeter* also than syrup or honey from the comb" were the ordinances of the Lord, the psalmist said. "For this substance of yours revealed your *sweetness* towards your children," the book of Wisdom read. And the epistle of Peter encouraged Francis: "Be as eager for milk as newborn babies—pure milk of the spirit to make you grow unto salvation, now that you have tasted that the Lord is *sweet*" (Ps. 34.9, 19.11; Wis. 16.21; 1 Pet. 2.2–3). In the story of the Israelites' pilgrimage, the "bitter" waters turned "sweet" when the wood was thrown into them. The "wood" that made the bitter waters of the encounter with lepers "sweet," as Francis interpreted it, was the wood of the cross, that place in his life where the Lord Jesus demonstrated for all to see the public spectacle of the humility and charity of a God of love in a disfigured body. The experience of engaging the lepers became for Francis a doorway into the experience of God's condescending love in the world. This insight illuminated many other areas of life.

During the course of the abuse crisis we Franciscan friars began to ponder the deeper dimensions of this conversion story of Francis of Assisi. The point was not the identification of the lepers with anyone, and certainly not with the survivors of abuse. Rather, the central point seemed to be that in the course of his own history Francis had in fact been led not to avoid "scandalous people or places" but to engage them in the light of God's Word. The engagement with the challenges of history became revelatory of a more penetrating experience of God's overwhelming mercy. This had been expressed in human history by the leading of the chosen people through the desert and the fulfillment of the promises in the Incarnation of Christ. "Bitter" experiences of life were subsumed into a much larger story of the "sweetness" of a loving and faithful Creator. When read from that perspective, events that were experienced as scandalous could become opportunities for a deeper discovery of who God is and how God works in the human relationships that mark our history. It seemed to some of us that this insight could also help us deal with the sometimes bitter experience of the Church itself. While the Church is composed of human beings whose vices could become all too evident, while its patterns of relational power could cause great suffering in others, it was still a human place in which God chooses to make a home.

As I have come to think about this conversion of Francis in its contemporary application, I put it this way. Particular areas of Church life call for moral vigilance and action; the sexual abuse of minors is intolerable, and this crime must be rooted out; institutional reforms are absolutely necessary. But that being accomplished and engaged, still the other deeper challenges remain. Flawed members, some of whom are leaders, and organizational patterns shot through with human vices elude even the most resolute of reformers. Positive relational power can easily be lost. There is a politics in the Church that can come to serve poor ends. At certain times in history and in the consciousness of some believers these moral disfigurements obscure and even make "incredible" the life of the Gospel in the Church.

In the same *Testament* to his followers that begins with the story of the lepers, Francis tries to answer the dilemma that many believers can experience. He connects the juxtaposition of human poverty (physical, mental, moral, relational) and God's sweet presence, which he had experienced among the lepers, with his own knowledge of a Church that is badly in need of repair. On a daily level, the question focuses itself in the experience of "the impoverished priests of this world." The term "impoverished" refers probably to the ignorance, lack of chastity, and greed often associated with the clergy of the day. Francis noted, "And I do not want to consider any sin in them because I discern the Son of God in them and they are my lords. And I act in this way because, in this world, I see nothing corporally of the most high Son of God except His most holy Body and Blood which they receive and they alone administer to others."[19] Why does God give the grace of office to sinful priests in the Church? This is the wrong question. Francis's intuition is simple. The creative power of God to act for good in "the grace of office" and in the Lord's Body and Blood in the Eucharist is greater than the weakness of its carriers to block that power for good. It is a question of faith in God and in the way in which God chooses to be, "as if a leper," in a world of brothers and sisters. The story of salvation that the Church carries is the story of God's fidelity in the midst of human beings.

Put in more sacramental and spiritual terms, the wood of Christ's love on the cross has been planted deeply in Francis's heart through the sweet waters of his Baptism. In those who so obviously demonstrate the flawed humanity of the members of the Church, he sees not their sin but the profound mystery of God's power and condescension. What makes disfigured bodies beautiful is love, the Lord's loving choice to be faithfully present and to offer forgiveness in the situation of human frailty and sin. This is not an excuse for the toleration of sin but the stimulus to repent and reform. It must always be recalled that the first step is the doing of penance. The question is not simply how its members disfigure the Body of Christ, but also what the Head of the Body of Christ, united to his members, is choosing to do among them and through them. Francis writes, "O how holy and how loving, gratifying, humbling, peace-giving, sweet, worthy of love, and above all things, desirable: to have such a Brother and such a Son, our Lord Jesus Christ, Who laid down His life for His sheep."[20] Married to the frailty of human flesh through Mary, in the Incarnation, along the pilgrim way, and on the Cross, the Word of God has taken the disfigured human condition in all of its poverty as his loved one. As Augustine puts it in reference to the Church: "Let the bride be happy, then, for she has been loved by God. And when was she loved? While she was still ugly, for as the apostle says, *All have sinned, and are in need of the glory of God*, and again, *Christ died for the impious*. She was loved in her ugliness, that she might not remain ugly. It was not because she was ugly that she was loved; her ugliness was not itself the object of his love. If he had loved that, he would have preserved it, but in fact he rid her of her ugliness and formed beauty in her."[21] For the disciple, the follower of Christ, love drives the desire to take up the cross of the Church's flawed humanity. For Francis, as I began to understand, this is true religion.[22]

The Mix of the Good and the Not-so-good in the Church

In an earlier portion of this work I referred to the experience of systemic trauma, which afflicted some communities and, I believe, some portions of the Church. Key to dealing with this type of reality is a frame of meaning that can relate that experience to the deepest wellsprings of core beliefs. From the Franciscan tradition, we began to understand our own story in a way that elicited confidence and hope. The insight revolved around the reality of belonging to a group of penitents. This insight helped us negotiate the perilous paths of scandal in the Church. The following represented one way of rereading our own sources and the theological tradition.

From the very beginning, adherents to the way of Francis of Assisi were perceived among the people and in the Church as a very mixed bag of the good and the not-so-good. The *Earlier Rule* of the Friars Minor encouraged the friars not to become "disturbed or angered at another's sin or evil." "As the Lord says, let them not consider the least sins of others; instead, let them reflect more upon their own sins in *the bitterness of their soul.*" The friars were "to know with certainty that nothing belongs to us except our vices and sins."[23] One of the early sources of the history of the fraternity consistently recalled the friars in difficult situations of both public shame and ecclesial rejection: "Many who saw and heard them considered them impostors or fools. Someone among them remarked: 'I wouldn't care to invite them into my house; they would probably steal my belongings.' And because of this, any number of insults were inflicted on them in many places."[24] It was this situation of public ridicule that gave rise to one of the earliest social names of the friars.

> Some people willingly and joyfully listened to the brothers; others, however, jeered at them, and it was extremely wearisome to answer so many questions because new situations often gave rise to new questions. Some asked them: "Where do you come from?" While others asked,

"To which Order do you belong?" They answered, simply, "We are penitents and we were born in Assisi."[25]

This acceptance of their identity as penitents did not mean that the members of the movement compromised with sin or failure or that some of their behaviors, for example, "straying in word or in deed from the Catholic faith and life," did not bear the weight of expulsion.[26] There was always an outward limit.[27] Instead, being a penitent meant constant reform, continual growth, an ever-deepening assimilation of what it meant to be turned toward God in a world and a Church that was poor. Even the difficult action of expulsion needed to be shaped by the knowledge that one too was a sinner. Those who erred continued to be in some fashion human beings, "brother" and "sister" lepers. It was a tall order in a world where people wished completely to expel the lepers from the human community and claim a social or ecclesial order based on a righteous health.

As the early biographers of Francis narrated it, the priests and laity, men and women, prelates and subjects who understood themselves as penitents gathered around the Franciscan movement.[28] They found the vision attractive and realistic. They believed the Church to be full of grace, holy in its sacraments and in its teaching. They also knew "scandal." Sensitive to hypocrisy, they had encountered many "pitiful priests of this world"; and they experienced at first hand the leprosarium of the Church. We could say today that the movement belonged to those who wished to pursue perfection in imperfection by placing in the middle of human frailty not only their own work for reform but also the primacy of God's condescension and the order of love.[29] In any given situation, a person always tried to make things better. But that being done, the chief sins to be avoided were institutional hypocrisy, greed, anger, and the personal and communal search for prestige or vainglory. This humble and poor religious way of being in the world, which coupled a penitential life with joy in the beauty of God's love, was meant to be medicinal in a society and Church that could too easily value *fama publica*, false prestige, outward impressions, and gloominess.[30]

Here, in this Christian world as Francis saw it, the only permanent state that produced Gospel prestige and holiness was not the state of appearing to be holy, nor the state one occupied by virtue of office, nor the state of being a priest, nor the state of having possessions and power, nor the state of religious life, but the state of choosing to be a penitent in one's heart, mind, and behavior because one was a member of a Body of Christ still struggling in time.[31] Scandal occurred in this world in three ways. First, scandal happened not when one sinned but when one refused to admit that one belonged to a community of people who sin. Second, scandal occurred when there was no purpose and action of amendment. And, third, admitting sin and repenting, scandal occurred because no one was proclaiming the goodness of God. That was why, to be a penitent was considered holy: It was an outward public sign that while recognizing the human community's state of limitation and sinfulness, one also had turned to the God who looks on the world and its peoples and proclaims them "good," sends the Son to "become leprous" and "to redeem us captives through His cross and blood and death," and finally to say to all those who had served in penance, "Come, you blessed of my Father, receive the kingdom prepared for you from the beginning of the world."[32]

As we have seen throughout this book, the Franciscan theological tradition eventually explained this Gospel faith of a penitent Church by turning to Saint Augustine. In his struggle against those who would demand perfection in the Church, the doctor of grace described a Body of Christ in which the good and the bad were mixed together. At times, in periods of real purification, the citizens of a worldly Babylon, those marked with avarice and pride, controlled the public affairs of the city of Jerusalem, the Church.[33] The biblical parables of the Church that served as guiding metaphors for this situation were those of the good seed and the weeds that were allowed to grow together until the final harvest, or the dragnet that contained both the worthwhile and the useless until the angels separated the wicked from the just at the end of the world.[34] In such a world the virtues of patience and charity took center stage.

Bonaventure expressed a similar spiritual and institutional experience very well when he responded to the perfectionistic tendencies embedded in the Church of his time. When the friars were attacked for bringing shame upon the Church because not all of them were good, for subverting its hierarchical order, or for identifying with those whom society discarded, he replied: "It pertains to the perfection of the mystical body of Christ that its members share with one another 'in giving and receiving,' so that they together might supply for one another's indigence."[35] He explained his vision of both the Franciscan Order and the Church with reference to the actions of Christ.

> Nevertheless, granted their large numbers, it can hardly be avoided that some, along with Judas, love money bags and turn aside from the right path. For if the Lord did not grant that his apostles, all twelve personally chosen, would be universally good, is it amazing that he does not grant the same assurance to other congregations? However, because of this those who are good must not be condemned along with the evil, just as the evil are not righteous, even though they are intermingled with the good.[36]

In this Augustinian-Franciscan vision it was important to capture two realities at the same time: The Church was holy as the Body of Christ. The life-giving influence and authority of the Head of the Body guaranteed the holiness of the sacramental and hierarchical elements, providing stability to the Church as it made its pilgrim way through history.[37] God gave the power of forgiveness even to sinful priests not because of their own merits but for the usefulness of the community.[38] But the Church was also a gathering of penitents, bound together by the mutual forgiveness of sins, held together, if you like, by practices of justice, mercy, and compassion, by the give and take of courtesy, humility, and mutual correction. People, no matter their state of life, needed each other in order to be followers of Christ. The Church was a sacrament of a God who enters human life, takes on the disfigured body of those who are poor, pilgrimages with them in history, and chooses to save people through the actions of other human beings who are flawed.

With respect to the inherited structures of the Christian world and its juridical and organizational views of holiness, there was a certain historical realism embedded in this Franciscan spiritual and theological inheritance. Invisible entanglements with partially sinful patterns of relationality and the struggle of the two loves—a private love directed to self-aggrandizement and a social love directed toward the neighbor—cut through everyone.[39] Those entanglements or loves could reside in ecclesial, political, cultural, legal, or economic relationships between people. Those blind to the entanglements and to the drives of the human heart were the most opaque to the Gospel. They distanced themselves from an experience of the goodness and mercy and power of God by refusing to engage reality as it came to them. They denied the necessity for both tears of repentance and tears of love. Life's center of gravity needed to become not the perfection of Christendom but the following of Christ and the embrace of his presence in his disfigured body on earth, the Church. If people made room for the poor in the Church, perhaps there would be more room for the poor in the universe.

Today, in a society where the maintenance of prestige is highly valued and often translates into a cultural demand for perfection (in technological control, professional expertise, sexual purity, economic success, and legal vindication) and in a public Church that can appear to stress separation in its ministers or to focus inordinately on ritual exactness, there is a need to develop a language and institutional practice that includes human weakness and diversity in virtue. I believe there is a need for people who, knowing institutional reality well, embrace its limitations and its flawed relational power and in their poverty and humility "show themselves joyful, cheerful and consistently gracious in the Lord."[40] This is the truth that the experience of sexual abuse taught many of us. We may not have always lived it well, and we still have a long way to go. But we began to understand the Church and its presence in the world in a way different from an identity fearful of scandal and the public acknowledgment of sin in its midst. Perhaps this is a learning that some may find helpful.

The Practice and Prayer of the Disfigured Body of Christ

When scandal came, genuine scandal, we did not know what to do. Understanding eluded us; the power to solve the collision of values in a completely satisfactory way exceeded everyone's capacity; the good could not be completely separated out from the not-so-good. As we have seen in our narration, the truthfulness of brothers and sisters both inside and outside the fraternity, the responsibilities of office, the pressure from those seeking more justice, and the advice of good counselors were blessed constraints. They prevented flight and dispelled the temptations to denial, inaction, or withdrawal. Perhaps, as with Francis, we could say it was the Lord who led us there. In such a situation, accompanied by the hurt of disaffection and the obscurity of questioning, the spiritual inheritance of Francis of Assisi told us to move forward through simple practice. A guiding principle became simply trying to bring a little more good out of the not-so-good. Reading our own sources from this experience, I began to name what I would like to call the "practice and prayer of the disfigured Body of Christ." It may be outlined in the following way.

As Francis engaged this place of the leper's body and the

leprous body of the Church, all he could initially do was practice penance, trying to perform small acts of mercy and compassion in the midst of his own anger and reluctance. The "law of constraints" hemmed him in, and the history of his own life was breaking apart the private crevices in his own heart. Looking back on it, he realized that he had been led into this place of disorder by the Holy Spirit; in it, he had been guided by the "fixed choice"[41] of his will to practice the Great Commandment, to subordinate himself to the "order of love." At the time, however, this sweetness lay hidden in the experience of the bitter. Later biographers of Francis, using more technical language, tried to capture the experience and give it some theological structure by speaking about the training in *pietas*, or "piety," which this school of patience and charity gave to him.[42] Eventually, they noted, "sweetness" would appear, but practice came first.

In his *Collations on the Seven Gifts of the Holy Spirit*, Bonaventure emphasized this starting point of practice. When people complained that they did not have the gift of piety—they could not conceive this gift in their hearts—he noted that the Scriptures instructed them: "Train yourself in piety."[43] "No, brother [sister], I could not lead you to the original source of piety except through the act and the exercise of piety."[44] This training in piety began with a most exalted reverence for God, something that conformed to a natural tendency in human beings. It applied to every human situation and answered the simple question: Do I believe in these circumstances that God's power is capable of bringing good out of that which is not-so-good? Bonaventure noted: "Concerning God's power and wisdom, if you think that God cannot restore bodies for a better or worse state, then you think poorly of God, and you do not think in the most exalted terms. Furthermore, if you do not believe in the divine condescensions and mercies by which God fills the creature that serves him with grace, forgiveness, and happiness, then you are not a worshipper of God."[45] This fear of God was then accompanied by the prodding of a good conscience in oneself, and an action of compassion toward one's neighbor. *Pietas* in this fashion found its beginning in practice and opened itself up to a gift of the Holy Spirit. It was unlocked through the willing acceptance of a necessity one could not avoid, an encounter with the disfigured neighbor. Training in *pietas* began with engagement in the real world and believing God could act there.

For both Francis and Bonaventure this practice of *pietas* had a very special relevance in the Church and the society of their day. In a world where hypocrisy, impatience, anger, judgment, and cruelty divided people from each other, the way of *pietas* led to facing the disfigured neighbor.[46] A person could not just feel "piety" or preach it; he could not functionally make it the responsibility of professional caregivers. He had to demonstrate it among brothers and sisters in the same way the Lord Jesus had, by entering the world of people's suffering and, from within this experience, working to alleviate it. The Gospel taught him that in social circumstances that tempted a person to flee into a private and safe enclave, scandal occurred not when someone sinned but when people ceased to be in contact with the suffering of their neighbors.

The companions of Francis testified repeatedly that he wished to avoid this scandal at all costs. He preferred always that words match deeds, that the example of virtue trump the imposition of virtue by force or authority.[47] The penitential life needed to go public.[48] For example, Bonaventure noted that while many criticized the "poor" clergy of the day, Francis practiced piety toward them, not criticizing but weeping over their sins.[49] This was the chief reason for his reverence for a minister of God's word "who in preaching seeks not the salvation of souls but his own praise, or who destroys with the depravity of his life what he builds up with the truth of teaching."[50] Through piety Francis called not only the lepers but all creatures "brothers" and "sisters." Piety even crossed the boundary between believers and unbelievers, creating a universal community of people.[51]

This practice of piety was connected with the other social

virtues (patience, charity, humility) that served as medicine for the disfigured bodies of both the society and the Church. The practice was needed precisely because the disease of social division was so deep. For Bonaventure the practice was especially necessary for soothing the wounds of the Body of Christ.

> Most beloved! See whether your piety is that of brother to brother; or brothers [and sisters] from the same womb. Who is our father? Certainly, God. Who is our mother? She is the church. She has begotten us in her womb through the Holy Spirit, and will give birth to us when we are brought to eternal light. Do you not see that as one member of a body suffers with another member, so we ought to have compassion for one another? We are all members of one body. We are fed with one food. We are brought forth from the same womb. We are moving toward the same inheritance. And our inheritance will be increased and not diminished in proportion to our number. We are one body. Therefore we should be related to each other through piety.[52]

"Piety" was more than gentleness, mildness, mercy, compassion.[53] It was not only a consideration of the suffering of the neighbor and attending to it. It was more than simply countering irritation with mildness. It moved beyond caring for others through the prudential sharing of resources. It was instead a being with the suffering, the moral weakness, the bodily disfigurement. The one who practiced piety saw through the disfigurement to something much deeper, to the image of God in the human being.[54] To practice *pietas* was to refuse to be trapped by scandal and to learn to acknowledge a God-given human dignity in those who were disfigured. To practice *pietas* in a world and Church where the good mixed with the not-so-good was to exemplify in one's own body the "sweet" presence of God. As

Bonaventure described it: "While God possesses all the noblest properties, yet God is most excellent in this property of piety. Thus it is said in a prayer: 'God, whose property is always to have mercy and to spare,' etc. Sirach 2.13 states, 'God is compassionate and merciful, and forgives sins in time of tribulation. God is a protector to all those who seek God in truth.'"[55] Piety could not be practiced without grace.

Finally, confronted by scandal in the Body of Christ and learning to practice piety led Francis and Bonaventure and their companions in their bitterness to pray the same prayer that has risen to the lips of many in the Church of our own day: "My God, my God, why have you forsaken me?"[56] Yet, to their own astonishment, it was in the saying of this prayer of penance and abandonment with others that "sweetness" came in the shape of a new enlightenment. Christ had been there before them and was with them now. The Lord himself, in his own disfigured body, had taken on the sufferings of those around him and from within that experience had enunciated a plea for mercy. In Christ, those who were suffering from a scandal that had muted them now found strength in the presence of someone greater than themselves.

There is a long tradition in the Church that has taken very seriously these words from the Epistle to the Hebrews: "In the days when he was in the flesh, he offered prayers and supplications with loud cries and tears to God, who was able to save him from death, and he was heard because of his reverence. Son though he was, he learned obedience from what he suffered; and when perfected, he became the source of eternal salvation for all who obey him, designated by God as high priest according to the order of Melchizedek" (Heb. 5.7–9). In this passage the Catholic tradition has found the Head of the Body that is the Church continually interceding for his own disfigured members. Bonaventure, following Augustine, describes Jesus saying the prayer of embodied *pietas* (Psalm 22) from the altar of the cross in this way:

The use of the words "My God" makes it clear that this word was spoken in the name of the assumed manhood of Jesus, though, of course, he was still one person with the Son of God. They could not have been said by one who was one with the Father unless he had assumed a human nature. But what does he say next? "Why hast thou forsaken me?" Could the Father ever forsake his only Son? God forbid. The most kind Jesus, therefore, must have spoken in this way on behalf of the whole Church, of which he is the Head. Desiring to commend the union and loving relation he had with his spouse the Church, he, who as the Head had already endured suffering in his own body, which he received from the Virgin, now shewed himself prepared to share the suffering of all the members of his body, the Church. So he, who in his own divine nature could not be forsaken, cried out that he was forsaken, because he knew that so many members of his body would endure great tribulation. This was the reason why he appeared to be inwardly forsaken by God.

The Franciscan leader concludes his meditation not by referring to his own suffering but by being grateful to a Lord who chooses to be with him in this suffering.

Blessed be our adorable God, our most kind Jesus, for condescending to share the tribulation, which we so justly suffer, first by himself on our behalf, but now both with us and in us! In order to ground our trust in him more firmly, mindful of our suffering, he cries, "I will be with him in trouble."[57]

Never willingly chosen, the experience of scandal brings great disruption to the life of faith and to the trust we bring to the human mediators of the presence of God in our lives. It touches both our intellectual comprehension and our affective loyalties. Throughout this book I have argued that one result of the crisis of sexual abuse has been the loss of mediating spaces of reciprocal exchange. In some measure the prevalence of scandal and its debilitating effects has contributed to this loss. A key means of healing this wound is the discovery of a framework for faith that releases our energies to love again. In this chapter I have tried to describe through the Franciscan sources a few elements that could be described as a "catechesis" of how this experience of scandal might be negotiated. The description is not meant to be a map but only to identify some signposts along the way. Central to recovery is the knowledge of the Word that endures forever and the great condescension of God's love for us in Christ. "Eternal life is this, to know you, the only true God and him whom you have sent, Jesus Christ" (John 17.3).[58] Coming to the Church, the Body of Christ, through the eyes of faith in God and the Incarnation reveals another type of beauty. The path is not discovered through intellectual parsing but through companionship, humility, dispossession, lamentation, and the practice of *pietas*. Being loved, we turn to love again and reconstruct our spaces of reciprocal exchange. Some of the existential dimensions of this task have been elucidated in the four reflections in Chapters 2 and 3. Here perhaps is a way of reconstructing faith for those who have been led to cross the Rubicon of scandal. With this challenge for the leader, we come full circle to begin again.

9. THE SOOTHING OF JERUSALEM

One homeland we have, one homeland most dear to us,
one only homeland; and compared with that whatever we
  have now
is nothing but a journey. . . . Jerusalem, God's kingdom,
  the holy city, the city of God;
it was established to be a sign or figure, foreshadowing
  what was to come.

SAINT AUGUSTINE OF HIPPO
Expositions of the Psalms[1]

It is God alone who is this fire, and God's *furnace is in
  Jerusalem.*
And it is Christ who starts the fire
with the white flame of his most intense passion.

SAINT BONAVENTURE
Itinerarium Mentis in Deum[2]

IN CHRISTIAN IMAGERY THE homeland from which we come
and the homeland to which we journey is described as "the
new Jerusalem, the holy city, coming down out of heaven from
God." It is a city that gleams with the "splendor of God," a city
with "the radiance of a precious jewel that sparkled like a dia-
mond." The city has no temple, for "the Lord God almighty is
the temple—he and the Lamb." It has no need of sun or moon;
its gates are always open. In the middle of the city flows an
abundant river on the sides of which grow fruit trees whose
"leaves serve as medicine for the nations." Through the process
of conversion, the foundations of this city have already been
established, its citizens already participate in the world which is
to come. They are invited to be bearers of the leaves that serve

as "medicine for the nations."[3] Here, now, even though they are not yet home, the citizens of the city live by faith. They have "the confident assurance concerning what we hope for, and conviction about things we do not see" (Heb. 11.1).[4] As the Second Vatican Council noted, "At the hour when Christ will appear, when the glorious resurrection of the dead will occur, the glory of God will light up the heavenly city, and the Lamb will be its lamp." Until that time, the Church sees "herself as an exile."[5]

Augustine, Francis of Assisi, Bonaventure, and their companions—our mentors who have served as guides and supports throughout the journey described in this book—believed in this city where God's justice would become fully realized. In the Church they were able to drink from the life-giving waters that flowed from the throne of God: the Scriptures and the sacraments. They also rejoiced that through faith and hope they themselves had been invited by God to become co-workers in the partial realization of this city on earth. They had learned over time to think of everyone, those in the Church and those outside of it, as their neighbor.[6] Yet too many experiences in their lives indicated to them that they were not simply co-workers but also pilgrims in a foreign land, struggling in their own hearts to establish the reign of charity. They lived in a Church and a world where the good and the not-so-good mixed on a daily basis. They knew the reality of scandal and had discovered an image of God and practices of the faith that would help them negotiate their pilgrimage. In God's providence, the course of history was continuously purifying this faith, reminding them that the Jerusalem above lay in the future; here they had no lasting home. They were co-workers, yes, but also pilgrims and penitents, members of the Body of Christ, following the path laid out for them by their one teacher, also a traveler, a "stranger who lived on alms—He, the Blessed Virgin and His disciples."[7] He had not disdained to call them "brothers" and "sisters." Through his birth and death they had been redeemed, their sins forgiven. Our own story, it seems to me, has great affinities with the pilgrimages of those who have gone before us. A challenge before us is to mine this past so that we might pave the path into the future with its gold.

The course of the scandal has brought to our present situation many institutional "vitamin deficiencies." The collision of values has revealed a central problem of relational power. A Pandora's box of complexities hidden in our hearts and "ambiguous human tendencies" hidden in the community of the Church has been opened. How we hold relational power in trust and use it for others in service to the Great Commandment has become a real challenge for leadership. The course of the scandal itself has also occluded on a public level previously established pathways of reciprocal exchange and mutual support between clergy and laity, celibate and married believers, men and women, religious and diocesan leaders, bishops, the clergy, and the people of God. Reestablishing places of relational power and mediating institutional structures will not be easy. Part of the purpose of this book has been to argue for their necessity, and remembering the full course of the abuse scandal may help us recover the importance of this vision of community.

In the course of this book I have tried to outline some of the qualities that will be necessary if we are to create new pathways of reciprocal exchange. As seen from the Franciscan point of view, leadership in the Church will be challenged in the future to create a consistent communal ethic of repentance, humility, the respect for a common human dignity dictated by the terms "brother" and "sister," obedience to the order of love, and the daily practice of *pietas*. This ethic will demand a thorough institutionalization of the evangelical law of "giving and receiving" and the creation of a shared space of mutual dispossession. We can do no better than appeal to a tradition articulated by Augustine. When asked who already is a citizen of the holy city, the bishop replies: "But all whose taste is schooled to the things above, who ponder the realities of heaven, who live with circumspection in this world, taking care not to offend God, who are wary of committing sin, but if they do sin are not ashamed to confess it, all who are humble, gentle, holy, just, devout and good—all these belong to the one city whose king is Christ."[8] It is my hope that the story told in these pages has contributed to this continuing task to live by an ethic of reciprocal exchange. Many other hopes also need to find a place within an international context and a Church in the United States that continues to do penance and search for better ways of giving witness to the Body of Christ. "The body is one and has many members, but all the members many though they are, are one body; and so it is with Christ. . . . The eye cannot say to the hand, 'I do not need you.'. . . If one member suffers, all the members suffer with it; if one member is honored, all the members share its joy" (cf. 1 Cor. 12.12–13.13). Here, I have tried to place some of the resources of the Franciscan spiritual and theological tradition in service to that mission that touches all aspects of Church life.

In conclusion, let me simply state that communities of people are shaped not only by their ideals and goals but also by the memory they construct of their experiences, both good and bad. In this reflection, I have attempted to construct a memory of the past that opens up for us a creative path for the future. The crisis over the sexual abuse of minors in the Church has begun to fade from the height of its institutional charge; but its consequences, our memory of it, and what it has taught us about our Church and our society, we need always to treasure. I do not believe we should bury the facts of our own history, the injuries done and the penances required. When not clouded by denial or retreat, memory can open us to a richer sense of Who God Is and who we are who encounter each other. What has been presented here has been an explicitly Franciscan take on the challenges and the possibilities for leadership inherent in the scandal of sexual abuse. Were one to examine the situation from the viewpoint of other spiritual traditions in the Church, that of Basil, Benedict, Ignatius, Teresa of Avila, or Francis de Sales, for example, I believe the vision might be very similar. One challenge before the Church is clearly the complete elimination of the crime of the sexual abuse of minors. There is also another task: To re-member the scandal, and by this re-membering to insert into our public discourse and life a Gospel vision of God's goodness and who we are called to be together. May the Lord give us peace.

Abbreviations

DQEP   Bonaventure, *Disputed Questions on Evangelical Perfection: Works of St. Bonaventure* XIII, introduction and notes by Robert J. Karris, O.F.M., translation by Thomas Reist, O.F.M. Conv., and Robert J. Karris, O.F.M. (St. Bonaventure, N.Y.: Franciscan Institute, 2008).

FAED   Regis J. Armstrong, O.F.M. Cap., J. A. Wayne Hellmann, O.F.M.Conv., and William J. Short, O.F.M., eds., *Francis of Assisi: Early Documents* (New York: New City Press, 1999).

Notes

Introduction

1. Augustine, Exposition of Psalm 99.12 in *The Works of Saint Augustine, Expositions of the Psalms IV*, ed. Boniface Ramsey, trans. Maria Boulding, O.S.B. (Hyde Park, N.Y.: New City Press, 2002), 23. The "evil aspects which are mingled with the good" refers to the parable of the wheat and the weeds in Matthew 13.24–30.

2. Dante, *The Divine Comedy*, The Inferno I.1–6.

3. Yves Congar, O.P., "Saintete et peche dans l'église," *La Vie Intellectuelle* 15 (Novembré 1947): 6–40, with citation from 36.

1. The Church in Relation to the Times

1. Saint Bonaventure, *Collations on the Six Days* (April 29–May 28, 1273), 20.27. For the actual text see *Doctoris Seraphici S. Bonaventurae Opera Omnia* (Quaracchi: Collegii Sancti Bonaventurae, 1882–1902, 10 volumes), V, 329–354: "*Unde non habetur illuminatio, nisi quando Ecclesia consideratur secundum sua tempora.*"

2. See *The Nature and Scope of Sexual Abuse of Minors by Catholic Priests in the United States, 1950–2002, 2006 Supplementary Report*, A Research Study Conducted by the John Jay College of Criminal Justice, The City University of New York, 2006 (Washington, D.C.: United States Conference of Catholic Bishops, 2006), 1–4; National Review Board for the Protection of Children and Young People, "Report: Causes and Context of the Sexual Abuse Crisis," *Origins* 33 (March 11, 2004).

3. National Review Board, United States Conference of Catholic Bishops, Office of Child and Youth Protection, *Report on the Implementation of the Charter for the Protection of Children and Young People, 2006 Annual Report, Findings and Recommendations*, 8, 12, 25–28.

4. BishopAccountability.org, established in 2003 and available on the internet, tries to keep a running cost and publishes numerous documents related to the history of the scandal.

5. Cf. *The Nature and Scope of Sexual Abuse of Minors, 2006 Supplementary Report*, passim.

6. National Review Board, *Report on the Implementation*, 2006, 12.

7. Ad Hoc Committee on Sexual Abuse, "Brief History: Handling Child Sex Abuse Claims," *Origins* 23 (March 10, 1994): 666–670.

8. I make no attempt here to present a full history. For standard accounts see Jason Berry, *Lead Us Not into Temptation: Catholic Priests and the Sexual Abuse of Children* (New York: Doubleday, 1992); A. W. Richard Sipe, *Sex, Priests, and Power, Anatomy of a Crisis* (New York: Brunner/Mazel Publications, 1995); Philip Jenkins, *Pedophiles and Priests: Anatomy of a Contemporary Crisis* (New York: Oxford University Press, 1996); Bishop Geoffrey Robinson, *Confronting Power and Sex in the Catholic Church: Reclaiming the Spirit of Jesus* (Collegeville, Minn.: The Liturgical Press, 2008); Nicholas P. Cafardi, *Before Dallas: The U.S. Bishops' Response to Clergy Sexual Abuse of Children* (New York/Mahwah, N.J.: Paulist Press, 2008).

9. The "public" sphere, essential to the emergence of modern participative government, was first defined by Jürgen Habermas as a free zone between the individual and the state where "individuals participate in discussions about matters of common concern." See Mark E. Warren, "The Self in Discursive Democracy," in *The Cambridge Companion to Habermas,* ed. Stephen K. White (New York: Cambridge University Press, 1995), 167–200, citation from 171. A historiographical overview of the much-debated meaning of "public" as religious interpreters see it is given in E. Harold Breitenberg Jr., "To Tell the Truth: Will the Real Public Theology Please Stand Up," *Journal of the Society of Christian Ethics* 23 (Fall/Winter 2003): 55–96. In this chapter I take "public" in the widest sense to refer to society's broader religious, institutional, social, economic, political, intellectual, and cultural values and means of organization. Issues surface publicly when they begin to have broad social charge, and the various dimensions of social organizations (the law, the press, churches, government, professional elites, etc.) are marshaled to address them. The surfacing itself indicates congealed patterns of social change.

10. For the institutional silence see John E. B. Myers, *Child Protection in America, Past, Present, and Future* (New York: Oxford University Press, 2006).

11. For some historical reflections on this problem see Yves Congar, "Saintete et peche dans l'église."

12. John L. Thomas, S.J., names the two competing sexual regulatory systems of the 1950s, the social order approach and the personalist approach, in an insightful article "Sex and Society," *Social Order* IV (June 1954): 243–248. For parallel comments on the culture see K. A. Cuordileone, "Politics in an Age of Anxiety: Cold War Political Culture and the Crisis in American Masculinity, 1945–1960," *Journal of American History* 87 (September 2000): 515–545.

13. Much insight can be gained into this institutional problem of invisibility from the recent study of communications media and Mary

Douglas's anthropological analysis of embedded "thought styles." See Paul Starr, *The Creation of the Media: Political Origins of Modern Communications* (New York: Basic Books, 2004); Mary Douglas, *How Institutions Think* (Syracuse, N.Y.: Syracuse University Press, 1986).

14. The context is well set in Beth Bailey, "Sexual Revolution(s)," and Kenneth Cmiel, "The Politics of Civility," in *The Sixties: From Memory to History*, ed. David Farber (Chapel Hill: University of North Carolina Press, 1994), 235–262, 263–290.

15. This analysis is confirmed in National Review Board, "Report: Causes and Context of the Sexual Abuse Crisis," 661.

16. For background see Jenkins, *Pedophiles and Priests*, 140–151; Sara M. Evans, "Beyond Declension: Feminist Radicalism in the 1970s and 1980s," in *The World the Sixties Made: Politics and Culture in Recent America*, ed. Van Gosse and Richard Moser (Philadelphia: Temple University Press, 2003), 52–66; and Jeffrey Escoffier, "Fabulous Politics, Gay, Lesbian, and Queer Movements, 1969–1999," also in *The World the Sixties Made: Politics and Culture in Recent America*, ed. Gosse and Moser, 191–218. The broader social movement is often identified as the "culture wars." See James Davison Hunter, *Culture Wars: The Struggle to Define America* (New York: Basic Books, 1991).

17. Anne Larabee, *Decade of Disaster* (Urbana: University of Illinois Press, 2000); Charles J. Sykes, *A Nation of Victims:, The Decay of the American Character* (New York: St. Martin's Press, 1992); John Taylor, "Don't Blame Me! The New Culture of Victimization," *This World* (August 18, 1991), which speaks cogently of the "rights inflation" and "litigation as panacea."

18. A good review of the mobilization of public forces after the mid-1970s is Philip Jenkins, *Decade of Nightmares: The End of the Sixties and the Making of the Eighties* (New York: Oxford University Press, 2006), chaps. 4, 5.

19. Cf. James M. O'Toole, *The Faithful: A History of Catholics in America* (Cambridge, Mass.: Harvard University Press, 2008), chaps. 4, 5.

20. There is general agreement as to this initial time frame. See Norbert J. Rigali, S.J., "Church Responses to Pedophilia," *Theological Studies* 55 (March 1994): 124–139; Berry, *Lead Us Not into Temptation;* Ad Hoc Committee, "Brief History"; National Review Board, "Report: Causes and Context of the Sexual Abuse Crisis"; Peter Steinfels, "The Church's Sex-Abuse Crisis," *Commonweal* LXXIX, April 19, 2002, 13–19; Jenkins, *Pedophiles and Priests;* Cafardi, *Before Dallas.*

21. Ad Hoc Committee on Sexual Abuse, "Brief History."

22. *National Catholic Reporter*, June 7, 1984, 4–6, 19–21.

23. F. Ray Mouton, J.D., and Thomas P. Doyle, O.P., "The Problem of

Sexual Molestation by Roman Catholic Clergy: Meeting the Problem in a Comprehensive and Responsible Manner." This report is reprinted in Thomas P. Doyle, A. W. R. Sipe, Patrick J. Wall, *Sex, Priests, and Secret Codes, The Catholic Church's 2,000-Year Paper Trail of Sexual Abuse* (Los Angeles: Volt Press, 2006), 99–174. It is available online through BishopAccountability.org.

24. There is a good statement of the canonical problems raised by the treatment centers and the difficulties with Roman authorities in Cafardi, *Before Dallas*, 124–127. A general analysis is beyond the scope of this chapter.

25. The prevalence of this model of response is admitted by the Ad Hoc Committee on Sexual Abuse, "Brief History." Cf. "USCC Pedophilia Statement," *Origins* 17 (February 18, 1988): 624.

26. For some of these conditioning elements see Mark Massa, *Anti-Catholicism in America: The Last Acceptable Prejudice* (New York: Crossroad, 2003); and Philip Jenkins, *The New Anti-Catholicism: The Last Acceptable Prejudice* (New York: Oxford University Press, 2003).

27. Cf. for some parallel historical reflections Steven Mintz and John Stauffer, eds., *The Problem of Evil: Slavery, Freedom, and the Ambiguities of American Reform* (Amherst: University of Massachusetts Press, 2007).

28. Cf. again Starr, *The Creation of the Media*, 1–12.

29. Ad Hoc Committee on Sexual Abuse, "Brief History."

30. For indications of the changing approaches in psychology and treatment see Archbishop Daniel Pilarczyk, "Painful Pastoral Question: Sexual Abuse of Minors," *Origins* 22 (August 6, 1992): 177–178; Servants of the Paraclete, "Statement on Therapy for Pedophilia," *Origins* 22 (October 1, 1992): 284. The background and changes are well covered in the research paper posted on the website of the United States Conference of Catholic Bishops (formerly National Conference of Catholic Bishops): Karen J. Terry and Jennifer Tallon, "Child Sexual Abuse: A Review of Literature."

31. Carl M. Cannon, "Local Dioceses Creating Guidelines on Abuse," *San Jose Mercury News*, December 31, 1987; "Church and Denominational Liability for the Sexual Misconduct of Clergy," *Church Law & Tax Report*, September/October 1991, 4–7.

32. See Jeffrey R. Anderson, "Sexual Abuse by Clergy: Affirming the Church's Responsibility," unpublished paper, no date; Donald C. Clark, "Sexual Abuse in the Church: The Law Steps In," *The Christian Century* 110 (April 14, 1993): 396–398.

33. Jason Berry, "Listening to the Survivors: Voices of People of God," *America* 169 (November 13, 1993): 4–9. For early activity of SNAP see flyer "Survivors of Sexual Abuse by Priests Hold Gathering for Personal Support and Political Action," which refers to the Chicago group holding meetings

in Oakland, San Francisco, Boston, St. Louis, and Chicago.

34. Philip E. Lawler, "Suffer the Children," *The Catholic World Report*, November 1993, 38–47.

35. Stephen Rossetti was a pioneer in this area. See "Broken Symbols: Child Sexual Abuse and the Priesthood," and "A Wounded Church: Child Sexual Abuse and the Catholic Church," *Today's Parish*, September 1992, 9–13; October 1992, 9–13; *Slayer of the Soul: Child Sexual Abuse and the Catholic Church* (Mystic, Conn.: Twenty-Third Publications, 1991).

36. A good summary and overview may be found in Cafardi, *Before Dallas*, 77–85.

37. "Chicago Policy Regarding Clerical Sexual Misconduct with Minors," *Origins* 22 (October 1, 1992): 274–281.

38. Pilarczyk, "Painful Pastoral Question."

39. Father Canice Connors, "Subcommittee Head Introduces Think Tank Recommendations," *Origins* 23 (July 1, 1993): 105–107; "NCCB Establishes Committee on Sexual Abuse," *Origins* 23 (July 1, 1993): 104–105; John Paul II, "Vatican–U.S. Bishops' Committee to Study Applying Canonical Norms," *Origins* 23 (July 1, 1993): 102–103.

40. See Cafardi, *Before Dallas*, for a summary of the committee's work.

41. Ad Hoc Committee, "Restoring Trust," 11/94, in author's possession.

42. "Charges Against Chicago Archbishop Dropped," *Origins* 23 (March 10, 1994).

43. Steinfels, "The Church's Sex-Abuse Crisis." The Bernardin case also coincided with increasing awareness on the part of psychological professionals of the complications of repressed and false memories. See Stephanie Salter, "Recalling Abuse in the Mind's Eye," *San Francisco Examiner,* April 4–9, 1993; Martha L. Rogers, "Evaluating Adult Litigants Who Allege Injuries from Sexual Abuse: Clinical Assessment Methods for Traumatic Memories," *Issues in Child Abuse Accusations* 4, no. 4 (1992): 221–238; Paul W. Simpson, "False Memory Syndrome: Research and Implications," White Paper, May 18, 1993.

44. Some significant titles are Stephen J. Rossetti, *A Tragic Grace: The Catholic Church and Child Sexual Abuse* (Collegeville, Minn.: The Liturgical Press, 1996); Sipe, *Sex, Priests, and Power*; Jenkins, *Pedophiles and Priests.*

45. National Review Board, "Report: Causes and Context of the Sexual Abuse Crisis," 662, 680–681.

46. It would be helpful to analyze the legal activity during this period in relationship to the series of essays in Austin Sarat and Stuart A. Scheingold, eds., *Cause Lawyers and Social Movements* (Stanford, Calif.: Stanford Law and Politics, 2006). Once again, as throughout the crisis, it

would show the convergence between social and ecclesial developments.

47. "Faith Betrayed," February 16, 1997; "The Bishop's Justice," February 17; "Abuse of the Collar," February 18; "Bishop Will Look to Chicago Archdiocese for Help," February 20.

48. For another example of the episcopal issue see Don Lattin, "Sex Scandals Bare Church's Sordid Secrets," *San Francisco Chronicle,* August 14, 1999, A1–A8.

49. This progress from institutional invisibility to systemic anger followed the pattern already established in the civil rights, feminist, and homosexual rights movements. For broad background see Van Gosse, *Rethinking the New Left: An Interpretive History* (New York: Palgrave Macmillan, 2005).

50. Linda Graham Caleca and Richard D. Walton, "The Bishop's Justice," *Indianapolis Star,* February 17, 1997, 1, 8; Will Higgins, "Bishop Will Look to Chicago Archdiocese for Help," *Indianapolis Star*, February 20, 1997, F1, 2.

51. Cf. Investigative Staff of *The Boston Globe, Betrayal: The Crisis in the Catholic Church* (Boston: Little, Brown, 2002); David France, *Our Fathers: The Secret Life of the Catholic Church in an Age of Scandal* (New York: Broadway Books, 2004).

52. National Review Board, "Report: Causes and Context of the Sexual Abuse Crisis," 663.

53. For an account of the birth of Voice of the Faithful see James E. Muller and Charles Kenney, *Keep the Faith, Change the Church* (Emmaus, Penn.: Rodale, 2004). This national group is well covered in William D'Antonio and Anthony Pogorelc, *Voices of the Faithful: Loyal Catholics Striving for Change* (New York: Crossroad, 2007).

54. Melinda Henneberger with James Sterngold, "Vatican Meeting on Abuse Issue Is Set to Confront Thorny Topics," *New York Times*, April 19, 2002, A1, A20; Laurie Goodstein, "On a Mission to Restore Credibility," *New York Times*, April 21, 2002, A28.

55. Geraldine Baum and Eric Slater, "Pope Accepts Resignation of Milwaukee Archbishop," *New York Times*, May 25, 2002, A23.

56. See the coverage in the *New York Times,* June 15, 2002, A1, 10–11.

57. Dean E. Murphy, "Egan Says He Might Have Mishandled Sex Abuse Cases," *New York Times*, April 21, 2002, 29; Sam Dillon, "In Dealing with Abusive Priests, Bishops Stood Along a Wide Spectrum," *New York Times*, April 23, 2002, A21; Marco R. della Cava, "Santa Fe Archdiocese Learned Lessons That Could Help Others," *USA Today*, March 26, 2002, 1–2A.

58. See *The Nature and Scope of Sexual Abuse of Minors, 2006 Supplementary Report, 9.*

59. For examples and an overview, see Laurie Goodstein, "Trail of Pain in Church Crisis Leads to Nearly Every Diocese," *New York Times*, January 12, 2003, A1, 20–21; for particular examples: Cincinnati, see Francis X. Clines, "Subpoenaed Archbishop Avoids Testifying," *New York Times*, April 19, 2002, A21; New Hampshire, see Sam Dillon, "New Hampshire Bishop Embroiled in Abuse Disputes," *New York Times*, October 22, 2002, A18; San Bernardino, see Nick Madigan, "Warning About Priest Didn't Prompt Inquiry," *New York Times*, April 10, 2002, A20; southern California, see "Catholics Grapple with Mixed Feelings on Church Scandals," *Los Angeles Times*, April 8, 2002, B1, B8.

60. A good representative is the highly partisan "Franciscan Friars Held Accountable for Decades of Childhood Sexual Abuse," *Santa Barbara Lawyer* #408 (September 2006): 7–8.

61. A good example of this interpretation is L. Martin Nussbaum, "Changing the Rules," *America* 194 (May 15, 2006): 13–15, which names in particular the lawyers Jeffrey Anderson of Minnesota and Laurence Drivon of California, in conjunction with the political action work of SNAP. For anti-Catholicism see Jenkins, *The New Anti-Catholicism*.

62. Sam Dillon and Leslie Wayne, "As Lawsuits Spread, Church Faces Questions of Finances," *New York Times*, June 13, 2002; Pam Belluck and Adam Liptak, "For Boston Archdiocese, Bankruptcy Would Have Drawbacks," *New York Times*, December 3, 2002, A26; Glenn F. Bunting, Ralph Frammolino, and Richard Winton, "Archdiocese for Years Kept Claims of Abuse from Priests," *Los Angeles Times*, August 10, 2002, A1, 28–31; Ron Russell, "Camp Ped," *Los Angeles New Times,* August 15–21, 2002; Ron Russell, "Bishop Bad Boy," *SF Weekly* 22 (March 19–25, 2003).

63. Laurie Goodstein, "California Dioceses Brace for a Wave of Suits," *New York Times*, December 6, 2002, A1, 26; Gillian Flaccus, "Civil Sexual-Abuse Cases Poised to Accelerate," *The Tribune* (San Luis Obispo, California), October 10, 2004, B7.

64. Nussbaum, "Changing the Rules," 14. The states include New York, Iowa, Mississippi, where the legislation was rejected; Connecticut, Illinois, Ohio, Kansas, where the statute was extended; and Colorado, Massachusetts, Maryland, Michigan, New Jersey, Pennsylvania, Tennessee, where it is being considered. For continued debate over this "window" legislation see Marci A. Hamilton, "What the Clergy Abuse Crisis Has Taught Us," *America* 195 (September 25, 2006): 17–20; Charles J. Chaput, O.F.M.Cap., "The False Promise of 'Window' Legislation," *America* 195 (October 9, 2006): 34; Paul Vitello, "Religious Leaders Fight Bill to Open Abuse Cases," *New York Times*, March 12, 2009, A1, 21; Vitello, "Passions Remain High as Child Victims Act Is

Derailed After Bruising Fight," *New York Times*, August 10, 2009, A11.

65. As of 2006 the dioceses that had declared bankruptcy were Tucson, Arizona; Spokane, Washington; Portland, Oregon; and Davenport, Iowa. See "Abuse Cases Lead Diocese in Iowa to File for Chapter 11," *New York Times*, October 11, 2006, A22.

2. Confessions

1. Augustine, *The Trinity, The Works of St. Augustine*, introduction, translation, and notes by Edmund Hill, O.P., ed., John E. Rotelle, O.S.A. (Hyde Park, N.Y.: New City Press, 2002), III.1.9.

2. Some of the complexities of interpreting the overall crisis are indicated in James D. Davidson and Dean R. Hoge, "Catholics after the Scandal: A New Study's Major Findings," *Commonweal* 131 (November 20, 2004): 13–19.

3. The change is narrated in "A Comprehensive Approach to Provincial Policy and a Pastoral Response to Instances of Sexual Abuse of Minors at St. Anthony's Seminary," Province of Saint Barbara, December 4, 1992, and is printed in Geoffrey Stearns et al., *Report to Father Joseph P. Chinnici, O.F.M., Provincial Minister, Province of Saint Barbara, Independent Board of Inquiry Regarding St. Anthony Seminary, November 1993*. Hereafter referred to as *Independent Board of Inquiry*.

4. See Province of Saint Barbara, "Accusations of Sexual Abuse of Children: Policies and Procedures," January 1992.

5. Augustine, *Confessions*, IX.8. The translation by R. S. Pine-Coffin (London: Penguin Books, 1961) will be used throughout.

6. One of the more prominent people to analyze the impact of sexual abuse on parochial life was Stephen J. Rossetti. See his *Slayer of the Soul*, and *A Tragic Grace: The Catholic Church and Child Sexual Abuse* (Collegeville, Minn.: Liturgical Press, 1996); "Broken Symbols: Child Sexual Abuse and the Priesthood," *Today's Parish*, September 1992, 9–13; "A Wounded Church: Child Sexual Abuse and the Catholic Church," *Today's Parish*, October 1992, 9–13. He would later be invited to Santa Barbara to address the local religious and lay community.

7. "Chicago Policy Regarding Clerical Sexual Misconduct with Minors," *Origins* 22 (October 1, 1992): 273–281. For St. John's, see letter of October 27, 1992: St. John's monastic community in Collegeville, Minnesota, accepts "responsibility of responding appropriately to charges of sexual abuse and sexual exploitation" (Letter of Br. Dietrich Reinhart, O.S.B., to Parents, Alumni, Friends). For further developments at St. John's see the establishment of the Interfaith Sexual Trauma Institute and the newsletter *The ISTI Sun*.

8. The meeting occurred at the annual meeting of the National Conference of Catholic Bishops, November 16–19, 1992, and was led by Cardinal Roger Mahony. See Knight-Ridder News Service, November 21, 1992.

9. Bonaventure, *Collations on the Six Days*, 20.27.

10. Nick Welch, "Franciscans Respond to Abuse Complaints," *Santa Barbara Independent,* November 5, 1992, 9.

11. The November 30, 1992, "Commission Requirements," which the laity developed were printed in the appendix to *Independent Board of Inquiry*. The paper also contained criteria for the composition of an investigative commission.

12. Joseph P. Chinnici, O.F.M., November 24, 1992.

13. "A Comprehensive Approach to Provincial Policy and a Pastoral Response to Instances of Sexual Abuse of Minors at St. Anthony's Seminary," December 4, 1992, reprinted in *Independent Board of Inquiry*.

14. Cf. the remarks in the *Santa Barbara News-Press,* December 10, 1992.

15. Cf. Augustine, *Confessions*, VII.10–21.

16. Václav Havel, *Summer Meditations*, trans. Paul Wilson (New York: Alfred A. Knopf, 1992), 1. "The Power of the Powerless," a significant commentary on how social change occurs, may be found in Václav Havel, *Open Letters: Selected Writings, 1965–1990* (New York: Alfred A. Knopf, 1991), 125–214.

17. For deeper reflections on this whole issue of the inherited Christian world and the emergent Christian world see Yves M.-J. Congar, *Vraie et fausse réforme dans l'église* (Paris: Éditions du Cerf, 1950, 1968).

18. The entire process and the guidelines given in *Independent Board of Inquiry*.

19. "A Comprehensive Approach to Provincial Policy and a Pastoral Response to Instances of Sexual Abuse of Minors at St. Anthony's Seminary," 4.

20. The full story of the Board of Inquiry, its composition and process, may be found in *Independent Board of Inquiry*, 3–17.

21. Joseph P. Chinnici, O.F.M., "Pastoral Response to Report," November 29, 1993.

22. The issues and questions surrounding the press and media during the sexual abuse crisis are well covered in David E. DeCosse, "Freedom of the Press and Catholic Social Thought: Reflections on the Sexual Abuse Scandal in the Catholic Church in the United States," *Theological Studies* 68 (December 2007): 865–899. Sorting out all the ethical issues involved here is beyond the competence of this writer. From my point of view the issue also involves the action of God in history: Is the free press with all its

difficulties part of this action? See also John R. Quinn, *The Reform of the Papacy* (New York: Crossroad, 1999), 51–57.

23. *Independent Board of Inquiry*, 8.

24. The press release is printed in the appendix to *Independent Board of Inquiry*. See pages 8–9.

25. See, for example, *The Independent*, February 18, 1993; February 28, 1993; June 3–10, 1993; *Santa Barbara News-Press,* March 19, 1993; April 23, 1993.

26. Flyer, "Breaking the Silence—Protecting the Innocent." Cf. "Summary of Talks on Child Sexual Abuse Sponsored by the Archdiocese of Los Angeles and the Friars of the Santa Barbara Province—Lent, 1993," in author's possession. The lectures were all by experts in child sexual abuse: Mrs. Cecilia Rodriguez, M.A., Dr. Robert Doughtery, Ph.D., and Fr. Stephen Rossetti, D.Min. They occurred on March 11, 24, and April 3, 1993. Perhaps two dozen attended the first meeting with declining attendance thereafter.

27. The process is identified in *Independent Board of Inquiry*, 14–15.

28. Ibid., 11.

29. Ibid., 14, 16.

30. In June 1993 the information available to the Provincial Minister and made available to the Board also was Francis G. Morrisey, O.M.I., "Issue of Confidentiality in Religious Life," *Bulletin on Issues of Religious Life* 4 (April 1988). Applicable canons at the time were 220, 630.5, 1352.2, 1390.2, etc. For difficulties in the penal law of the Church see the review by Cafardi, *Before Dallas*, 15–46, 146–56. See also *Selected Studies Relative to Clergy Sexual Abuse and Related Issues*, privately distributed reprints from *The Jurist* (Washington, D.C., 1993).

31. As a careful reading of *Independent Board of Inquiry*, 14–17, indicates.

32. I refer here to the case of one priest who had been accused of some misconduct at the time of the Independent Board of Inquiry, who had undergone the necessary professional evaluations, but against whom there was no corroborating evidence at the time. Still, in favor of the victim, his ministry with minors was restricted. In 2002, when other individuals came forward, he was removed completely from ministry. See Rhonda Parks Manville, "Former Local Priest Loses Oregon Post," *Santa Barbara News-Press*, May 26, 2002.

33. Morgan Green, *Santa Barbara News-Press*, October 28, 1993, B1, B3.

34. *Independent Board of Inquiry*, 17.

35. For the law of "constraints" see Augustine, *Expositions of the Psalms I* (New York: New City Press, 2000), Psalm 30, Exposition 2.13.

Augustine gives a classic example of the judge who asks to be delivered from his "necessities," in *City of God*, XIX.6. For commentary see R. A. Markus, *Saeculum, History and Society in the Theology of St. Augustine* (Cambridge: Cambridge University Press, 1970), 99–100. Cf. *Confessions*, X.36–41.

36. I will pursue this theme in a later chapter.

37. Augustine, *Expositions of the Psalms III* (Hyde Park, N.Y.: New City Press, 2001), 54.8, and the whole passage for parallel comments. For very pertinent reflections see Michael C. McCarthy, S.J., "The Ecclesiology of Groaning: Augustine, The Psalms, and the Making of Church," *Theological Studies* 66 (2005): 23–48.

38. Irenaeus *Adversus Haereses* 4.64 as cited in Irénée Hausherr, S.J., *The Doctrine of Compunction in the Christian East* (Kalamazoo, Mich.: Cistercian Publications, 1982), 158.

3. Intersections in the Church and Society

1. Saint Augustine, *Expositions of the Psalms I*, Ps. 30, exp. 2, 13.

2. For recollections see Joseph Cardinal Bernardin, *The Gift of Peace, Personal Reflections* (Chicago: Loyola Press, 1997). See *Origins* 23 (March 10, 1994) for the complete story and court documents.

3. Cafardi, *Before Dallas*, 91–94.

4. March 22, 1993.

5. Paul Wilkes, "Unholy Acts," *New Yorker*, June 7, 1993, 62–77.

6. As cited in Cafardi, *Before Dallas*, 92.

7. The intense national atmosphere at this time is well captured in Jason Berry, "Fathers," *Los Angeles Times Magazine*, June 13, 1993, 24, 26–27, 56–57. For actions of the bishops see Bishops' Committee Report, "Brief History: Handling Child Sex Abuse Claims," *Origins* 23 (March 10, 1994): 666–670.

8. Cf. Philip F. Lawler, "Suffer the Children," *Catholic World Report*, November 1993, 38–42.

9. It is beyond the purpose and competence of this book to trace this movement for broader social and ecclesial justice among the laity. Chapter 1 has referred to the period after 1994 as one of "Percolation and Institutional Splitting." For some evidence of this trend as it links to St. Anthony Seminary see the Associated Press report, June 22, 1993; Wally Newman, "Can Tremblor Here Rock the Vatican," *Santa Barbara News-Press* (December 29, 1993), where he writes: "Fed up with rampant crime, the public forces passage of the Brady Bill. So, too, a lay public disgusted with revelations of the sexual abuses of many Catholic clergy may force

church authorities to look again at the efficacy of celibacy in the '90s." On July 29, 1994, the *News-Press* reported the passage of a new law in California, lobbied by a statewide coalition of lawyers and engaged parents, which relaxed the existing statutes regarding civil suits. See also Rhonda Parks Manville, "Bitterness Remains over Local Clergy Case," *News-Press*, April 1, 2002, A1, 12. For the precise contemporary context see Jason Berry, "Listening to the Survivors: Voices of the People of God," *America*, November 13, 1993, 4–9.

10. Citation is from Andrew Rice, "Franciscans Admit 34 Boys Were Molested at St. Anthony's," *The Independent*, December 2, 1993. Cf. *Independent Board of Inquiry*, section on "Findings"; "Press Release," Santa Barbara, California, November 29, 1993.

11. Stearns, "Presentation of Board's Report."

12. *Independent Board of Inquiry*, 32–38. For a precise listing of the psychological and relational impact, which is great, see page 41.

13. "Presentation of Board's Report," remarks by Geoffrey Stearns, chairperson.

14. Seth Adams, "11 Friars at California Seminary Molested Students, Inquiry Finds," *New York Times*, December 1, 1993, A1, 12.

15. Press release, Santa Barbara, California, November 29, 1993. The dispositions of the friars in question are listed in *Independent Board of Inquiry*, 29–31. One was deceased; one served six months in jail and left the Order; a third left the Order before final profession. Seven "were sent to highly respected professionals, experienced in working with sexual offenders and recommended by the Board, where they are currently in various stages of assessment and treatment." One friar, "where the facts are disputed by the friar," continues "in ministry with monitoring and restrictions on his contact with minors." For a last friar, not directly implicated in abusive behavior, more information was needed before any final disposition.

16. Joseph P. Chinnici, O.F.M., "Pastoral Response to Report," document made publicly available at the time and later reprinted as "Commentary," in *Santa Barbara News-Press,* December 14, 1993.

17. See *New York Times*, December 1, 1993, A12; cf. *Santa Barbara News-Press*, December 5, 1993; *New York Times*, December 2, 1993, for other reactions from survivors and family members.

18. The writer has a small collection of these public documents from Los Angeles, Santa Barbara, Oakland, San Francisco, Contra Costa, California; Minneapolis; Philadelphia; Arizona; and the national publications, *New York Times, Business Insurance, U.S.A. Today*; religious press, the *National Catholic Reporter*. Events were covered in Ireland, England, Canada, etc.

19. The citation is from *La Repubblica,* December 1, 1993; cf. *Corriere della Sera and Messaggero di Roma* for the same day.

20. This passage from Francis of Assisi came to the memory of the Provincial Minister December 7, 1993. Cf. *Office of the Passion,* V.8–10, Regis J. Armstrong, O.F.M.Cap., and Ignatius C. Brady, O.F.M., *Francis and Clare: The Complete Works* (New York: Paulist Press, 1982), 86.

21. The interview, which is a matter of record, will not be covered here. See "One Pastoral Response to Abuse, Interview with Joseph P. Chinnici, O.F.M.," *America* 170 (January 15, 1994): 4–8. The interview took place December 6, 1993.

22. Letter of December 5, 1993, in author's possession.

23. Larry B. Stammer, "Priest Abuse Inquiry Finds 'Terrible Truths,'" *Los Angeles Times,* December 1, 1993, A3, A22.

24. Ibid. See also "No Church Is All Saints," an editorial in same issue of *Los Angeles Times,* December 1, 1993; "Seminary Praised for Fast Response to Sexual Abuse," *Oakland Tribune,* December 1, 1993.

25. The writer, a man of great experience, refers to Romans 5.15.

26. Cf. *Lumen Gentium 8:* "Just as Christ carried out the work of redemption in poverty and oppression, so the Church is called to follow the same path if she is to communicate the fruits of salvation to men. . . . Similarly, the Church encompasses with her love all those who are afflicted by human misery and she recognizes in those who are poor and who suffer, the image of her poor and suffering founder. . . . [T]he Church, however, clasping sinners to her bosom, at once holy and in need of purification, follows constantly the path of penance and renewal."

27. Augustine, *The Trinity,* III.2.16.

28. Augustine, *Expositions of the Psalms VI,* Ps. 122.2 (Hyde Park, N.Y.: New City Press, 2006), 30.

29. Augustine refers to this passage and others as marking the pilgrim nature of those who belong to the city of God in this world. See *City of God,* XV.6.

30. Bonaventure, *Vitus Mystica,* X.2, *Opera Omnia,* VIII (176). Augustine, *Expositions of the Psalms* I, 22.2.2. See Chapter 8 of this book for the implications.

31. Cf. the biblical images of the Church presented in *Lumen Gentium,* 5–6.

32. The Vulgate reads *quasi leprosus* at verse 4. As we shall see later, this became an important icon for Francis of Assisi. Cf. Bonaventure, *Collations on the Seven Gifts of the Holy Spirit, Works of St. Bonaventure* XIV, trans. Zachary Hayes, O.F.M., notes by Robert J. Karris, O.F.M.,

Collation IV.22 (St. Bonaventure, N.Y.: Franciscan Institute Publications, 2008), 101–102.

33. Chhinnici, "Pastoral Response to Report," 1.

34. See *IRT-BULLETIN* April 1995; *IRT-BULLETIN* May 1998; Newsletter, Province of Saint Barbara; "A Response to Sexual Abuse of Minors, Province of Saint Barbara" (brochure).

35. Franciscan Friars, Province of Saint Barbara, *Therapeutic Guidelines for the Return to Limited Ministry in Cases of Child Sexual Abuse*.

36. For background and the nonreception of the Ad Hoc Committee's recommendations see Cafardi, *Before Dallas*, 100–114.

37. Nationally the switch of course predates November 29, 1993, but this general trend becomes more pronounced during this period. See Donald C. Clark Jr., "Sexual Abuse in the Church: The Law Steps In," *Christian Century* 110 (April 14, 1993): 396–398. I am speaking here of the Santa Barbara situation. For broader dimensions see Jo Renee Formicola, "The Vatican, the American Bishops, and the Church-State Ramifications of Clerical Sexual Abuse," *Journal of Church and State* 46 (Summer 2004): 479–502.

38. Morgan Green, "Second Man Sues for Abuse at Seminary," *Santa Barbara News-Press*, December 17, 1993, B1, B3.

39. The change in terminology is best described as a "professional thicket" of continuances, depositions, requirements forbidding contact between litigants, objectified definitions of misconduct, corporate exposure, piercing the veil, arbitration, mediation, privacy law, accuracy, employer-employee relationships, *respondeat superior*, case law, delayed discovery, disclosure, admissible and nonadmissible evidence, burdensome actions, motions to compel, information beyond the scope of discovery, objections, denial of motions, to give a partial listing.

40. For just two broad examples of the thicket of questions arising from insurance see "Church and Denominational Liability for the Sexual Misconduct of Clergy," *Church Law & Tax Report*, September/October 1991, 4–7; and implications for a diocese, Jean Guccione, "Priest Abuse Payout May Be Costly," *Los Angeles Times*, August 29, 2004; William Lobdell and Jean Guccione, "Diocese's Deal Raises the Bar across the U.S.," *Los Angeles Times*, December 4, 2004, A1, A24.

41. Some interesting comments on another intersection between law, causes, and the economic culture of the United States may be found in Lynn Jones, "The Haves Come Out Ahead: How Cause Lawyers Frame the Legal System for Movements," in *Cause Lawyers and Social Movements*, ed. Sarat and Scheingold, 182–196.

42. For a recent attempt to do this for the universal Church from the per-

spective of Benedict XVI, see *Charity in Truth, Caritas in Veritate* (Washington D.C.: United States Conference of Catholic Bishops, 2009), especially chapter 3, which shows considerable affinity with the Franciscan tradition.

43. See Giacomo Todeschini, *Franciscan Wealth: From Voluntary Poverty to Market Society* (St. Bonaventure, N.Y.: Franciscan Institute, 2009), for general background.

44. Armstrong and Brady, *Francis and Clare*, 141.

45. *The Rule and the General Constitutions of the Order of Friars Minor* (Pulaski, Wisc.: Franciscan Publishers, 1988), Article 72.1–3: "The brothers are pilgrims and strangers in this world. They give up personal ownership and hold on to nothing as their own, neither a house nor a place nor anything else, according to the Rule. They devote themselves and whatever they have for their life and work to the service of the Church and the world in poverty and humility. Buildings that are constructed for the brothers and everything they acquire or use should be in harmony with poverty according to circumstances of place and time. Goods that are given to the brothers for their use shall be shared with the poor, according to the prescriptions in particular statutes."

46. Bonaventure, *Apologia Pauperum [Defense of the Mendicants]*, XII.20, translation furnished by Robert J. Karris, O.F.M., in Franciscan Institute Publications. Cf. Question 2, article 1, ad 2 of *Disputed Questions on Evangelical Perfection, Works of Saint Bonaventure* XIII (St. Bonaventure, N.Y.: Franciscan Institute, 2008), 77–79.

47. For a good introduction to the social consequences of the adherence to poverty see Ovidio Capitani, *Figure e motivi del francescanesimo medievale* (Bologna: Pàtrum Editore, 2000), 11–30.

48. California statutes governing civil suits in cases of child molestation as they applied to or were interpreted for our situation changed in 1986, 1990, 1994, and 1998. The 2002 law dissolved all statutory limits for lapsed cases for the calendar year 2003.

49. Augustine, *The Trinity*, III.2.16.

50. I have been helped considerably in identifying the elements in this analysis by Ronnie Janoff-Bulman, *Shattered Assumptions: Towards a New Psychology of Trauma* (New York: Free Press, 1992); George S. Everly Jr. and Jeffrey M. Lating, *Psychotraumatology: Key Papers and Core Concepts in Post-Traumatic Stress* (New York: Plenum Press, 1995); Rossetti, *Tragic Grace*.

51. See Janoff-Bulman, *Shattered Assumptions*, chap. 6.

52. The Fraternity-in-Mission program is extensively described and analyzed in Richard McManus, "Franciscan Conversatio Process: A Faith Story-based Dialogue Method" (D.Min. thesis, Pacific School of Religion, Berkeley, California, 2009).

53. See, for example, Marco R. della Cava, "Santa Fe Archdiocese Learned Lessons That Could Help Others," *USA Today*, March 26, 2002, 1A–2A.

54. See, for example, Laurie Goodstein, "On a Mission to Restore Credibility," *New York Times*, April 21, 2002, A1, 28–29; Liptak, "U.S. Laws Pose Risk of Steep Penalties"; Sara Rimer and Anthony De Palma, "Doubt Tempers Catholics' Hopes," *New York Times*, April 23, 2002, A20; "Subpoenaed Archbishop Avoids Testifying," *New York Times*, April 19, 2002, A21; Ron Russell, "Bishop Bad Boy," *San Francisco Weekly*, March 19–25, 2003, 25–36. For a critique of some of the *New York Times* coverage see Andrew M. Greeley, "The *Times* and Sexual Abuse by Priests," *America* 188 (February 10, 2003): 16–17.

55. Cf. Larry B. Stammer, "No Easy Solution to Priest Problem," and Patrick Giles, "The Cross and the Cover-up," *Los Angeles Times*, April 14, 2002, A26, M2. See, for example, some of the articles in *America* 190 (March 22, 2004), which critique the John Jay Report; special issue of *St. Anthony Messenger*, "Crisis in the Church," 111 (June 2003); Stephen J. Rossetti, "The Catholic Church and Child Sexual Abuse," *America* 186 (April 22, 2002), 8–15.

56. See Rhonda Parks Manville, "Bitterness Remains over Local Clergy Case," *Santa Barbara News-Press*, April 1, 2002, A1, A12; Rhonda Parks Manville, "Former Local Priest Loses Oregon Post," *News-Press*, May 26, 2002, A1, A16; Rhonda Parks Manville, "Man Files Lawsuit under New State Abuse Law," *News-Press*, January 3, 2003. There is a fine analysis of the influence of a national media profile of sexual abuse cases up to the mid-1990s in Philip Jenkins, *Pedophiles and Priests: Anatomy of a Contemporary Crisis*, 53ff. Jenkins counts over five hundred articles. See also the pertinent remarks of Peter Steinfels following the Boston revelations: "Catholic Church's Sex-Abuse Crisis," *Commonweal*, April 19, 2002. See David E. DeCosse, "Freedom of the Press and Catholic Social Thought: Reflections on the Sexual Abuse Scandal in the Catholic Church in the United States," for comments on various interpretations of press coverage. Here I simply want to note its consistent role in the public life of the Church.

57. Carole McGraw, "Church Knew of Case against Priest," *Orange County Register*, May 18, 2003; Rhonda Parks Manville, "Former Local Priest Loses Oregon Post," *Santa Barbara News-Press*, May 26, 2002, A1, A16.

58. For examples see "Franciscan Friars Held Accountable for Decades of Childhood Sexual Abuse," *Santa Barbara Lawyer* 408 (September 2006): 7–8; Rhonda Parks Manville, "Abuse Group Spreads Word about New Law," *News-Press*, January 2, 2003, local news.

4. Community and Power in the Church

1. Augustine, Letter LXI, to Theodorus, in Philip Schaff, ed., *Nicene and Post-Nicene Fathers of the Christian Church*, I (Buffalo, N.Y.: Christian Literature Company, 1886), 318. For reference and commentary see John Burnaby, *Amor Dei: A Study of the Religion of St. Augustine* (1983; Eugene, Ore.: Wipf & Stock, 2007), 103.

2. Definition taken from William Morris, ed., *The American Heritage Dictionary of the English Language* (Boston: American Heritage and Houghton Mifflin, 1969).

3. This definition of power is taken from Rollo May, *Power and Innocence: A Search for the Sources of Violence* (New York: W. W. Norton, 1972), 99, combined with Richard Gula, "The Dynamics of Power," in *Just Ministry: Professional Ethics for Pastoral Ministries* (New York/Mahwah, N.J.: Paulist Press, 2010), 117–55, who identifies "social power" in reliance on the work of James D. Whitehead and Evelyn Eaton Whitehead, *The Emerging Laity* (New York: Doubleday, 1988), 35–49, and Edgar H. Schein, *Organizational Culture and Leadership* (San Francisco: Jossey-Bass, 1986). For another type of psychological approach see Adolf Guggenbuhl-Craig, *Power and the Healing Professions* (Dallas: Spring Publications, 1982). Sociologically, power could be defined as "the possibility of imposing one's will upon the behavior of other persons." This definition is taken from Max Weber as cited by James J. Gill, S.J., "Priests, Power, and Sexual Abuse," a paper contained in the first install-ment of Ad Hoc Committee on Sexual Abuse (NCCB, 1994), *Restoring Trust: A Pastoral Response to Sexual Abuse*. Using John Kenneth Galbraith's *The Anatomy of Power*, Gill provides a good introduction to power as it touches this particular scandal of sexual abuse.

4. Most notably Richard Sipe, *Sex, Priests, and Power: Anatomy of a Crisis;* Bishop Geoffrey Robinson, *Confronting Power and Sex in the Catholic Church;* Thomas P. Doyle, "Roman Catholic Clericalism, Religious Duress, and Clergy Sexual Abuse," *Pastoral Psychology* 51 (January 2003): 189–231; Gill, "Priests, Power, and Sexual Abuse." While not addressing power directly, the National Review Board, "Report: Causes and Context of the Sexual Abuse Crisis" speaks about issues of authority, clericalism, and "haughty attitude." For a fine analysis of power in the pastoral relationship see Gula, "The Dynamics of Power."

5. I have dealt with the questions of authority and power related to reli-gious women in "Hierarchy, Power, and the Franciscan Family in the American Church: A Dialogue with St. Bonaventure," *Cord* 54 (September/October 2004): 222–262. For the immediate postconciliar development of the problem of power see Joseph P. Chinnici, O.F.M., "An

Historian's Creed and the Emergence of Postconciliar Culture Wars," *Catholic Historical Review* 94 (April 2008): 219–244; "The Impact of Clericalization on Franciscan Evangelization," in *Franciscan Evangelization, Striving to Preach the Gospel, Washington Theological Union Symposium Papers, 2007,* ed. Elise Saggau, O.S.F. (St. Bonaventure, N.Y.: Franciscan Institute, 2008), 79–122; "A Pluriform Unity: An Historical View of the Contemporary Church," paper prepared for Greenberg Center, Trinity College, Hartford (forthcoming).

6. Analyzing the general context for the emergence into the public of the sexual abuse crisis in the mid-1980s would take this work too far afield. Significant indicators of the tense emotional atmosphere may be found in Priestly Life and Ministry Committee, "Reflections on the Morale of Priests," *Origins* 18 (January 12, 1989): 499–505; The Bishops' Committee on Priestly Life and Ministry, "Women Religious and Priests: A Brief Reflection," November 1, 1985; "Response of NCCB Priestly Life and Ministry Committee to *Attitudes of American Priests in 1970 and 1985 on the Church and Priesthood,* September 22–23, 1986," Bishops' Committee on Priestly Life and Ministry, February 2, 1987, Archives of the Archdiocese of San Francisco; Conference of Major Superiors of Men, Task Force Report, "In Solidarity and Service, Reflections on the Problem of Clericalism in the Church," 1983, manuscript in author's possession; Constance FitzGerald, O.C.D., "Impasse and Dark Night," in *Women's Spirituality: Resources for Christian Development,* ed. Joann Wolski Conn (New York: Paulist Press, 1986), 287–311.

7. On the side of the liberal reformers are Jason Berry, *Lead Us Not into Temptation*; Elinor Burkett and Frank Bruni, *A Gospel of Shame: Children, Sexual Abuse and the Catholic Church* (New York: Viking, 1993); Sipe, *Sex, Priests, and Power.* One of the primary spokesmen for seminary reform is the social commentator George Weigel, *The Courage to Be Catholic: Crisis, Reform, and the Future of the Church* (New York: Basic Books, 2002). For international comments see Robinson, *Confronting Power and Sex in the Catholic Church.* For the disjunctive reassertion of the clerical and lay poles see below.

8. For parallel examples of the formulation of "charged social symbols" see Jason C. Bivins, *The Fracture of Good Order: Christian Antiliberalism and the Challenge to American Politics* (Chapel Hill: University of North Carolina Press, 2003). Bivins speaks of a "sacred register" as a manifestation of the tendency to politicize what is most intimate to people, their very identity and self-understanding as religious practitioners. Also see the analysis of the Equal Rights Amendment in Donald G. Mathews, "'Spiritual Warfare': Cultural Fundamentalism and the Equal Rights Amendment," *Religion and American Culture* 3, no. 1 (1993): 129–154;

Donald Mathews and Jane Sherron De Hart, *Sex, Gender, and the Politics of ERA: A State and the Nation* (New York: Oxford University Press, 1990). The multiple meanings involved in the right to life struggle serve as a third parallel example. See Kristin Luker, *Abortion and the Politics of Motherhood* (Berkeley: University of California Press, 1984). For general background, T. V. Reed, *The Art of Protest, Culture and Activism from the Civil Rights Movement to the Streets of Seattle* (Minneapolis: University of Minnesota Press, 2005).

9. For examples, see James E. Muller and Charles Kenney, *Keep the Faith: Change the Church*; William D'Antonio and Anthony Pogorelc, *Voices of the Faithful*; Grant Gallicho, "Are the Bishops Listening? An Interview with VOTF's James E. Post," *Commonweal* 130 (June 6, 2003): 12–17; "Voice of the Faithful Leaders Studied," *CARA Report* 12 (Summer 2006): 9; James D. Davidson and Dean R. Hoge, "Catholics after the Scandal: A New Study's Major Findings," *Commonweal* 131 (November 19, 2004): 13–19; Mark M. Gray and Paul Perl, *Catholic Reactions to the News of Sexual Abuse Cases Involving Catholic Clergy, CARA Working Paper* 8 (April 2006). The episcopal divisions come through very strongly in National Review Board, "Report: Causes and Context of the Sexual Abuse Crisis."

10. Dean R. Hoge and Jacqueline G. Wenger, *Evolving Visions of the Priesthood* (Collegeville, Minn.: Liturgical Press, 2003), 69.

11. National Review Board, "Report: Causes and Context of the Sexual Abuse Crisis," IV.2 (669).

12. This oscillation between hierarchical and communal poles of the Church can be traced in the reception of John Paul II, *Pastores Dabo Vobis* (1992) and the Vatican Instruction, "Some Questions Regarding Collaboration of Nonordained Faithful in Priests' Sacred Ministry" (August 15, 1997), printed in *Origins* 27 (November 27, 1997): 397–407, 409–410. In both its introduction and the "Explanatory Note" that accompanied it, the latter document called attention to the role of the laity and the other communal values mentioned above. The focus on the onto-logical was not meant to dissolve these values; it was instead seen as a much-needed counterpoint to an excessively functional view of the Church, one moving away from the mystery of its sacramental structure and reducing relationships to "competition, power, efficiency." In 2000 the third *General Instruction of the Roman Missal* ritually prescribed a stronger separation between the clergy and laity; in 2001 *Liturgiam Authenticam* on the translation of the liturgical texts appeared; and in 2004 *Redemptionis Sacramentum* called attention to liturgical abuses and defined as "reprobate" the practice of the priest present at the celebration of the Eucharist refraining from distributing communion and handing the

function over to the laity. The point here is not the actions themselves, really directed to a world Church, but the context in the United States in which they were received. See J. Kerkhofs, "Vatican II: Twenty Years Later," *Pro Mundi Vita* (1985) for a review in the wake of the Council of a world situation that reflected the tension between the ministerial priesthood and the priesthood of all believers. For commentary on the documents see John M. Huels, "The New General Instruction of the Roman Missal: Subsidiarity or Uniformity," *Worship* 75 (November 2001): 482–511, with listing of new developments on page 506; Helen Hull Hitchcock, "A New Era in the Renewal of the Liturgy," in *The Catholic Imagination, Proceedings from the Twenty-fourth Annual Convention of the Fellowship of Catholic Scholars*, ed. Kenneth D. Whitehead (South Bend, Ind.: St. Augustine's Press, 2003), 140–150, and subsequent articles by others, 151–158; for a critical review see Peter Jeffery, Obl.S.B., *Translating Tradition: A Chant Historian Reads* Liturgiam Authenticam (Collegeville, Minn.: Liturgical Press, 2005).

13. Cf. United States Conference of Catholic Bishops, *Program of Priestly Formation* (Washington, D.C.: USCCB, 2006). Compare its treatment of priestly identity with *Lumen Gentium* (II.10–12, IV.34–36), the decree on the Apostolate of the Laity, *Apostolicam Actuositatem* (I2), and with "Co-workers in the Vineyard of the Lord," *Origins* 35 (December 4, 2005); Rose McDermott, S.S.J., "Co-Workers in the Vineyard of the Lord: A Canonical Analysis," *Jurist* 67 (2007): 432–460.

14. Cf. *Lumen Gentium*, 10.

15. It would be good in the light of the sexual abuse crisis to reread Bishops Committee on Priestly Life and Ministry, *A Reflection Guide on Human Sexuality and the Ordained Priesthood* (Washington, D.C.: United States Catholic Conference, 1983), which points to the importance of self-esteem and relationships in the proper functioning of the priest. This was on the eve of the public scandal.

16. Cf. James H. Provost, "Ministry: Reflections on Some Canonical Issues," *The Heythrop Journal* 29 (July 1988): 285–299; John P. Beal, "The Exercise of the Power of Governance by Lay People: State of the Question," *The Jurist* 55 (1995): 1–92; Luigi Sabbarese, *I Fideli Constituti Popolo Di Dio* (Rome: Urbaniana University Press, 2000), 67–72. For multiple perspectives see James Provost and Knaut Walf, eds., *Power in the Church* (Edinburgh: T & T Clark, 1988).

17. Most helpful in understanding Augustine is R. A. Markus, "Conversion and Disenchantment in Augustine's Spiritual Career," Saint Augustine Lecture, Villanova University, 1984, reprinted in *Sacred and Secular: Studies on Augustine and Latin Christianity* (Aldershot, Hampshire, Great Britain: Variorum, 1994). Cf. also Robert Dodaro,

Christ and the Just Society in the Thought of Saint Augustine (Cambridge: Cambridge University Press, 2004), 68–69, on the turn to the private and the illusion of self-sufficiency.

18. Augustine, *Expositions of the Psalms.I*, Ps. 8.13. For commentary on Augustine's view of the Church composed of sinners and saints see T. Johannes van Bavel, O.S.A., "What Kind of Church Do You Want? The Breadth of Augustine's Ecclesiology," *Louvain Studies* 7 (Spring 1979): 147–171.

19. Augustine, *Expositions of the Psalms III*, Ps. 63.9.

20. National Review Board, "Report: Causes and Context of the Sexual Abuse Crisis," 681–682.

21. For the social and political world see Bill Bishop, *The Big Sort: Why the Clustering of Like-minded America Is Tearing Us Apart* (Boston: Houghton Mifflin, 2008); for an ecclesial parallel see the comparison of the dioceses of Saginaw and Lincoln in Charles R. Morris, *American Catholic: The Saints and Sinners Who Built America's Most Powerful Church* (New York: Random House, 1997; Vintage Books, 1998).

22. The image is taken from Peter Brown, *Augustine of Hippo: A Biography* (Berkeley, Calif.: University of California Press, 2000), 505.

23. I have been helped in thinking of this problem as the creation of a "new ethical space" by Gregory Baum, *Amazing Church: A Catholic Theologian Remembers a Half-Century of Change* (Maryknoll, N.Y.: Orbis Books, 2005).

24. Bonaventure cites this "law of reciprocity" from Philippians 4.15 several times in his writings. Cf. *Disputed Questions on Evangelical Perfection: Works of St. Bonaventure* XIII, introduction and notes by Robert J. Karris, O.F.M., translation by Thomas Reist, O.F.M.Conv., and Robert J. Karris, O.F.M. (St. Bonaventure, N.Y.: Franciscan Institute, 2008), QII, a2, d8 and rep. neg. d15 (97, 129). Hereafter *DQEP*.

5. Power, Relationships, and the Franciscan Tradition I

1. Francis of Assisi, "Earlier Exhortation to the Brothers and Sisters of Penance," in Regis J. Armstrong, O.F.M. Cap., J. A. Wayne Hellmann, O.F.M.Conv., and William J. Short, O.F.M., eds., *Francis of Assisi: Early Documents* I (New York: New City Press, 1999), I.42. Hereafter *FAED*.

2. I am not alone in trying to search within the Franciscan tradition for some answers to our contemporary dilemmas, and it is best here when we begin our specifically Franciscan reflections to mention some of the major foreign studies that have helped in articulating my own understanding of the tradition and its current application. See in particular for questions of poverty, Roberto Lambertini, *La povertà pensata: Evoluzione storica della*

definizione dell'idntità minoretica da Bonaventura ad Occam (Modena: Mucchi Editore, 2000); Lambertini, *"Pecunia, possessio, proprietas* alle origini di Minori e Predicatori: Osservazioni sul filo della terminologia," in *L'economia dei conventi dei frati minori e predicatori fina alla metà del Trecento, Atti del XXXI Covegno internazionale, Assisi, 9–11 Ottobre 2003* (Spoleto: Centro Italiano di Studi sull'alto Medioevo, 2004), 3–42; Alain Boureau and Sylvain Piron, eds., *Pierre de Jean Olivi (1248–1298): Pensée scolastique, dissidence spirituelle et société* (Paris: Librairie Philosophique J. Vrin, 1999). For overall philosophy, theology, and ethics, see Orlando Todisco, *Lo stupore della ragione: Il pensare francescano e la filosofia moderna* (Padova: Messaggero di Sant'Antonio, 2003); "L'etica francescana e la soggettività moderna," *Miscellanea Francescana* 102 (Gennaio-Giugno 2002): 84–142; Alfonso Pompei, "San Bonaventura e La Chiesa, Oggi," in *Bonaventura da Bagnoregio: Il pensare francescano* (Rome: Miscellanea Francescana, 1993), 317–334.

3. For a structural approach to the issues considered here see Jacques LeGoff, "Francis of Assisi between the Renewal and Restraints of Feudal Society," in *Saint Francis of Assisi,* trans. Christine Rhone (New York: Routledge, 2004), 1–12. By a master historian of medieval society, this work on Francis is one of the best guides for understanding his importance as it touches the issues considered in this book. See also Daniela Rando, " 'Laicus religiosus': Tra strutture civili ed ecclesiastiche: l'ospedale di Ognissanti in Treviso (sec. XIII)," *Studi Medievali* 24 (1983): 617–656.

4. A classic statement is that of the First Lateran Council (1123), canon 17: "We forbid abbots and monks to impose public penances, to visit the sick, to administer extreme unction, and to sing public masses. The chrism, holy oil, consecration of altars, and ordination of clerics they shall obtain from the bishops in whose dioceses they reside." H. J. Schroeder, O.P., *Disciplinary Decrees of the General Councils, Text, Translation, and Commentary* (St. Louis: B. Herder, 1937), 189. For the importance of this legal codification as background for the structural relevance of the Franciscan movement see C. Colt Anderson, *A Call to Piety: Saint Bonaventure's Collations on the Six Days* (Quincy, Ill.: Franciscan Press, 2002), 16ff.

5. References may be found in "The Later Rule" I.2, IX.1, XII.4 and "Testament" 6 in Armstrong et al., *FAED,* 100, 104, 106, 125. For specific interpretation of Francis's relationship to the Roman Church see Michele Maccarrone, "S. Francesco e la Chiesa di Innocenzo III," in *Approccio Storico-Critico alle Fonti Francescane* (Rome: Antonianum, 1979), 31–43; Pietro Zerbi, "San Francesco d'Assisi e la Chiesa Romana," in *"Ecclesia in hoc mundo posita": Studi di storia e di storiografia medio-*

evale racolti in occasione del 70 genetliacao dell'autore, a cura di Maria Pia Alberzoni (Milan, 1993), 355–384.

6. The literature here is vast, but see as beginning points Giovanni Gonnet, "La Donna Presso I Movimenti Pauperistico-Evangelici," in *Movimento religioso femminile e Francescanesimo nel secolo XIII, Atti del VII Covegno Internazionale, Assisi, 11–13 Ottobre 1979* (Assisi, 1980), 103–129; Kurt-Victor Selge, "I movimenti religiosi laici del XII sec., in partolare I Valdesi, quale sfondo e premessa del movimento francescano," *Protestantesimo* 43 (1988): 71–92; Raul Manselli, "Evangelismo e povertá," in Manselli, *Il Secolo XII: Religione popolare ed eresia* (Jouvence, 1983).

7. *Admonition* XVI in Armstrong et al., *FAED*, I.

8. Dominic V. Monti, O.F.M., ed., *Breviloquium, Works of St. Bonaventure*, IX (St. Bonaventure, N.Y.: Franciscan Institute, 2005), VI.5, VI.9, VI.10, VI.12. For Bonaventure's ecclesiology see Peter D. Fehlner, O.F.M.Conv., *The Role of Charity in the Ecclesiology of St. Bonaventure* (Rome: Miscellanea Francescana, 1965).

9. Some of the best reflections on the evangelical movement of the times remain those of M. D. Chenu in *Nature, Man, and Society in the Twelfth Century: Essays on New Theological Perspectives in the Latin West*, selected, edited and translated by Jerome Taylor and Lester K. Little (Chicago: University of Chicago Press, 1968), 202–269. For background on the commune see J. K. Hyde, *Society and Politics in Medieval Italy: The Evolution of the Civil Life* (New York: St. Martin's Press, 1973); Augustine Thompson, O.P., *Cities of God: The Religion of the Italian Communes, 1125–1325* (University Park: Pennsylvania State University Press, 2005).

10. See, for example, Daniela Rando, " 'Laicus religiosus': Tra strutture civili ed ecclesiastiche: l'ospedale di Ognissanti in Treviso (sec. XIII)"; Grado Merlo, "La conversione alla povertá nell'Italia dei secoli XII–XIV," in *La conversione alla povertá nell Italia dei secoli XII–XIV, Atti del XXVII Covegno storico internazionale, Todi, 14–17 Ottobre 1990* (Spoleto: Centro Italiano di Studi sull'Alto Medioeve, 1991), 3–32.

11. The subsequent difficult history of the Friars Minor has borne testimony to its contentious birth between these two warring factions. See Roberto Lambertini and Andrea Tabarroni, *Dopo Francesco: L'eredità difficile* (Turin, 1989).

12. *Testament* 23 in Armstrong et al., *FAED*, I, 126. For important comments related to Francis's social task see Ovidio Capitani, "Verso una nuova antropologia e una nuova religiositá," in *La conversione alla povertá,* 447–471.

13. For more extensive comments and explanation see Yves Congar, "Les laics et l'ecclesiologie des 'ordines' chex theologiens des XIe et XIIe

siècles," in *I laici nella "societas Christiana" dei secoli IX e XII* (Milan, 1968), 83–117; Théophile Desbonnets, *From Intuition to Institution: The Franciscans* (Chicago: Franciscan Herald Press, 1988), 57–71.

14. *Earlier Exhortation* 1.13, Armstrong et al., *FAED*, I, 42, with reference to Hebrews 2.11.

15. For clear examples of both mutual obedience and reciprocal charity, see *The Earlier Rule* IV–VI, *Admonitions* III–IV, Armstrong et al., *FAED*, I, 66–68, 130. For "sisters" see Clare, *Rule* I.1, X.4, *Testament* 19 in Armstrong and Brady, *Francis and Clare*, 211, 222, 231. For important background in the society see Felice Accrocca and Antonio Ciceri, *Francesco e I suoi frati* (Milan: Biblioteca Francescana, 1998), chap. 2.

16. For various interpretations of Francis's clothing see above all Chiara Frugoni, *Francis of Assisi*, trans. John Bowden (New York: Continuum, 1999), 42–50; Desbonnets, *From Intuition to Institution: The Franciscans*, 20–21. The original title of Frugoni's book is *Vita di un uomo: Francesco d'Assisi*. The theme of the universality of Francis's message is well treated in Jacques Dalarun, *Francesco: Un passaggio, donni e donne negli scritti e nella leggenda di Francesco d'Assisi* (Rome: Viella, 1994).

17. "A Letter to the Entire Order," Armstrong et al., *FAED*, I, 116–118. For commentary on this vision of "brothers who are priests" see Bernhard Holter, "'Sacerdotes Fraternitatis in Christo Humiles,' (Ep.Ord. 2), Il sacerdozio minoritico nella vision di S. Francesco," in *"Minores et Subditi Omnibus": Tratti caratterizzanti dell'identitá francescana*, ed. L. Padovese (Rome, 2003), 161–174.

18. For the significance of the Gospel as the primary referent see Yves Congar, "The Gospel as an Absolute in Christendom" (1952), reprinted in *St. Francis of Assisi: Essays in Commemoration*, ed. Maurice W. Sheehan, O.F.M.Cap. (St. Bonaventure, N.Y.: Franciscan Institute, 1982), 59–76.

19. *Admonition* IV in Armstrong et al., *FAED*, I, 130.

20. Two of the best articles are Francis de Beer, O.F.M., "La genesis de la fraternidad Franciscana segun algunas fuentes primitivas," *Selecciones de Franciscanismo* 31 (1982): 49–74; Marie Dominique Chenu, "'Fraternitas' evangile et condition socio-culturelle," *Revue d'Histoire de Spiritualité* 49 (1973): 385–400. For explicit reflections on power see Jacques Dalarun, *Francesco d'Assisi, il potere in questione e la questione del potere* (Milan: Edizioni Biblioteca Francescana, 1999), 21–49. See also Grado Giovanni Merlo, "Intorno a frate Francesco: Uomini e identita di una nuova 'fraternitas.'" in *I compagni di Francesco e la prima generazione minoritica, Atti del XIX Covegno internazionale* (Spoleto: Centro Italiano di Studi sull'Alto Medioevo, 1992), 315–338. There is important background information on the feminization of authority for this period in

Caroline Walker Bynum, *Jesus as Mother: Studies in the Spirituality of the High Middle Ages* (Berkeley: University of California Press, 1982).
21. LeGoff, "The Vocabulary of Social Categories in Saint Francis of Assisi and His Thirteenth-Century Biographers," in *Saint Francis of Assisi*, 63–96, with exposition and citation from 74–75.
22. I have tried to deal with this social mission in "Penitential Humanism: Rereading the Sources to Develop a Franciscan Urban Spirituality," in *Franciscans in Urban Ministry*, ed. Kenneth Himes, O.F.M. (St. Bonaventure, N.Y.: Franciscan Institute, 2002), 109–128. For broader background see Lester K. Little, *Religious Poverty and the Profit Economy in Medieval Europe* (Ithaca, N.Y.: Cornell University Press, 1978). The "tranquility of order" is taken from Augustine, *City of God*, XIX.13, a definition used by Bonaventure. See *DQEP* with references to Augustine, p. 347. "Order" encompassed both hierarchical and communal structures of life.
23. *Earlier Rule* XXI.4–6, Armstrong et al., *FAED*, I, 78, citing Luke 6.38; Matt. 6.14, 11.25.
24. Caroline Walker Bynum, in *Jesus as Mother*, notes how the period saw a revival of interest in the Pauline concept of the Body of Christ and unity through conformity to the one model of Jesus (82–109).
25. *Earlier Exhortation* 8–10, in Armstrong et al., *FAED*, I, 42. For commentary see Enríco Menestò, "A Re-reading of Francis of Assisi's Letter to the Faithful," *Greyfriars Review* 14, no. 2 (2000): 97–110. Clare uses the terms "sister," "mother," "spouse," "daughter" in reference to the Lord in her *Letters to Agnes of Prague* in *Francis and Clare*, III.1 (199), IV.4 (203).
26. Augustine, "Holy Virginity," 5.5, in *Marriage and Virginity*, ed. John E. Rotelle, O.S.A. (Hyde Park, N.Y.: New City Press, 1999), 70.
27. For the significance of reciprocity as a new spiritual term deriving from the Augustinian canonical reform see Caroline Walker Bynum, *Docere Verbo et Exemplo: An Aspect of Twelfth-Century Spirituality* (Missoula, Mont.: Scholars Press, 1979). Francis applies this tradition of reciprocity to the new circumstances of a *fraternitas* and moves the experience into the marketplace of life.
28. *Earlier Rule* 17.11–12, 11.6, *Letter to the Entire Order*, 9, *Admonition* VIII, in Armstrong et al., *FAED*, I, 75, 72, 117.
29. See Damien Isabell, O.F.M., *The Practice and Meaning of Confession in the Primitive Franciscan Community according to the Writings of Saint Francis of Assisi and Thomas of Celano* (Assisi, 1973).
30. *Rule of Clare* 9.4–5 in Armstrong and Brady, *Francis and Clare*, 221. For the encouragement of the forgiveness of sins and confession within the social context see *Earlier Rule*, 21.4–7; *Later Exhortation*, 38, 42–44.

31. See the insightful study by David Flood, O.F.M., *Work for Everyone: Francis of Assisi and the Ethic of Service* (Quezon City, Philippines: CCFMC Office for Asia/Oceania, 1997). For later developments see Lambertini, *La povertà pensata*, chap. 2. *Habere pro aliis* is central for how one interprets ecclesiastical office as service.

32. *Earlier Rule* XXIII.7, *FAED*, I, 84, with commentary by LeGoff, *Saint Francis of Assisi*, 74–79.

6. Power, Relationships, and the Franciscan Tradition II

1. Bonaventure, *Disputed Questions on Evangelical Perfection, Works of St. Bonaventure* XIII, trans.Thomas Reist, O.F.M.Conv., and Robert J. Karris, O.F.M. (Saint Bonaventure, N.Y.: Franciscan Institute Publications, 2008), QI, rep. neg. 2 (48–49).

2. For pertinent comments see Andre Vauchez, "L'utopie franciscaine dans l'église medievale," *Lumiere & Vie* 33 (April–June 1984): 39–47.

3. For introductions see Ilia Delio, O.S.F., *Simply Bonaventure: An Introduction to His Life, Thought, and Writings* (New York: New City Press, 2001); and above all Zachary Hayes, *The Hidden Center: Spirituality and Speculative Christology in St. Bonaventure* (St. Bonaventure, N.Y.: Franciscan Institute, 1992).

4. For a fine analysis see Lambertini, *La povertà pensata*; Alfonso Pompei, "'L'apologia pauperum' e lo scontro tra maestri secolari e mendicanti in seno all'università di Parigi," in *Bonaventura da Bagnoregio*, 194–222; M.-M. Dufeil, *Guillaume de Saint-Amour et la polémique universitaire parisienne, 1250–1259* (Paris: Éditions A. et J. Picard, 1972); K. Schleyer, "Disputes scolastiques sur les états de perfection," *Recherches de Théologie ancienne et médievale* 10 (1938): 279–293. It is interesting to note that Cardinal Joseph Ratzinger makes reference to the relevance of this dispute for the contemporary Church in "The Theological Locus of Ecclesial Movements," *Communio* 25 (Fall 1998): 480–504.

5. Bonaventure's five major works, written during the controversy: *Disputed Questions on Evangelical Perfection* (1255–56), *Collations on the Ten Commandments* (1267), *Collations on Seven Gifts of the Holy Spirit* (1268), *Defense of the Mendicants* (1269), and his final work, *Collations on the Six Days of Creation or Hexaemeron* (1273).

6. *Collations on the Seven Gifts of the Holy Spirit, Works of St. Bonaventure*, XIV, introduction and translation by Zachary Hayes, O.F.M., notes by Robert J. Karris, O.F.M. (St. Bonaventure, N.Y.: Franciscan Institute, 2008), III.9 (74). For the misbehavior and anger of the brothers see the encyclical letters by Bonaventure in 1257 and 1266 in

Writings Concerning the Franciscan Order, Works of Saint Bonaventure V, by Dominici Monti, O.F.M (St. Bonaventure, N.Y.: Franciscan Institute, 1994). Bonaventure will repeat again in the *Hexaemeron* 23.23: "For some men are pious zealots, and later they turn to the fire of impatience."

7. *Collations on the Ten Commandments, Works of St. Bonaventure* VI, introduction and translation by Paul J. Spaeth (St. Bonaventure, N.Y.: Franciscan Institute, 1995), II.29 (42–43).

8. Augustine, *The Trinity,* XII.14 (330).

9. For quotes and references see *DQEP,* QII, a2, rep. neg. 20 (133), QIV, a2, rep. neg. 12 (241); *Collations on the Seven Gifts* I.10 (35), III.14 (79), VI.13 (131), VII.15, 17 (152–156), VIII.4 (164), IX.11, 16 (190, 195).

10. Second Encyclical Letter (1266), 2 in *Writings Concerning the Franciscan Order,* 227.

11. Most notably in Bonaventure's last work, the *Hexaemeron.* See Anderson, *A Call to Piety;* Joseph Ratzinger, *The Theology of History in St. Bonaventure* (Chicago: Franciscan Herald Press, 1971).

12. See *DQEP,* QII, a2, rep. neg. 11 (125–126) where the abuses inflicted on the mendicants by "prelates and others" are listed. See also Luigi Pellegrini, "Mendicanti e parroci: Coesistenza e conflitti di due structture organizative della 'cura animarum,'" in *Francescanesimo e vita religosa dei laici nel 1200, Atti dell VIII covegno internazionale* (Assisi, 1981), 131–167.

13. See, for example, *DQEP,* QII, a2, d 15 (91), and in the same volume William of Saint-Amour, *Quaestio de mendicitate,* d.13 (285); *Defense of the Mendicants,* X.13–16, on common ownership.

14. See contrast between *Etsi animarum* (1254) of Innocent IV and *Quasi lignum vitae* (1255) of Alexander IV, which sided with the mendicants. Cf. Pompei, "L'apologia pauperum," 206. For an older but good beginning summary of these issues see A. G. Little, *Studies in English Franciscan History: Being the Ford Lectures Delivered in the University of Oxford in 1916* (Manchester: University Press, 1917), 92–122.

15. For a good overview of the problems of the friars see Jay M. Hammond III, "An Historical Analysis of the Concept of Peace in Bonaventure's *Itinerariuim Mentis in Deum*" (Ph.D. diss., St. Louis University, 1998).

16. For a very clear contemporary example see Martin Luther King Jr., "A Challenge to the Churches and Synagogues," in *Race: Challenge to Religion,* ed. Mathew Ahmann (Chicago: Henry Regnery, 1963), 155–169.

17. Historians and theologians have noted how Bonaventure argued for the plentitude of papal jurisdictional power so the Friars Minor could be approved over the opposition of local bishoprics. This was a theological and jurisdictional solution to a systemic problem of Franciscan homeless-

ness that was to have lasting influence in the Church. Only through papal approval could the friars' right to witness to the Gospel and evangelize society be universally recognized. This approach, however, leaves aside the motivating force of the Franciscan movement as a new structural path in the Church of the thirteenth century. Cf. Ratzinger, "The Theological Locus of Ecclesial Movements" for the importance of Bonaventure's defense of the universal pole of apostolicity. From a historical point of view see Brian Tierney, "From Thomas of York to William of Ockham: The Franciscans and the Papal *Sollicitudo Omnium Ecclesiarum 1250–1350*," in Joseph D'Ercole and Alphonso M. Stickler, *Communione interecclesiale collegialità—primato ecumenismo, acta conventus internationalis de historia sollicitudinis omnium ecclesiarum, Romae 1967* (Rome: Communio, 1972), 607–658.

18. Bonaventure, *DQEP*, QIIaII, d36 (105). See Luke 11.5–8. Cf. Donald X. Burt, O.S.A., *Friendship and Society: An Introduction to Augustine's Practical Philosophy* (Grand Rapids, Mich.: William B. Eerdmans, 1999), 56: "Augustine believed that our social nature is a true good. We are perfected as humans by our love for other humans. We are made happy when that love is returned, and the most important expression of such reciprocal love is the love of friendship."

19. William of Saint-Amour, *Quaestio de mendicitate*, d.1, d.25 (288–303). For background on William's ecclesiology see John Thomas Marrone, "The Ecclesiology of the Parisian Secular Masters, 1250–1320" (Ph.D. diss., Cornell University, 1972).

20. *DQEP*, QI, Concl. (42–43). For a beautiful passage from Augustine see Letter CXVIII in *The Confessions and Letters of St. Augustine*, I, ed. Phil Schaff: "[U]nless humility precede, accompany, and follow every good action which we perform, being at once the object which we keep before our eyes, the support to which we cling, and the monitor by which we are restrained, pride wrests wholly from our hand any good work on which we are congratulating ourselves. All other vices are to be apprehended when we are doing wrong; but pride is to be feared even when we do right actions, lest those things which are done in a praiseworthy manner be spoiled by the desire for praise itself." For humility as a public virtue see Augustine, *City of God* 5.19–20, 26. Humility, justice, and power seem to be a triad. See Augustine, *The Trinity* XIII.17, where Christ presents a picture of the "justice of humility."

21. *DQEP*, QII, a2, rep. to subsequent neg., 3 (146).

22. *DQEP*, QI, rep. neg. 2 (48–49). The argument relies on St. Augustine. From the latter's views on the "order of love" expressed in the Great Commandment see *City of God*, XV.22: "We must, in fact, observe the right order even in our love for the very love with which we love what

is deserving love, so that there may be in us the virtue which is the condition of the good life. Hence, as it seems to me, a brief and true definition of virtue is 'rightly ordered love.'" See the foundational passage in *On Christian Teaching* I.22–23, and Bonaventure's commentary on the Sentences III, dXXIX, Q1: *De ordine caritatis.*

23. *DQEP*, Q4, a2, concl. (233–234).

24. For Augustine on the "order of love" see Hannah Arendt, *Love and Saint Augustine*, ed. Joanna Becchiarelli Scott and Judith Chelius Stark (Chicago: University of Chicago Press, 1996); John von Heyking, *Augustine and Politics as Longing in the World* (Columbia: University of Missouri Press, 2001); and most importantly, Eric Gregory, *Politics and the Order of Love: An Augustinian Ethic of Democratic Citizenship* (Chicago: University of Chicago Press, 2008).

25. The scheme of Bonaventure's whole theology is beyond the scope of this book. For his Christology see Hayes, *The Hidden Center*; Ilia Delio, *Crucified Love: Bonaventure's Mysticism of the Crucified Christ* (Quincy, Ill.: Franciscan Press, 1998). For the Holy Spirit see Zachary Hayes, "The Doctrine of the Spirit in the Early Writings of St. Bonaventure," in *Doors of Understanding: Conversations in Global Spirituality in Honor of Ewert Cousins*, ed. Steven Chase (Quincy, Ill.: Franciscan Press, 1997), 179–198. For background as to the social nature of the Christology see Dodaro, *Christ and the Just Society in the Thought of St. Augustine*, passim; Brian E. Daley, SJ, "A Humble Mediator: The Distinctive Elements in Saint Augustine's Christology," *Word and Spirit* 9 (1987): 100–117.

26. *Collations on the Seven Gifts*, III.13 (77).

27. The healing of contraries by contraries is central to Bonaventure's redemptive schema. See *Breviloquium*, IV.3.3, fn. 28; IV.9.4.

28. Cf. *Collations on the Seven Gifts*, III.2–8 (66–73). Cf. *Breviloquium*, Part V, for the action of grace.

29. *DQEP*, QI, resp. to neg. 3, 7 (50, 51–52).

30. *Itinerariuim Mentis in Deum, Works of St. Bonaventure*, II, ed. Philotheus Boehner, O.F.M., and Zachary Hayes, O.F.M. (St. Bonaventure, N.Y.: Franciscan Institute, 2002), VII.2 (135).

31. Bonaventure, *Collations on the Seven Gifts of the Holy Spirit*, IV.18–19 (97–99). Cf. Augustine, *The Literal Meaning of Genesis*, in John E. Rotelle, O.S.A., ed., *On Genesis* (Hyde Park, N.Y.: New City Press, 2002), XI.14.18, XI.15.19 (438–439).

32. Cf. *Collations on the Six Days*, XX.28, XX.7. See J.A. Wayne Hellmann, *Divine and Created Order in Bonaventure's Theology* (St. Bonaventure, N.Y.: Franciscan Institute, 2001), 156–160, for very significant commentary.

33. See A. Pompei, "Ecclesiología Franciscana," in *Manual de Teología franciscana*, 226–234 (Madrid: BAC, 2003), for reflections on the Holy Spirit, Mary, and the individual Christian. Cf. *Collations on the Seven Gifts of the Holy Spirit*, V–VI.

34. See Luc Mathieu, O.F.M., "Le ministere des religieux-pretres, d'apres Saint Bonaventure (*Apologia Pauperum*, XII, nn. 3–13)," in Francisco de Asís Chvero Blanco, O.F.M., *Bonaventuriana, Miscellanea in onore di Jacques Guy Bougerol OFM* (Rome: Edizioni Antonianum, 1988), 431–447.

35. Hellmann, *Divine and Created Order*; Fehlner, *The Role of Charity in the Ecclesiology of St. Bonaventure*; Marietta Jenicek, O.S.F., "Franciscan Vision of Hierarchy," *Analecta* TOR 34 (2003): 811–30; Pompei, "San Bonaventura e La Chiesa, Oggi," 329–334. For a fine analysis of his concept of God's liberality see Maria Calisi, *Trinitarian Perspectives in the Franciscan Theological Tradition* (St. Bonaventure, N.Y.: Franciscan Institute, 2008).

36. *Breviloquium* I.2.2 (30); *Itinerarium*, VI.2–3.

37. Fehlner refers to the centrality of the image of one heart in a multitude of believers (*The Role of Charity*, 72). See also Bonaventure, *The Mystical Vine: A Treatise on the Passion* (London: A. R. Mowbray, 1955), 3.4 (19–20).

38. *DQEP*, QIV, a1, rep. neg. 6 (221).

39. *Defense of the Mendicants*, II.12.

40. Ibid., VI.4, with citation from 1 Cor. 7.7.

41. *Com. Sent.*, IV, dXXIV, P.I, aII, q1 (614–615).

42. *De Reductione Artium ad Theologiam: A Commentary with an Introduction and Translation*, ed. Sister Emma Thérèse Healy (St. Bonaventure, N.Y.: Franciscan Institute, 1955), 26 (40).

43. Cf. the section titled "A Reflection on the Church as the Pilgrim Christ in the Modern World," in Chapter 3.

44. Bonaventure, *Collations on the Ten Commandments*, 7.16 (100–101).

45. Augustine, *Expositions of the Psalms IV*, ed. John E. Rotelle, O.S.A. (Hyde Park, N.Y.: New City Press, 2002), Ps 98.13 (480). Cf. Bonaventure, *Collations on the Seven Gifts of the Holy Spirit*, IV.22 (101), with reference to Augustine, *On Christian Doctrine* II.7.16ff.

7. Ownership and Freedom

1. Bonaventure, *Defense of the Mendicants*, IX.4.

2. *DQEP*, Q I, concl. (40–47).

3. "Report: Causes and Context of the Sexual Abuse Crisis," III.E, 662.

4. Bishops' Committee Report, "Brief History: Handling Child Sex

Abuse Claims," *Origins* 23 (March 10, 1994): 666–670; National Review Board, "Report: Causes and Context of Sexual Abuse Crisis"; Norbert Rigali, "Church Responses to Pedophilia," *Theological Studies* 55 (March 1994): 124–139; for Boston, Philip F. Lawler, *The Faithful Departed: The Collapse of Boston's Catholic Culture* (New York: Encounter Books, 2008); France, *Our Fathers*.

5. Cf. as some examples L. Martin Nussbaum, "Changing the Rules: Selective Justice for Catholic Institutions," *America* 194 (May 15, 2006): 13–15; Sam Dillon and Leslie Wayne, "As Lawsuits Spread, Church Faces Questions of Finances," *New York Times*, June 13, 2002; Jean Guccione, "Priest Abuse Payout May Be Costly," *Los Angeles Times*, August 29, 2004; William Lobdell and Jean Guccione, "Diocese's Deal Raises the Bar Across the U.S.," *Los Angeles Times*, December 4, 2004, A1, A24.

6. *Rule*, VI.1, in Armstrong et al., *FAED*, I, 103.

7. For a description of one diocese that declared bankruptcy and the subsequent positive developments see Most Rev. Gerald F. Kicanas, "Healing through Bankruptcy," *America* 193 (September 26, 2005): 10–13.

8. The phrase is Augustine's in *Confessions*, IX.2.

9. See Little, *Religious Poverty and the Profit Economy*; Lauro Martines, *Power and Imagination: City-States in Renaissance Italy* (New York: Vintage Books, 1981); Arnaldo Fortini, *Francis of Assisi*, trans. Helen Moak (New York: Crossroad, 1981).

10. Pope Benedict XVI, *Charity in Truth, Caritas in Veritate* (Vatican City: Libreria Editrice Vaticana, 2009), 38. I want to suggest a deep connection between this vision and Benedict's call for the "logic of the gift" within a world dominated by the "logic of the market" and the "logic of the State."

11. The following stories need to be placed within the context of the Church described in Susan Wood, *The Proprietary Church in the Medieval West* (New York: Oxford University Press, 2006). See also Todeschini, *Franciscan Wealth*, passim.

12. *The Legend of the Three Companions*, IX.35, in Regis J. Armstrong, O.F.M.Cap., J.A. Wayne Hellmann, O.F.M.Conv., and William J. Short, O.F.M., eds., *Francis of Assisi: Early Documents*, II (Hyde Park, N.Y.: New City Press, 2000), 89.

13. Thomas of Celano, *The Remembrance of the Desire of a Soul*, #67 in Armstrong et al., *FAED*, II, 291–292.

14. The entirety of the spiritual vision cannot be seen outside of these roots in desert monasticism communicated to the middle ages particularly through the writings of John Cassian, the Rule of Benedict, and the teaching of Gregory the Great. See, for background, Philip Rousseau, *Ascetics,*

Authority, and the Church in the Age of Jerome and Cassian (New York: Oxford University Press, 1978); Columba Stewart, *Cassian the Monk* (New York: Oxford University Press, 1998); Carole Straw, *Gregory the Great: Perfection in Imperfection* (Berkeley: University of California Press, 1988).

15. *Earlier Rule* XXII.7, citing Mark 7.21–23; Matt. 15.19, *FAED*, I, 79.

16. Ibid., XXII.20, *FAED*, I, 80.

17. For general commentary see Ovidio Capitani, *Figure e motive del francescanesimo medievale* (Bologna: Pàtron Editore, 2000), 11–30, 31–45; Lambertini, *La povertà pensata*; Virpi Makinen, *Property Rights in the Late Medieval Discussion on Franciscan Poverty* (Leuven, Belgium: Peeters, 2001); Kevin Madigan, "Aquinas and Olivi on Evangelical Poverty: A Medieval Debate and Its Modern Significance," *The Thomist* 61 (1997): 567–586.

18. *Defense of the Mendicants*, VII.1. See the confirming passages in Matthew 19.23: "Only with difficulty will a rich man enter into the kingdom of God"; and the teaching of Jesus in Matthew 10.9–10, "Do not take gold or silver or money in your belts, no bag for your journey, nor two tunics, nor sandals." See *DQEP* QII, arg. for affirmative, d.1 (93, 77). The theological reason for the rootage of evil in avarice was its connection with pride, the sin of Lucifer, and the fall of Adam and Eve. These abstract explanations were ultimately revelatory of the experience of real life in a contentious and proprietary society. Bonaventure writes in *Breviloquium* III.3 (106), Adam and Eve "fell into disobedience and were enticed by greed because both had risen up in pride, the woman by seeking and desiring what she did not possess, the man by too greatly loving and clinging to what he had." Cf. *Collations on the Six Days*, 21.10; Augustine, *The Literal Meaning of Genesis* XI.15.19 (439).

19. For background on the "will" as central to the Augustinian inheritance see *The Trinity*, books X–XI and passim; Burnaby, *Amor Dei*, 92–100.

20. See, for example, his two encyclical letters of 1257 or 1266 in Monti, *Writings Concerning the Franciscan Order*, 57–63, 226–229; *Defense of the Mendicants*, XII.6 where he compares the Christian people to a "deteriorating building"; Luigi Pellegrini, O.F.M.Cap., "L'Ordine Franciscano e la societá Cittadina in Epoca Bonaventuriana: Un analisi del *Determinationes questionum super Regulam Fratrum Minorum*," *Laurentianum* 1–2 (1974): 154–200.

21. *Collations on the Seven Gifts of the Holy Spirit* IX.15 (194); *DQEP*, QII, a2, rep. neg. d20 (133).

22. *Confessions*, XIII.9. the weight of custom and habit, embedded in

the memory, in the interior of the person, runs throughout the *Confessions*.

23. *Collations on the Seven Gifts of the Holy Spirit* III.5 (68–69).

24. Bonaventure, "Prologue: Book II of the Sentences," as translated in *Writings on the Spiritual Life, Works of St. Bonaventure* X, Introduction and Notes by Edward F. Coughlin, O.F.M. (Saint Bonaventure, N.Y.: Franciscan Institute, 2006), 355, with reference to Prov. 30.16; Eccles. 5.9; cf. *The Threefold Way*, I.4, fn. 17 (92).

25. *DQEP*, QII, a1, concl. (70), referring to the *Rule* of the Friars Minor 6.1.

26. *DQEP*, QII, a1, d27 (65).

27. *DQEP*, QII, a1, concl. (71), citing Augustine's *Eighty Three Different Questions*, 36.1.

28. *Confessions*, X.32; for Bonaventure cf. *Soliloquium*, which begins with the devout soul in the course of its journey "depressed by its struggles," "seduced by error," "overcome by weariness." Prologue 1 (218), and II.2 on the "threefold vanity of earthy things" experienced or witnessed in life, in *Writings on the Spiritual Life*.

29. *Defense of the Mendicants*, VII.7.

30. Cf. *Defense of the Mendicants*, IX.3, VII.30; *Collations on the Six Days* XVIII.7: "If indeed man had not sinned, there would not have been a division of lands, but all would have been in common."

31. *DQEP*, AII, a2, rep. to neg. 15 (129), citing Rom. 13.8.

32. Ibid.

33. *Defense of the Mendicants*, X.10–16. For background see Odd Langholm, *Economics in the Medieval Schools: Wealth, Exchange, Value, Money and Usury according to the Paris Theological Tradition, 1200–1350* (Leiden: Brill, 1992).

34. *Defense of the Mendicants*, X.24.

35. *Defense of the Mendicants*, VIII.17.

36. *Defense of the Mendicants*, X.15, X.11.

37. *Defense of the Mendicants*, IX.29. Cf. *Soliloquium*, chap. 2, in Coughlin, ed., *Writings on the Spiritual Life*, 271–295.

38. *Defense of the Mendicants*, XII.26, where Bonaventure talks about "begging" which "stems from cupidity."

39. *Defense of the Mendicants*, II.8–9.

40. *Collations on the Six Days*, 22.23 (352).

41. *Defense of the Mendicants*, II.8, citing one of Bonaventure's favorite descriptions of the Church from 1 Cor. 12.11.

42. I have been influenced in this interpretation of Bonaventure by the fine work on Augustine by Paula Fredriksen, *Augustine and the Jews: A Christian Defense of Judaism* (New York: Doubleday, 2008), with its

interpretation of *City of God* and the "de-materialization" of evil, pages 331ff; cf. "Beyond the Body/Soul Dichotomy: Augustine on Paul against the Manichees and the Pelagians," *Recherches Augustiniennes* 23 (1988): 87–114. Once Bonaventure is placed in argument with both the "manichees" of his day and those committed to a completely purified society created through the imposition of law, the interpretive connection appears clear.

43. *Collations on the Six Days*, 22.23 (352).

44. *Defense of the Mendicants* III.22, referring to Philippians 2.3. Bonaventure is following in this analysis the approach of Augustine in *The Excellence of Marriage*, 3.29, "It is better to have only good things, even though lesser ones, than to have a great good together with a great evil." See Rotelle, O.S.A., ed., Saint Augustine, *Marriage and Virginity*, 55.

45. John E. Rotelle, O.S.A., ed., *Saint Augustine, On Genesis* (Hyde Park, N.Y.: New City Press, 2002), *The Literal Meaning of Genesis* XI.15.20 (439–440). Cf. also *Expositions of the Psalms III*, Ps. 64.2 (266). For Bonaventure's use of Augustine's motif see *DQEP*, QII, a1, d26–27 (64–65), QI, d19 (35) citing *City of God*, XIV.28; *Commentary on Ecclesiastes, Works of St. Bonaventure* VII, Robert J. Karris, O.F.M., Campion Murray, O.F.M., eds. (Saint Bonaventure, N.Y.: Franciscan Institute, 2005), "General Introduction," 1.

46. Francis, "Salutation of the Virtues," 11–12, *FAED*, I, 165.

47. *DQEP* QII. a1 concl. (70–71). For background in Augustine see *City of God*, XIV.28; *Expositions of the Psalms III*, Ps. 64.2 (265–267).

48. The basic principle is well enunciated in *DQEP*, QII, a1 resp. 6 (83): "Indeed when one is dispensing the goods of the Church, it does not violate perfection to hold to moderation."

49. Benedict XVI, *Charity in Truth*, Ch. III.

8. Scandal and the Church

1. Bonaventure, Com. Sent. IV, d10, a1, q1, concl. (IV, 218). See also *Commentary on the Gospel of John, Works of St. Bonaventure* XI, introduction, translation, and notes by Robert J. Karris (Saint Bonaventure, N.Y.: Franciscan Institute, 2007), chap. 21, Q4 (997).

2. See Rev. Michael A. McGuire, *The New Baltimore Catechism, No. 1, Official Revised Edition* (New York: Benziger Brothers, 1942), passim, for use of the term "holy" as a mark of the Church and its actions.

3. Waldemar Molinski, "Scandal," in Adolph Darlap, General Editor, *Sacramentum Mundi: An Encyclopedia of Theology* VI (New York: Herder and Herder, 1970), 1–5, with citation on 1.

4. Cf. James A. Morone, *Hellfire Nation: The Politics of Sin in American History* (New Haven, Conn.: Yale University Press, 2003).

5. National Review Board, "Report: Causes and Context of the Sexual Abuse Crisis," IV.4 (677).

6. Ibid.

7. For the speech of John Paul II see "Vatican–U.S. Bishops' Committee to Study Applying Canonical Norms," *Origins* 23 (July 1, 1993): 102–103.

8. "Report: Causes and Context of the Sexual Abuse Crisis," IV.5 (673).

9. Cf. Heribert Jone, O.F.M.Cap., and Urban Adelman, O.F.M.Cap., *Moral Theology* (Cork, Ireland: Mercier Press, 1955), nos. 372–376.

10. "Report: Causes and Context of the Sexual Abuse Crisis," IV.5 (673).

11. Cf. the significant commentary by Augustine, *On Christian Doctrine* II.7.10, cited by Bonaventure, *Collations on Seven Gifts of the Holy Spirit*, IV.22 (101).

12. A classic reflection with much theological depth may be found in Henri de Lubac, S.J., *The Splendour of the Church* (New York: Sheed and Ward, 1956), in which the author addresses directly the flaws and sins of the members of the Church: "The very thing that makes sanctity possible is also what opens the way to fakes of the most horrible kind. It is the fate of men to make one another suffer even while they help one another" (59). See also the very perceptive comments about the Church's humanity in Yves M.-J. Congar, O.P., *Christ, Our Lady and the Church: A Study in Eirenic Theology* (Westminster, Md.: Newman Press, 1957), 43–68.

13. Francis of Assisi, The *Earlier Rule*, 23.9, *FAED*, I, 85.

14. Armstrong et al., *FAED*, I, 124. See Fr. Francisco Manuel Romero Garcia, O.F.M., "*Videre Leprosos*": *Contenido y significado de la experiencia de Francisco de Asís entre los leprosos, segun sus Escritos* (Rome: Antonianum, 1989); Raul Manselli, "San Francesco dal Dolore Degli Uomini al Cristo Crociffiso," *Analecta Tertius Ordinis Regularis* XVI (1983): 191–210 for very significant interpretive comments.

15. There is a fine parallel example of Francis's hermeneutical method for interpreting experience in Marilyn Hammond, "Saint Francis as Struggling Hermeneut," in *Francis of Assisi: History, Hagiography and Hermeneutics in the Early Documents*, ed. Jay M. Hammond (Hyde Park, N.Y.: New City Press, 2004), 210–228.

16. For just one example of the extensive literature on this topic see Saul Nathaniel Brody, *The Disease of the Soul: Leprosy in Medieval Literature* (Ithaca, N.Y.: Cornell University Press, 1974).

17. For the ritual see Arnaldo Fortini, *Francis of Assisi*, 209–210. See

also Mark Gregory Pegg, "Le corps et l'autorite: la lepre de Baudouin IV," *Annales ESC* (March–April 1990): 265–287.

18. *The Assisi Compilation*, 64, *FAED*, II, 166.

19. *Testament*, 9–10, *FAED*, I, 125.

20. *Earlier Exhortation*, I.13, *FAED*, I, 42.

21. Augustine, *Expositions of the Psalms II*, translation and notes by Maria Boulding, O.S.B., ed. John E. Rotelle, O.S.A. (Hyde Park, N.Y.: New City Press, 2000), Ps 44.3 (282–283). Citations from Romans 3.23, 5.6.

22. Cf. *Later Admonition and Exhortation*, 4, *FAED*, I (46).

23. *Earlier Rule*, 9.2–6, 5.7, 11.11–12, 17.7, *Later Rule* 7.3, *FAED*, I, 67, 70, 72, 75, 104.

24. John of Perugia, *The Beginning or Founding of the Order*, 20, in Armstrong et al., *FAED*, II, 43. For ecclesial rejection see the chronicle of Roger of Wendover in *FAED*, I, 598–599.

25. *The Beginning or the Founding of the Order*, 19, page 43.

26. *Earlier Rule* XIX.1, XIII, *FAED*, I, 77, 73.

27. See, for example, the codification of the "outward limits" in *The Constitutions of Narbonne* (1260), VII.1–26, in *Writings Concerning the Franciscan Order*, 105–111. Today, of course, the sexual abuse of minors is an "outward limit," not to be tolerated.

28. Thomas of Celano, *Life of Saint Francis*, XII.31, XV.37, *FAED*, I, 209, 216–217. Cf. Giovanna Casagrande, *Religiosita penitentiziale e citta al tempo dei communi* (Rome: Instituto Storico dei Cappuccini, 1995); Casagrande, "Un ordine per I laici: Penitenza e penitenti nel duecento," in Maria Pia Alberzoni et al., *Francesco d'Assisi e il primo secolo di storia francescana* (Turin: Einaudi, 1997), 237–255.

29. The description is partially taken from Straw, *Gregory the Great*. Straw quotes from Gregory's *Homilies on Ezekiel*, where he comments on why God permitted Peter to betray the Savior: "This we recognize certainly as an act performed by [God's] dispensation of great mercy, so that he who was to be shepherd of the Church might discern in his own sin how he should have compassion for others. And so first [the Lord] shows [Peter] to himself and then sets him over others, so that from his own weakness he might recognize how to bear mercifully with the weaknesses of others" (*H.Ez.* 2.21.4, as cited on p. 256). Once again we see the importance here of ancient spiritual traditions.

30. *Earlier Rule*, 2.13–15, 5.9–12, 7.15–16, 15, 17.5, *FAED*, I, 65, 67, 69, 73, 75–76.

31. *Earlier Rule* 21.7, 23.8, *FAED*, I, 78, 84. For a fine commentary on this interpretation of "status" in the Church see *St. Bonaventure's Commentary on the Gospel of Luke, Chapters 17–24, Works of St.*

Bonaventure, introduction, translation, and notes by Robert J. Karris, O.F.M. (St. Bonaventure, N.Y.: Franciscan Institute, 2004), chapter 17.58–60 (1692–1697).

32. *Earlier Rule* 23.1–5, *FAED*, I, 82–83, known as the "Franciscan Creed." See Thadée Matura, O.F.M., *Francis of Assisi: The Message in His Writings* (St. Bonaventure, N.Y.: Franciscan Institute Publications, 1997, 2004).

33. See, in particular, Augustine's comments on Psalm 61 in John E. Rotelle, O.S.A., ed., *Expositions of the Psalms*, 51–72, III (Hyde Park, N.Y.: New City Press, 2001), 202–228. Cf. Pasquale Borgomeo, *L'église de ce temps dans la prédication de Saint Augustin* (Paris: Études Augustiniennes, 1972), 279–374. I have been repeatedly struck throughout the course of researching this material by the parallels between Bonaventure's views and those of Augustine. For background see Dodaro, *Christ and the Just Society in the Thought of St. Augustine*; R. A. Markus, *Saeculum: History and Society in the Theology of St. Augustine* (Cambridge: Cambridge University Press, 1970), where he elucidates Augustine's notion of the *corpus permixtum* and the eschatological drive of this ecclesiological vision (chap. 6).

34. Cf. St. Bonaventure's *Commentary on the Gospel of Luke, Chapters 1–8, Works of St. Bonaventure*, introduction, translation, and notes by Robert J. Karris, O.F.M. (St. Bonaventure, N.Y.: Franciscan Institute, 2001), 6.33, citing Matt. 13.30, 13.47. Augustine uses these and other similes to explain this mix of good and bad in the Church in *Expositions of the Psalms I*, Ps. 8.13 (137). For a significant commentary on the importance of these images see Gaetano Lettieri, "Tollerare or sradicare? Il dilemma del discernimento: La parabola della zizzania nell'Occidente latino da Ambrogio a Leone Magno," *Cristianesimo nella storia* XXVI (Gennaio, 2005), 65–121.

35. *DQEP*, QII, a2, resp. 15. Cf. C. Colt Anderson, "Bonaventure and the Sin of the Church," *Theological Studies* 63 (2002): 667–689.

36. *DQEP*, QII, a2, resp. 18.

37. See Bonaventure, *Breviloquium*, VI.4.4 (227): "Therefore, it was fitting that the administration of the sacraments be entrusted to persons, not by reason of their sanctity, which varies according to the condition of their will, but by reason of their authority, which always remains what it is. It was therefore fitting that this power was given to good and bad alike, to those within the Church and those without." Also, VI.6.3, VI.12.1–6. The sacramental and hierarchical elements are well described in Fehlner, *The Role of Charity in the Ecclesiology of St. Bonaventure*.

38. *Com. Sent.* IV.dXIX, a1, q2, in *Opera Theologica Selecta* (Florence: Quaracchi, 1949), 485–487.

39. I use the term "patterns of relationality" instead of "structures." For an analogous concept of "structures of sin" see John Paul II, *On Social Concern* (Boston: Daughters of St. Paul, 1987), 36.
40. The *Earlier Rule* XII.16, *FAED*, I, 69.
41. Thomas of Celano, *The Life of Saint Francis*, VII, 17, *FAED*, I, 196.
42. Ibid., I, 195; Bonaventure, *The Major Life of Saint Francis*, II.6, *FAED*, II, 539.
43. 1 Tim. 4.7 cited in *Collations on the Seven Gifts of the Holy Spirit*, III.1, 2, 10 (65, 66, 74).
44. *Collations on the Seven Gifts of the Holy Spirit*, III.10 (74).
45. Ibid., III.5 (68). Cf. III.6–8 for conscience and compassion (69–73).
46. Ibid., III.6, 8 (69, 73–74).
47. Ibid., 50, *FAED*, II, 149. For a brilliant analysis of the significance of Francis's approach see Raul Manselli, *Nos qui cum eo fuimus, contributo alla questione francescana* (Rome: Instituto Storico dei Cappucccini, 1980).
48. *The Assisi Compilation*, 80–82, *FAED*, II, 181–184.
49. *The Major Legend of Saint Francis*, I.6, *FAED*, II, 534.
50. Ibid., 8.1–2, *FAED*, II, 587.
51. Ibid., 8.6, *FAED*, II, 590; 4.7 (555), where piety is demonstrated by the Saracen.
52. *Collations on the Seven Gifts of the Holy Spirit*, III, with special reference to the church in number 13 (77).
53. "*Pietas*" was the preferred term in the Franciscan lexicon; it obviously built on the monastic inheritance of "mercy," outlined by Edith Scholl, OCSO, in "Mercy within Mercy, *Misericordia and Miseria*," in *Cistercian Studies Quarterly* 42, no. 1 (2007): 63–82. I am indebted to Regis J. Armstrong, O.F.M.Cap., who many years ago pointed out the importance of "piety" in the Franciscan self-understanding.
54. Bonaventure, *Com. Sent.* III, QVI (784–786).
55. *Collations on the Seven Gifts of the Holy Spirit*, III.11 (74–75).
56. For a fine contemporary exposition see Kathleen M. O'Connor, *Lamentations and the Tears of the World* (Maryknoll, N.Y.: Orbis Books, 2002).
57. *The Mystical Vine, A Treatise on the Passion of Our Lord by S. Bonaventure*, translated from the Latin by A Friar of S.S.F. (London: A. R. Mowbray, 1955), X (40–41). For a similar prayer of Francis of Assisi see *Office of the Passion*, VI, *FAED*, I, 146. For Augustine see *Expositions of the Psalms* I, Exp. 2 of Psalm 21, 227–243, Exp. 2 of Psalm 30, 321–325.
58. For extended reflections on faith see Bonaventure, *Breviloquium*, V.7.1–6; *Itinerarium* I.10–13. Cf. George H. Tavard, A.A., *Transiency and Permanence: The Nature of Theology According to St. Bonaventure* (St. Bonaventure, N.Y.: Franciscan Institute, 1954), 31–55.

9. The Soothing of Jerusalem

1. Augustine, *Expositions of the Psalms III*, Ps. 61.7 (208–209).

2. Bonaventure, *Itinerarium Mentis in Deum* VII.6 (139).

3. The imagery is taken from Augustine, *Exposition of the Psalms* 3, Ps 61.207–215. For significant commentary as it applies to the Church see Pasquale Borgomeo, *L'église de ce temps dans la prédication de Saint Augustin*, 301–324.

4. For commentary on this verse (Heb. 11.1) and faith as both an intellectual and affective virtue in the thought of St. Bonaventure see A. Menard, "Traité de Bonaventure su la foi," *Etudes Franciscaines* 24 (1974): 113–226, especially 142–145. Cf. Benedict XVI, *On Christian Hope, Spe Salvi* (Vatican City: Libreria Editrice Vaticana, 2007), nos. 1–13.

5. *Lumen Gentium*, VI.51, and for references to the Church as "that Jerusalem which is above," I.6.

6. Cf. Augustine, *Expositions of the Psalms I*, Ps 25.2.2 "None of you, dear brothers and sisters, should conclude that 'speaking with your neighbor' means that you must tell the truth to a Christian but are allowed to lie to a pagan. No, your neighbor is anyone descended like yourself from Adam and Eve. We are all neighbors by the fact of our earthly birth, but in quite another sense we are brothers and sisters by the hope of our heavenly inheritance. You should think of everyone as your neighbor, even before he or she is a Christian, for you do not know what that person is in God's sight, or what God's foreknowledge of him or her may be."

7. Francis, *Earlier Rule*, 9.5 (70).

8. *Expositions of the Psalms III*, Ps. 61.6 (208).

Index